SCHOOL READINESS

Behavior Tests Used at the
Gesell Institute

children, explaining how to give tests, how to evaluate them, and how to use the results. Tabular norms are presented for each test. For the first time, in this edition, preschool data are given in the instructions and tables where appropriate. This makes possible the accurate diagnosis of those five-year-olds who may be responding at a younger-than-five level.

A final section introduces much new material, including a discussion of significant overflow behavior and the importance of preschool testing. A completely new chapter discusses many currently controversial topics, such as mainstreaming versus special classes, early cognitive training, remedial reading, learning disabilities, a shortened first-grade day, and sex differences in school behavior.

The authors contend that the substitution of an individual examination to determine readiness in terms of behavior would have far-reaching benefits for both child and community.

SCHOOL READINESS

Behavior Tests Used
at the
Gesell Institute

|||||||||||||||||||||||||||||||||||||||||||||||||||||||||||||||||||||||||||||||||||||||

Revised Edition

FRANCES L. ILG, M.D.
LOUISE BATES AMES, Ph.D.
JACQUELINE HAINES, A.B.
CLYDE GILLESPIE, M.S.A.
Gesell Institute of Child Development

HARPER & ROW, PUBLISHERS
NEW YORK, HAGERSTOWN, SAN FRANCISCO, LONDON

Library of Congress Cataloging in Publication Data

Gesell Institute of Child Development, New Haven.
    School readiness.
    Includes index.
    1. Readiness for school.   2. Educational tests and
measurements.   I.   Ilg, Frances Lillian, 1902–
II.   Title.
LB1132.G4   1978   372.1'2'6   77–11826
ISBN 0–06–012146–7

78 79 80 81 82 10 9 8 7 6 5 4 3 2 1

CONTENTS

v

LIST OF TABLES

PREFACE

For considerably more than fifty years, the Gesell Institute has been primarily concerned with outlining and describing the patterned stages through which different aspects of human behavior develop. Though it is our position that virtually all human behaviors develop in a patterned, predictable way, we have always been fully aware that not every individual behaves in a manner strictly in keeping with behavior normative for one of his or her exact chronological age. Obviously, any norm implies that some individuals will be ahead of normative expectations, some behind.

In spite of the fact that such a concept has been basic to much of our work, it is only within the past few decades that we have applied this kind of thinking to children in school. Once our eyes were opened, however, it became clear and reasonable that though most communities behave *as if* all 5-year-olds were ready for kindergarten, all 6-year-olds for first grade, the mere fact of having reached a fifth or sixth birthday did not of itself guarantee any given level of behavior.

Thus, though many schools all over the country continue to assume that a certain birthday age of itself guarantees readiness for the work of some given grade, that is by no means the case.

This light dawned on us back in the 1950s when a check on our own clinical service for school-age children revealed that the youngsters brought to this service because of failure or poor performance in school were nearly all overplaced—that is, nearly all were in a grade ahead of the one for which their developmental or behavior age suited them.

Chapter Two describes in some detail the stages in our growing conviction that a book for parents and teachers was needed, a book that would present our ideas about the importance of having children fully ready for beginning school and for subsequent promotion, based on their behavior age and not merely their age in years or their level of intelligence or their reading ability.

School Readiness was such a book and it has served well to make known our feelings and findings in this area. So far as we know, before its publication, though certainly many educators and some parents had long been aware of the fact that many students were simply not up to the work of the grade to which fate and state laws had assigned them, the *general concept* of the need for readiness was not fully accepted.

Actually, it is not fully accepted by everyone even today. But there has come to be, in the dozen or so years since our book's publication, a general feeling in many school communities that it should be behavior age, not birthday age or IQ, which determines the time of school entrance and subsequent promotion.

We ourselves go so far as to believe that perhaps 50 percent of school failure could be prevented or cured by having every child in the grade for which his behavior age suits him.

The whole idea seems so simple and sensible that it is sometimes hard for us to understand why not everyone sees things this way. That many do is, encouragingly, indicated by the fact that a number of school communities all over this country are now instituting what are called *kindergarten screening programs*. Using our own or other behavior measures, many communities actually make the effort to determine in advance whether children are ready to begin the work of kindergarten.

Unfortunately, accepting the idea is not enough. It takes several people working together to put into practice the concept of having each child *ready* when he starts school. Possibly, the group most accepting of this notion is made up of kindergarten teachers. Many a kindergarten teacher has commented: "Half the children in my class are just not going to be ready for first grade next year."

If kindergarten teachers, as a rule, have this degree of insight, one might ask then, what holds things up? Why are so many unready children still promoted into first grade?

The answer is that it is not the kindergarten teacher alone who makes this kind of decision. For things to go smoothly, the child's parents must agree that readiness is important and that the unready child should not be pushed along. Mothers quite often share the teacher's insight; fathers are less likely to do so. And there is always the administrator who may feel that the whole business of readiness is quite superfluous.

When we talk to the many parents who have *tried* to have their children start later than the law allows, we sometimes get the impression that there are all these good parents who would respect a concept of unreadiness, but that they are being thwarted by schools which do not understand.

But when we talk to teachers or administrators trying desperately to carry out a developmental program, only to be thwarted by a handful of militant parents, we must face the fact that no single group is all *for* or all *against* having children ready before they start school. It requires teachers, parents, and administrators all working together to see to it that all children in a system are placed where they belong in school.

We are encouraged that gradually, as other panaceas fail and as problems continue to plague our schools, a concept of readiness does seem to be gaining ground. We have been pleased with the acceptance and use of our book *School Readiness*.

The present revision comes now that the book has been in print for somewhat more than a dozen years. Changes to be found in this new edition are the direct result of our experience in consulting with school systems which have chosen to attempt what we call *developmental placement programs*, and in giving workshops in which teachers, psychologists, guidance personnel, and administrators have been taught the use and value of our battery of developmental tests.

These changes include the following:

To begin with, we have simplified our directions for the giving and interpreting of the tests. We have done this chiefly by leaving out much of the minute detail of both findings and interpretation which we initially found so beautifully revealing. Experience has indicated that too much detail, rather than clarifying what we are trying to convey, has proved more confusing than enlightening.

Second, we have projected each of our tests downward into the preschool years. Experience has shown that, predictably, not all 5-year-olds examined in a kindergarten screening program are fully up to a 5-year-old level of behavior. Many are just slightly below, but some are shockingly far behind. Thus a sprinkling of preschool norms, though not amounting to a full preschool examination as such, can at least give an examiner a good clue as to where any immature 5-year-old is actually functioning.

More than this, acquaintance with preschool responses, even when a child being examined is fully up to age expectation, gives the examiner a better understanding of what the behavior being tested is like in its longitudinal flow. It is often useful to know what kind of response comes *before* the one expected.

A further inclusion is a somewhat greater emphasis on what may be called *overflow patterns of behavior*—that is, ways a child behaves that are not strictly related to the test in question. Patterns of eye, mouth, and even whole body behavior expressed in addition to specific test responses can often tell us a good deal about what a child is like and at what level he is responding.

We have also described briefly some of the ways in which children who are overplaced reveal that overplacement in their school behavior.

Because we believe that an understanding, or at least a minimal appreciation, of the way in which a child's functioning or malfunctioning with respect to his visual behavior is important to those concerned with his academic performance, we have included a simple explanation of the way effective vision contributes to school success.

And also, more than in our earlier editions—since currently more is known about these things—we emphasize the importance of diet and nutrition and the significance of at least a beginning understanding of any child's body chemistry by all parents and educators.

Hopefully the general thesis of this work will be of interest to parents as well as to educators. For those parents who may be interested in the general thesis but not in the technical detail given here, we suggest a companion book, *Is Your Child in the Wrong Grade?* by one of the co-authors.

Fortunately, most psychologists have gone beyond the notion that all or most child behavior problems—at home and at school—are the result of something that parents or other adults have or have not done to or for the child. At this moment in history, those who blame everything that goes wrong on inadequate environmental factors are decreasing in number. Increasingly, parents, teachers, psychologists, and even psychiatrists are beginning to respect the fact that much of any individual's functioning or malfunctioning depends on the individual mechanism.

Different bodies, at different stages in their development, require different environments in order to function most effectively. An understanding of any child's behavior age (which may be quite different from his or her chronological age) will help all concerned to provide the school environment that will be most effective for any given boy or girl.

PART I
INTRODUCTION

CHAPTER *1*

ORIENTATION

||||||||||||||||||||||||||||||||||||||||||||||||||||||||||||||||||||||||||||

How can we best get at that bundle of vitality which is the child? How can we distill the essence of a growing human being at a certain age and as a unique individual who can reflect age and make it into his very own? This is not an easy task. And yet if we use effective tools, the child reveals himself* to all who will stop and listen to what he says, and who with seeing eyes will watch what he does.

Discovering and perfecting such tools was the life work of Dr. Arnold Gesell, a work that has been carried on by his colleagues. It was Dr. Gesell's contention that "Mind manifests itself" in whatever infant and child may do. He also contended that behavior develops in a patterned, largely predictable way, which with skill can be measured.

Though not everyone appreciates this fact, Dr. Gesell showed great respect for the child's life experiences. He stated very early[25]†: "The organism always participates in the creation of its environment, and the growth characteristics of the child are really the end-product expressions of an interaction between intrinsic and extrinsic determiners. *Because the interaction is the crux,* the distinction between these two sets of determiners should not be drawn too heavily."

Nevertheless, it was his belief that regardless of environment and regardless of individual differences, many behaviors do develop through basic stages, common to all. It was to check on this patterned development that he devised his infant and preschool behavior tests. These were presented through a series of publications,[23, 24, 26, 27] the first of which, *Infancy and Human Growth*, appeared as early as 1928. These tests have

* In general, though not consistently, we have referred to the child as "he" and the examiner as "she." However, obviously, the children we refer to are in real life often girls; examiners may be men as well as women. No sexism is intended by the fact that we have not, at every turn, emphasized this fact.

† Numbered list of references appears at end of book.

been imitated, copied, and elaborated by many others, but we at the Gesell Institute still use them in not too great a variation from their original form.

The beauty of the Gesell developmental tests lies in their simplicity, and in the fact that they are so devised that any child, no matter what his or her capability or lack of capability, can succeed at some level. That is, ours are not tests to which there is a specifically right or wrong response. Nearly all can be responded to in *some* way, revealing the child's true behavior level even when that level is far below what might be expected at his chronological age.

Dr. Gesell's original Copy Forms test shows how simple a test can be and still be revealing. He merely seriated six forms of increasing difficulty, from circle to cross to square to triangle to divided rectangle, and finally to diamond. We still use this test in its original form, though at the earliest ages we include a vertical and a horizontal line, and at the older ages, two three-dimensional forms—a cylinder and a cube. This test reveals behavior-age level from $2\frac{1}{2}$ through 9 years of age.

We have gradually come to realize that the significance of such a test as Copy Forms is not simply in the success of copying. It is also in the *way* the child copies, the size form he makes, the place on the paper where he chooses to draw his forms. All these and many other qualifying categories tell us more fully about the child than do his mere success or failure in copying the forms in question.

But—and here is their beauty so far as the child is concerned—if a given 5-year-old cannot copy a triangle, as our norms predict, chances are that he will be able to copy a square (a $4\frac{1}{2}$-year-old level of behavior), or at least a cross (a $3\frac{1}{2}$-year-old product). Thus he will be able to succeed on this test, even though not at his chronological age level.

Similarly, the Incomplete Man test has a wide age range of usefulness—also from 2 through 9 years of age. It, too, can be judged by the quality of the child's response as well as by the actual number of parts he adds. And here, too, an immature child does not have to face failure. If he cannot, for instance, add the upward-pointing arm typical of the 6-year-old, even though he may be fully 6, he can very likely add a straight-out or even a downward-pointing arm, more characteristic of a younger age. But he himself does not know that he is not up to age expectation.

Though there are only a small number of formal verbal tests in the school-age section of our battery, an examiner is able to observe verbal behavior throughout the entire examination. We especially attempt to record everything the child says in the short interviews at the beginning and end of the test, in the naming of parts of the body, and in the carrying out of commands on the Right and Left tests.

In addition to these basic tests, we have included in our school-age battery adaptations of Jacobson's Right and Left test, Visual One and

Visual Three from Marion Monroe's Reading Readiness test, and another Binet item—the naming of animals for one minute.

The initial and concluding interviews that we give in school-age examinations cannot be considered tests, but they tell us a great deal about the child. They suggest his level of intelligence, his powers of organization, his interests. These short interviews also help the child to feel the freedom of easy movement and may in part determine his enjoyment of the situation. Some of the enjoyment many seem to experience at all ages may be attributed to the feeling of success they get from being allowed to succeed at whatever level they are functioning.

And this, in essence, is what our tests aim to disclose—the level at which any given child is functioning. It should be emphasized here that our tests are not intelligence tests. Rather they are tests of maturity level—they attempt to reveal the child's behavior or maturity age.

This revision of our book *School Readiness*, as indicated in the Preface, differs from the earlier editions in several ways. Though it covers the same battery of tests originally proposed, practical experience has shown us that some of the fine detail, which we originally considered so entrancing and useful, has served in many instances merely to confuse readers and examiners. Thus we have streamlined our original presentation to quite an extent.

Also, since many 5-year-old boys and girls, when examined, proved not to be up to what we considered a normative performance, we have included for every test some information about the responses of preschoolers. This book does not pretend to be a preschool manual,* but it will give readers a taste of the beginnings of some of the behaviors which come to full fruit during the school years.

Though age level 10 was included in the original edition of *School Readiness*, we have omitted it here because of our growing feeling that sheer behavior tests are not entirely revealing for the 10-year-old *unless* there is a suspicion that the child in question is immature and thus is behaving more like an 8- or 9-year-old individual. Though, as our earlier editions show, predictable changes do occur in the test behavior of 10-year-olds which differentiate them from 9-year-olds, these changes are not striking or substantial enough for us to recommend routine developmental testing of children 10 years old and older.

---

* Gesell preschool tests are described in detail in *The First Five Years of Life*, by Gesell et al. (Harper & Row, 1940). A revision of these preschool tests is forthcoming in a volume by Walker and others.

CHAPTER 2

SCHOOL READINESS

Our clinical service at the Gesell Institute has for many, many years been consulted regarding boys and girls who are having trouble in school. But not until the middle 1950s did we become aware that a major cause of school failure was simple unreadiness for the work of the grade the child was placed in.

In 1956 Dr. Frances L. Ilg, then director of the Institute, acted as a consultant for the Fund for the Advancement of Education of the Ford Foundation. She observed that many children in the schools she visited seemed to be overplaced—that is, not ready for the grades in which the current custom of starting children in school on the basis of their chronological age had placed them.

A review of the most recent 100 cases we had seen on our clinical service revealed that every one of these children was overplaced and unready for the work demanded of him.

Fortunately, the Ford Foundation came to our aid again and made it possible for us to conduct a three-year study in the Hurlbutt School in Weston, Connecticut. We examined, by means of the Gesell developmental tests, standard intelligence tests, projective tests (the Rorschach and the Lowenfeld Mosaic), and technical visual tests, one entire kindergarten population (three different classes), one first-grade class, and one second-grade class. All children were followed for three subsequent years, with all but the intelligence tests repeated each year.

This investigation aimed at answering three specific questions: (1) How many, if any, of these children appeared on the basis of our testing to be too immature to meet the requirements of the grade in which they had been placed on the basis of their chronological age? (2) How consistent were the examiners' ratings from year to year? That is, did the children initially considered to be unready continue to be unready, or did

6

some of them catch up? (3) How well did our examination findings correlate with the teachers' ratings? In other words, did the children whom we considered unready in the fall of any given school year (when the testing was carried out) turn out to be those whom the teachers considered unready for promotion the following June?

Table 1 gives our findings on the first question: How many children were ready for the work of the grade in which they had been placed on the basis of their birthday age? As the table shows, this number ranged from a low of 34.5% to a high of 68%. Clearly, substantial numbers of children were not ready for the work of their grade.

TABLE 1 *Percentage of All Cases Seen Consistently Which Are Ready, Questionable, or Not Ready*

Grade	Number of Subjects	Ready		Questionable		Unready	
		Test 1	Test 4*	Test 1	Test 4	Test 1	Test 4
Developmental							
Kindergarten	69	46%	58%	40%	30%	14%	12%
First grade	22	55	59	36	32	9	9
Second grade	29*	38	34.5	38	34.5	24	31
Visual							
Kindergarten	69	44	54	36	30	20	16
First grade	22	50	68	36	23	14	9
Second grade	29	45	52	34.5	28	21	20
Rorschach							
Kindergarten	69	38	43	40	41	22	16
First grade	22	59	59	27	32	14	9
Second grade	29	59	52	27	20	14	28
Mosaic							
Kindergarten	69	45	51	30	33	25	16
First grade	22	68	73	18	18	14	9
Second grade	29	50	56	34.5	24	14	20

* For second grade there are only three, not four, successive tests.

For comparison, we examined in the spring of 1963 a group of North Haven, Connecticut, children at the end of their kindergarten year. Table 2 tabulates the percentage of North Haven kindergarten subjects ready for their grade as compared with the Weston subjects. These figures show more unready children in the North Haven than in the Weston groups, perhaps largely because this evaluation was made in a later year and at a time when we were more sure of our judgments. Possibly we were more ready to accept the evidence of unreadiness as revealed in our testing.

Regarding question 2, consistency of an examiner's ratings from year

TABLE 2   *Developmental Appraisal of Two Kindergarten Groups*

	Weston	North Haven	Recommendation for North Haven for the Following Year
Ready	46%	32%	Promote to regular first
Questionable	40	50	Promote to pre-primary or 5½-year-old group
Not ready	14	18	Repeat kindergarten

to year was highest for the developmental examination, on which 78% of kindergarten, 95% of first-grade, and 79% of second-grade subjects rated the same on first and final examinations. Next in consistency were the Rorschach ratings, which remained the same, from first to final tests, in 70%, 91%, and 76% of the three class groups.

Visual findings came next, with 81%, 73%, and 76% of kindergarten, first-, and second-grade groups consistent throughout the years of the study. Finally, in the Mosaic findings, only 65%, 77%, and 79% of the three groups showed consistency.

Correspondence between predictions based on the developmental examination response and the teachers' ratings at the end of any given school year (question 3) was reasonably high for kindergarten subjects. With minor exceptions, this agreement decreased with added age and higher grade placement. Thus, for comparisons made during the first year of this study, there was 83% agreement between results of the developmental examination and the teachers' estimates for kindergarten subjects. For first-grade subjects seen the first year of the study, the agreement was 68%; for second-graders, only 59%. In following years, as Table 3 shows, there was agreement in the majority of cases, but less impressively so than for kindergarten subjects.

TABLE 3   *Extent to Which Teachers' Judgments Agree with Developmental Ratings*

Class	Number	First Year		Second Year		Third Year	
		Agree (%)	Disagree (%)	Agree (%)	Disagree (%)	Agree (%)	Disagree (%)
Kindergarten	69	83	17	68	32	73	27
First grade	22	68	32	82	18	No discrimination in teachers' ratings	
Second grade	29	59	41	No data		52	48

Our interpretation of this decreasing correspondence is that kindergarten teachers look at the child's performance with relatively fresh and objective eyes. It appears to be quite within the average kindergarten teacher's ability to consider that a child is questionably ready for promotion to first grade, or that he might even need to be retained in kindergarten.

Even by the end of first grade the possibility of retention is less frequently entertained. By second grade and following, it appears to be the exceptional teacher who will recommend that a child repeat a grade.

However, at all grade levels, agreement between the developmental rating and teacher's judgment was very close for the fully ready (+) and the fully unready (−) children. The major area of disagreement was that group of children rated by us as questionable (±).

Even here, agreement was closer than might appear from the table. Though in many instances teachers gave our questionable children a + rating, and thus passed them on to the next grade, they often qualified this + rating with such statements as the following:

> A bit of a puzzle. Tests poorly.
> Have to just get after him and after him.
> Question of his reading, and not ready in arithmetic. Very slow but a good worker. At least he tries. No comprehension.

As this research was set up, we were not to discuss our findings with the teachers until all testing had been completed and all evaluations and predictions regarding school progress had been made. Once the work was completed, however, we were free to confer with teachers. We found that, in general, it was the kindergarten teacher who was the most perceptive, or at least seemed able to see the child most clearly in his current stage of development. But as soon as a teacher became more involved in and responsible for the child's learning, as happened with the older children, clarity of judgment became mixed up with excuses for poor behavior and anticipation of better behavior.

As a follow-up to our original three-year Weston study, in the spring of 1964 we checked the actual grade and group placement of all members of the original kindergarten group who were still in the Hurlbutt School. With the exception of two who had been double-promoted into seventh grade and two who had been left behind in fifth, all were in sixth grade. The grade had been divided, on the basis of general ability and school performance, into four groups, with the most excellent students in group 1, the least excellent in group 4.

Correlation between our original kindergarten predictions, made in the fall of 1957, and the school performance of these children as judged by this school placement six years later showed a correlation of .74 between our prediction of readiness and grade placement. Table 4 gives these data.

TABLE 4   *Correlation Between Kindergarten Prediction and Later Sixth-Grade Placement of Weston Subjects (Percentages)*

Kindergarten Prediction	Grades 7 and 6–1	Grade 6–2	Grade 6–3	Grades 6–4 and 5	
9 ready by 3*	67	11	22	0	= 100%
15 ready by 2*	40	47	13	0	= 100%
17 questionable	6	47	35	12	= 100%
11 unready	0	0	36	64	= 100%

* 3 of 3 examiners and 2 of 3 examiners, respectively.

A Developmental Placement Program

Our findings in Weston were substantial enough to convince us that many children started in school on the basis of chronological age alone turned out to be overplaced even in a community with good schools and middle- or upper-middle-class children. As a result, we published our discoveries and also described our tests and how to give and score them in the first edition of *School Readiness* (1964).

We have also presented these findings and taught the use of our tests through workshops and in personal consultations with school systems throughout the country. As a result of our preliminary work in this field, we have proposed what we call a system of *Developmental Placement Programs,* which we recommend for all elementary schools.

Such programs consist simply of starting children in school and subsequently promoting them on the basis of behavior age rather than intellectual level or chronological age. The procedure is simply to screen all applicants before kindergarten entrance by means of our behavior examination, made up of tests presented in this volume. Many of the children screened will undoubtedly show themselves ready for kindergarten and for probable promotion to first grade the next year.

Others will show themselves ready for a pre-kindergarten, but will give evidence that in all likelihood they will need a year in kindergarten also. Still others may show, by their immature response on our test battery, that they are not yet ready for even a pre-kindergarten.

All children will be given a second examination in the following spring, again to determine what their correct placement should be. (Some schools will even go so far as to provide a pre-first grade, just preceding the usual first grade.) And, one hopes, each child will also be examined prior to first-grade entrance, and again before second-grade entrance.

Thus a full developmental placement program might provide three levels of schooling *before* the regular first grade: pre-kindergarten, kindergarten, and pre-first grade. Perhaps a majority of children will need *only* kindergarten, before first grade. But some of the more slowly developing children, especially boys, may need three years of school before first grade. Though this may seem like undue caution, it has been our experience that not only do children get a better start in school, but also relatively few then fail first grade, *if* they are fully ready for first at the time they enter.

Requirements for Setting Up a Developmental Placement Program

Regardless of detail, the chief requirement for an effective developmental placement program is a developmental philosophy, shared by administration, teachers, and, hopefully, parents. A developmental philosophy maintains that behavior develops in a patterned, predictable way and that any child needs to have reached a certain level of maturity before he or she will be ready for the work of any given grade. It holds that teaching or training or preschool experiences do not speed up growth.[4]

That is, it maintains that the level of an individual's own behavior development—which depends on the level of bodily development rather than on something that somebody has or has not done to or for him—will determine the level at which he is performing and the school grade for which he is suited.

A second requirement is a developmental examiner (or examiners). A fully dedicated school system might provide a full-time developmental examiner for each elementary school. Others might be more sparing. The important thing is to have sufficient developmental examiners so that every child can be screened before entering kindergarten, and again in the spring of each school year, at least until he or she is surely placed in second or third grade.

(A minimum requirement would be enough personnel to carry out a preschool screening program so that no child will enter the system until ready at the very least for pre-kindergarten placement.)

As to who might best fill the role of developmental examiner, this varies tremendously from one school system to another. We have seen effective examiners come from the ranks of psychologists, guidance persons, remedial reading teachers, or grade school teachers released for this special work.

And in answer to the objection made by some school systems that providing a developmental examiner would require an extra expenditure of money, not available, there is the finding that a developmental placement program can indeed *save* money. This saving can be accomplished partly through the reduction in the need for a remedial staff, consequent on proper grade placement. Further, the number of children who fail a grade and thus need to repeat will be sharply reduced.

It is our position that through proper school placement, perhaps 50%

of school failures can be remedied or prevented. The financial as well as the emotional and academic saving is obvious.

A third essential of a successful developmental placement program is a willingness by parents and teachers and administrative personnel to have any child who was inadvertently overplaced *repeat a grade.* This basic part of any effective placement program will be discussed separately. (See page 15.)

And finally it is essential not to confuse a high intelligence quotient with readiness to start school or for subsequent promotion. It is extremely important for parents and teachers alike to appreciate the fact that an elevated IQ does not guarantee maturity or readiness for the work of any particular grade. A highly intelligent infant quite obviously would not be ready for school of any sort.

Less obvious but equally true, a 5-year-old with an IQ of 120 or over is not necessarily ready to use this intelligence at a 5-year-old level. The IQ can function effectively only when it is integrated with social, emotional, and general behavior development. The old-fashioned notion of "early entrance"—allowing children who are under age chronologically or developmentally to start school if they demonstrate high intelligence on an IQ test—has fortunately been given up in most communities.

Schools That Have Used Developmental Placement

Developmental placement programs such as we describe have been tried in many towns and cities in the United States, for the most part with success—especially on the east and west coasts. States showing the strongest interest are New Hampshire, Connecticut, Pennsylvania, Georgia, Montana, California, and Washington. Our closest contacts have been through our regional training workshops and those at the Gesell Institute. Workshop participants have come from various walks of life, but each of them was bound up in some way with the educational welfare of the child.

Two or three examples of cities or towns which have used developmental placement successfully should suffice.

Unpublished research from Visalia, California, has shown that through developmental placement, *a school can sharply reduce the number of children who need remedial help.* In one primary school of 500 children, before developmental placement was undertaken, there were 58 referrals outside the school for special help in one year. The next year, with developmental placement, there were only eight such referrals.

In Garden Grove, California, at the Genevieve M. Crosby school, the 1966–67 first-graders were kept as a bench mark or control group and all kindergarten children the next year were placed developmentally. There were sharp contrasts in the performance of the two groups: 65% of the control group had read below grade level, in contrast to only 8% of the developmentally placed children.

A report from the developmental examiner in the Gwinnet County, Georgia, elementary schools indicates that:

> For the educator, grasping the developmental point of view could be the beginning of a new way of life. In September, 1971, approximately 1800 Scott Foresman Reading Readiness tests were given to incoming first graders. On the basis of this test, it was determined that *only three out of ten* children would most likely be successful in a first grade reading program and would read on a first grade level. It also seemed that fall birthday children and boys more than girls would have trouble.
>
> This led to the realization that maturity was a major factor that had not been taken into account. Many of the children were in trouble not because they were slow, not because they had not had adequate preschool experience, but because they needed time to grow.
>
> Thus the school provided not only a readiness class for all who needed it, but also gave all children readiness tests before their placement was determined.
>
> Using age (six years) as a criterion for first grade entrance, the Scott Foresman survey showed that only 54% would be ready for reading. Using developmental age as a criterion, 71% would be ready to read. There was a greater predictive rate between behavior readiness and reading success than between chronological age and reading success.

Furthermore, a recent report from a town in California describes a developmental program which has been in force for a period of two years. Three schools were compared, one with a traditional program, a second with an Elementary and Secondary Education Act program, and a third with a developmental placement program.

The traditional school started out highest in reading in kindergarten. The ESEA and the developmental placement schools were closely matched. By the beginning of first grade, however, the ESEA school had definitely lost ground and the developmental placement program was far out in front, especially in the extended first-grade program. The traditional school, which had been in the lead to begin with, had lost considerable ground.

This particular community is planning to extend the developmental placement program to all its elementary schools. We must emphasize, however, that the success of such a program is dependent upon the groundwork laid down and the inclusion and cooperation of all those involved—teachers, parents, administrators.

Research

In actual practice, then, many communities have indeed found that developmental placement "works." Research is beginning to support this conclusion. In fact, we are not alone in our research findings regarding the importance of behavior age in determining school placement. Confirmation of the usefulness of the Gesell developmental tests comes from a number of sources. Arthur R. Jensen,[35] of California, comments that:

> Readiness in the cognitive sphere is largely the ability to conceptualize the learning task, to grasp the aim of one's efforts long before achieving mastery of the task.
> The relative ineffectiveness of shaping one's behavior to external requirements as compared with internal requirements is perhaps seen most dramatically in the child's efforts to copy geometric figures of varying difficulty. Unless the child can internalize conceptual representations of the figure, he cannot copy it, even though the model is directly before him.
> Partly for this reason, as well as for its correlations with school readiness, the Ilg and Ames figure copying test is probably one of the most convincing and valuable measures of cognitive development in the preschool years and throughout the primary grades. It shows very clearcut age differences, and the ten figures come close to being a true scale in the Gutman sense.

Alan Kaufman,[36] formerly of the Psychological Corporation, carried out a study to determine whether the clinically developed tasks of Gesell and Piaget stand up to the rigors of psychometric analysis, and also to check on their reliability. In addition to verifying the reliability of the Gesell developmental scale, he found a rather high correlation (.64) between performance on a battery of Piaget tests and on the Gesell scale. Follow-up studies by Kaufman are now checking on the predictive validity of our tests. Preliminary work suggests that they do provide an effective prediction of school readiness.

If we ourselves had to choose a single part of our test battery to determine a child's readiness, we could select the Incomplete Man test. One distraught developmental examiner, deluged with thirty-seven new pupils in the early grades on the first day of school, tested them with the Incomplete Man. Before the day was out, she had placed all thirty-seven by means of this test alone, and later discovered that she had missed out on the placement of only two children.

This developmental examiner's success has been corroborated by Joan Ames Chase,[19] of the Columbus Guidance Center East, Ohio, in a computerized attempt to determine which clinical measures correlated most highly with the actual promotion decisions of a group of first-grade teachers. The clinical data reviewed by her were voluminous. The most highly predictive of all measures used was the Gesell Incomplete Man test.

Repeating

An important requirement of an effective developmental placement program is that until or unless *all* children can be correctly placed to begin with, schools and parents alike will need to accept the practice of permitting children who have failed a grade because they were too immature for the work to repeat.

Ideally, if all children were entered in school at exactly the right time, if their growth proceeded evenly (as it does in most cases), and if class instruction fitted the requirements of each child, there would be very little need for any child to repeat a grade.

In actual practice, even within a developmental placement program, a few children still do need to repeat. The necessity occurs most, however, with children in a system where developmental placement was started just recently and some children in the higher grades were not properly placed—that is, started school too soon.

(Nongraded primaries made an effort to alleviate the need for repeating, but as things turned out, "more experience at this level" meant the same thing as repeating a grade. The need for repeating on the part of some children still remained.)

If all children are to be properly placed, the possibility of an initial incorrect placement must be faced, as must an uneven growth rate which results in what seemed like a correct placement not working out. And in our experience, the best solution in such cases is that the child repeat a grade. Not only would much remedial work become unnecessary if all children were properly placed, but also many children who are now diverted, full or part time, to the so-called learning disability classes, which are becoming so popular, could remain in the regular stream of education.

Our own experience with hundreds of cases of repeating has been extremely favorable, and research by ourselves and others bears out the value of having a child repeat when the necessity is indicated. In practical experience, we find that if parents and school present the situation in a favorable light, most children do accept the idea positively. Parents, for example, can point out that they made a mistake and started their child too soon.

Parents report, as a rule, that not only does schoolwork improve, but: "He is a changed child"; "Now he goes around the house singing"; "It is as if the weight of the world had been lifted from his shoulders"; "Except that he's in the same skin, I wouldn't know it was my own son—he is so happy and successful now that he has repeated."

Recent research findings bear out the effectiveness of repeating. In some early reports which indicated that repeating "didn't work," investigators had assumed that repeating should work for everybody, should cure all problems. Obviously it didn't. Our position is that repeating is an effective remedy when students are immature and thus overplaced, but that it should not be expected to solve all school problems. It is not a remedy when children are of very low intelligence, are dyslexic, psychotic, emotionally disturbed, or otherwise handicapped.

Recent, more careful research, which included only those children whose chief problem (according to their teachers) was immaturity, appears to show convincingly that in a majority of cases, repeating is effective and does improve school performance. Such studies as those by Stringer[50] in 1960, Chase[18] in 1968, and Scott and Ames in 1969,[47] all find that repeating can help a significant proportion of failing children *if careful criteria for selection are respected.*

A more recent study (unpublished) by Verne Lewis of Jefferson, Iowa,[40] further confirms the effectiveness of repeating, in the opinion of parents as well as of school and teachers. Lewis reports his findings from a questionnaire given to parents of 406 repeated children.

In response to such statements as "Good effects outweighed bad," Lewis asked parents to give a rating of 1 if they agreed completely, 2 if they were in partial agreement, 3 if they had no opinion, 4 if in partial disagreement, and 5 if in complete disagreement. His findings were as follows:

"Good effects outweighed bad"	77%—1;	10%—2
"Retention was justified"	80%—1;	10%—2
"Has done better academically"	70%—1;	10%—2
"Has done better emotionally"	58%—1;	16%—2
"I have never regretted this"	81%—1;	8%—2
"I would make same decision again"	82%—1;	6%—2

Dr. Richard N. Walker, of our own staff, followed the 1966–67 second-graders in Chesire, Connecticut, who had repeated second grade on the basis of their immaturity. For these 48 children, the average report card grade went from C— to B, and 73% of the children had higher grades after re-placement.

Age

It should be pointed out that some children unready for the work of the grade to which custom and the law assign them are not so much immature as merely too young by birthday age to do the work of their grade. Our own experience has been that the average girl does best if *fully* 5 before she begins kindergarten, fully 6 before she starts first grade. Boys on the average develop more slowly than do girls, and do best if fully 5½ before starting kindergarten, fully 6½ before beginning first grade.

Fortunately, many states are appreciating the importance to the child of having age on his side. States that have a September 1 cut-off date do their children a real service. Some states, however, have a cut-off date as late as January 31.

And even with a September 1 cut-off date there are many children who are still behind and need extra time—six months, one year, or even two. That is why each child needs to be examined individually. If a child is still functioning at a 5-year-old level although he is 6 or even 6½, he belongs in an advanced kindergarten only. If he is two years behind, he should not enter first grade until he is 8 years of age.

Beyond a two-year gap in maturity, corrected grade placement in all likelihood cannot solve a child's problems and special class placement must be considered.

Publications Can Help

One of our New Hampshire contingents, the New Hampshire School Readiness Project, Title III of ESEA 1965, has published an excellent pamphlet entitled *One Piece of the Puzzle: A School Readiness Manual*,[17] in which not only is the readiness concept discussed, but a full accounting is given of the 5½-year-old groups (which it calls pre-first grade). Some very specific ideas are presented on facilitating an environment for learning at this pre-first grade level. We recommend the pamphlet to anyone seriously interested in starting a developmental placement program.

Also, to assist the developmental examiner in her long, slow self-training, we have made available two sets of cards*—one on the Copy Forms, the other on the Incomplete Man test. These cards depict typical responses from preschool through 10 years of age and should prove a useful supplement to this text.

The volume *Is Your Child in the Wrong Grade?*, by Ames,[3] was written primarily for parents, but has also proved helpful to teachers who need to make parents aware of the importance of school readiness and correct grade placement. Another book, *Stop School Failure*, by Ames, Gillespie, and Streff,[5] may, with its chapters on perception and vision, add a new dimension to this total field.

---

* Both cards and pamphlet are available through Programs for Education, 101 Park Ave., Suite 1236, New York, N.Y. 10017.

In our initial 1957 survey of 100 consecutive clinical cases seen at the Institute because of trouble in school, *all* children were by our standards overplaced in school. Thirteen years later, in 1970, we made another such survey. Of the 100 clinical cases checked, 67% needed, in our estimation, to repeat a grade; 61% needed glasses; 34% required visual training; 12% could be helped by psychotherapy; 10% should attend a special school; 9% required endocrine therapy or at least a checkup; 7% should be in a special class; and 7% were referred to a specialist because of allergies or dietary problems. (All parents were, of course, counseled on the spot regardless of the problem.)

Thus the number of children who were overplaced, at least in our sample, was reduced from what it was earlier but amounted still to a substantial number. We continue to be of the opinion that one of the most easily spotted, most easily remedied, and most *serious* reasons for school failure in the primary grades is overplacement; and that such overplacement could to a large extent be done away with by a good developmental placement program.

Some generalizations which we have arrived at in our years of working with children who are having trouble in school may be helpful:

1. Boys in the early years develop more slowly than do girls, the lag amounting, as a rule, to about six months in the age zone of 5 to 7 years.
2. Even without a developmental examination, chronological age gives some clues as to possible readiness for school. We like to see girls fully 5, boys 5½ before they start kindergarten; girls fully 6 and boys 6½ before first grade.
3. Children younger than this should be carefully screened to make sure they are ready to begin kindergarten (or first grade), even when the law permits such early entrance.
4. Girls whose birthdays are in September and October should also be carefully screened to determine if they might not be ready for the grade in question, even though they miss a September 1 deadline (when such exists).
5. Some boys need to progress eighteen months more slowly than the average. At this slower rate they may be expected to keep up with a regular class group.
6. Few boys, or girls, who are more than two years behind can be expected to keep up with a regular class group. Such children need to be sidetracked into a special group in which they can receive individual attention and can progress both at their own rate and through their special interests.
7. Certain children who are advanced intellectually and who score high on both reading and achievement tests may still be functioning at an

immature level and may need to progress at a slower rate than their chronological age would suggest.

8. A kindergarten teacher's judgment about a child and his readiness should be listened to, since most such judgments correlate very well with developmental findings.

9. Any parent who wishes a child to go at a slower rate should be listened to. No parent wishes to hold a child back without a good reason. Therefore it may be assumed that real evidence of immaturity lies behind such a parental request.

10. The educator should, within reason, hold to his own decision about keeping a child back and should try to convince the parents of the wisdom of such a move if they should question it, as some do. When an educator feels that a child should be held back, the evidence for this feeling is usually quite strong. However, if a parent absolutely refuses to go along with the school's decision to retain a child, it is usually best not to insist.

11. Decisions should be made as problems arise. If a child needs to be re-placed, this change should not be delayed till the end of the year, or until some future year, especially in the early grades. Educators are too apt to put up with bad situations, hoping for a change for the better.

PART II
THE DEVELOPMENTAL
EXAMINATION

CHAPTER *3*

INTERVIEW

IIIIIIIIIIIIIIIIIIIHIIIIIIIIIIIIIIIFIIIIIIIIIIIIIIIIIIIIIIIIIIIII

Administration

A short initial interview not only puts the child at his ease, since the questions are within the realm of his immediate knowledge and experience, but also gives the examiner a quick glimpse of the child's level of performance and of his powers of organization. It is often surprising to look back over these short interviews to see how fully the child has revealed himself. Some children have their answers at their tongue's tip, ready to give, whereas with others each item has to be teased out bit by bit.

The examiner's questioning needs to be both deft and fluid. The child is being asked to specify as far as he can without being pressured. If he hits an impasse, it is up to the examiner to shift her questioning or to proceed with the next item. It is essential to get down what the child says exactly as he says it. Even his sentence construction, grammatical errors, pronunciation, tell a story about this specific child in this specific situation. Thus it is extremely important to record well and accurately.

QUESTIONS ASKED ROUTINELY

Name (Preschoolers Only). Ask: "Tell me your name." If the child gives only his first name, ask: "David what?" or "What's the rest of it?" or "What's your other name?"

Age (Preschool and School Age). Ask: "How old are you?" If fingers are shown, the child is asked: "How many does that make?" If he still does not answer, he may be asked to count his fingers—if he can— and give the total.

Sex (Preschoolers Only). Be sure the child's attention is secured and then ask casually (if the child is a boy): "Are you a boy or a girl?" If the child is a girl, ask: "Are you a girl or a boy?" If the answer is "No," ask: "Then what are you?"

23

Birthday (Preschool and School Age). Ask: "When is your birthday?" If the child holds up his fingers, as the preschooler is likely to do, ask: "How many is that?" If he names a season, or mentions proximity to a holiday, this suggests that he is not yet thinking in terms of months. If he gives the month, he should be asked further: "What day of the month?"

Brothers and Sisters (Preschool and School Age). Ask: "Do you have any brothers or sisters?" If the child says "Yes," but does not elaborate, ask: "How many brothers and how many sisters?" Regardless of whether the child gives a total number or separates them into boys and girls, or brothers and sisters, he should (at 5 years and older) then be asked: "What are their names and how old are they?" If he cannot give ages, he is asked whether they are bigger or smaller than he is. If this proves too difficult, he can be asked whether they stay at home or go to school, or what school they go to.

Father's Work (School Age Only). Ask: "What does your daddy do?" If the answer is a simple "He works," a further question, such as "Where does he work?" often elicits further detail.

Each examiner should feel free to build up his or her own battery of interview questions. However, the examiner needs a sufficient stability of repetitive questions so that he can compare one child with another. This short interview allows the examiner to become acquainted with the child and sets up an ease of relationship for the examination that is to follow.

Findings

1. Tell me your name. Even at 3 years of age, the average girl or boy can give first name, but even by 4½ giving first *and* last name is not normative, though nearly half at this age can tell both names, as Table 5 indicates.

TABLE 5   *Name*
(Percentage of Responses)

	3 years		3½ years		4 years		4½ years	
	G	B	G	B	G	B	G	B
No response	22	12	8	22	8	8	2	5
General statement	0	18	2	0	5	0	5	2
First name only	**62**	**58**	**55**	**58**	**57**	**60**	50	48
First and last	15	12	35	20	30	32	43	45

NOTE: Boldface figures in tables represent normative numbers—that is, those over 50%.

2. How old are you? Even by 3 years of age, giving correct age is normative in girls, and by 4 it is normative in both sexes. We sometimes ask this question as late as 7 years, but even by 5½ a correct answer is in the 90th percentile. A few at 5 may gesture by showing their five fingers, but can readily respond verbally when questioned further. Preschoolers very often just show their fingers and if the number shown is correct, the test is considered as passed successfully. Some at 5 may refer to the previous year, when they *were* 4. Table 6 gives data from 3 through 6 years of age.

TABLE 6   *Age*
(Percentage of Responses)

	3 years		3½ years		4 years		4½ years		5 years		5½ years		6 years	
	G	B	G	B	G	B	G	B	G	B	G	B	G	B
No answer or "I don't know"	18	27	15	32	8	10	10	5	4	9	2	4	2	2
"I was 2/3/4"	0	2	0	0	0	0	0	0	4	4	0	0	0	0
Incorrect	32	35	12	25	8	10	0	5	4	6	4	2	0	8
Correct	**50**	**35**	**73**	**43**	**85**	**80**	**90**	**90**	**88**	**81**	**94**	**94**	**93**	**90**

3. *Are you a boy or a girl?*   Even by 3 years of age, a successful—that is, correct—response to this question is normative, and by 4 years of age, a correct response is in the 90th percentile. There are virtually no incorrect responses after 3 years of age. Those who fail on this question fail merely by not giving a reply. (See Table 7.)

TABLE 7   *Sex*
(Percentage of Responses)

	3 years		3½ years		4 years		4½ years	
	G	B	G	B	G	B	G	B
No response	12	18	15	20	5	2	5	7
Incorrect	10	7	2	2	0	2	0	0
Correct	**78**	**75**	**83**	**78**	**95**	**95**	**95**	**93**

4. *When is your birthday?*   A correct response to this question comes rather late, in spite of the preschooler's great interest in birthdays and birthday parties. Giving the month correctly is normative in both boys and girls at 6 years of age, but day and month both correct are not normative until 7 years. The 5- and the 5½-year-old are likely to reply that they don't know, that they forgot, or that they had it already. A few even report that their mothers didn't tell them.

The very small number who respond correctly to this question at 4 and 4½ years (see Table 8) suggests that though it may be asked in the preschool years if the examiner so wishes, not much success should be expected before 5 years of age.

TABLE 8 *Birthday*
(Percentage of Responses)

	4 years		4½ years		5 years		5½ years		6 years		7 years		8 years		9 years	
	G	B	G	B	G	B	G	B	G	B	G	B	G	B	G	B
Month:																
Don't know	0	0	0	0	44	60	40	58	30	26	16	16	4	4	6	2
Incorrect	2	10	2	8	0	9	0	0	6	4	4	0	0	0	2	0
Correct	23	13	20	18	40	30	46	32	60	58	80	84	96	96	92	98
*	—	—	—	—	12	0	14	10	4	12	0	0	0	0	0	0
Day:																
Don't know	0	0	0	0	72	87	60	74	40	42	20	18	6	8	2	2
Incorrect	2	10	2	8	8	4	0	0	6	8	2	4	2	2	4	2
Correct	23	13	20	18	8	9	26	16	50	38	78	76	92	90	92	94
*	—	—	—	—	12	0	14	10	4	12	0	2	0	0	2	2
General reply, as "I had it"	32	42	28	32	12	24	16	18	10	0	4	2	0	0	0	0
No answer or "I forgot"	28	28	28	32	32	36	18	34	20	28	14	14	2	4	0	0
Day, month both correct	0	0	0	0	8	9	26	16	43	38	78	74	92	88	89	96

* A correct but general answer, such as "Halloween," "First day of summer," etc.

TABLE 9 *Siblings*
(Percentage of Responses)

	3 years		3½ years		4 years		4½ years		5 years		5½ years		6 years		7 years	
	G	B	G	B	G	B	G	B	G	B	G	B	G	B	G	B
No answer	18	27	10	30	13	15	5	15	4	0	0	0	0	0	0	0
Fails all ages	82	73	88	70	87	85	80	75	28	27	12	20	2	8	0	0
Fails some ages	0	0	0	0	0	0	2	0	8	13	6	10	2	14	0	0
Ages correct	0	0	2	0	0	0	13	10	60	60	82	70	96	78	97	100
Names correct	45	38	43	32	32	35	32	25	96	100	100	100	100	100	100	100

5. How many brothers and sisters do you have? This question is very difficult for most preschoolers, as Table 9 shows. In fact, it is not till 5 years of age that most children can give ages and names of siblings correctly. According to our table, there is a big jump in ability between 4½ and 5 years of age. However, it must be remembered that our pre-schoolers are of a different group, somewhat lower socioeconomically than our 5-to-9-year-olds. Thus with middle- or upper-middle-class children, more success than our table shows would be expected at 4½ years of age.

As the table indicates, our 5-year-olds report well on siblings, as to both their names and their ages. Some report on the family group more easily than do others. Many FIVES are so concerned about their family group that they include themselves along with siblings. Some even include their parents and household pets.

A reference to girls or boys is common at 5, even though the child has been asked about "brothers" and "sisters." Children in the 5-to-6-year-old range often report about siblings they don't have, as "I don't have any brothers, just sisters."

It is interesting to note the way children organize their siblings in their minds, whether they separate the boys from the girls, seriate them from oldest to youngest or vice versa, name their favorites first, etc. Those who have trouble with age are apt to refer to size, as "big" and "little." As they become able to grasp age, they may refer to "older" or "younger."

6. What does your daddy do? Replies to this question do not lend themselves well to tabular analysis. The important thing is to find out if the child has a concept of his father going out of the home to work. Many 5-year-olds still refer to their immediate knowledge of their father as they see him around the house: "He works down in the cellar"; "He eats dinner"; "He digs in the garden." Preschoolers, obviously, have even less concept of their father's business or profession.

A fair number of FIVES do know that their father goes to some special place to work, such as a farm, a garage, a bank, an office building. By 5½, many are more aware of what he does: "He makes telephones"; "He prints"; "He makes plans for boats"; "He fixes things." Even at 5 a child may be able to report that his or her father is a dentist, an engineer, or an electrician.

It almost seems that understanding of what father does is more an individual matter than a question of the child's age. Thus some even at 5½ appear to have only the vaguest notion of what their fathers do. Others may report such professions as draftsman, police auxiliary, or bank executive. It is often the quality of response which tells us about the child's notion of father and what father does rather than whether or not the child can give *some* reply.

CHAPTER *4*

PAPER AND PENCIL TESTS

|||||||||||||||||||||||||||||||||||||||||||||||||||||||||||||||||||||||||||||||||||||||

NAME AND ADDRESS

Administration

When the initial interview has been completed (or for preschoolers, after the subject has finished with the cubes), the examiner directs the child's attention to the green 8½-by-11-inch paper and the pencil on the table.

The examiner asks the child: "Can you write your name?" If the child cannot, say: "Can you write any letters, like the letter *A* or the first letter of your own name?" Do not push beyond this point if the child cannot respond, and most 2½- and 3-year-olds cannot.

If the child *is* able to write or print his name with his dominant hand, he is asked to write his first name with his nondominant hand. The examiner requests: "Now write your first name with your other hand." The child may say that he cannot. If so, he is asked to write only the first letter of his name.

By 8 years of age, the child is initially asked to write his *name and address*. If he says he can't write his address, he is asked to tell it. Then he is asked to write any part of it that he can. Often he stops after writing his street address. He is then asked if there is anything more to his address. This may remind him of the rest, but more often he will need to be asked specifically about the town and state.

The examiner will record responses on a separate recording sheet (test page 3).

Findings

WRITING NAME (OR LETTERS)

As Table 10 shows, few 2½-year-olds, 3-year-olds, or even 3½-year-olds make even random letters, let alone show any ability to print their

29

first name, but by 4 years of age slightly over one quarter of our subjects do make random letters. By 4½, about one third can manage random letters (only) and nearly another third can print their first name. Few go beyond that until 5 years of age.

The 4-year-old dashes out his strokes and may make his letters in a lying-down position. But by 5, most have grasped the concept of their own name, and 70% of the girls, 56% of the boys, can make at least their first name. A substantial number of these also can make at least the first letter of their last name and a scattering can print their full name. At 5, then, first name or better becomes normative. By 5½, first name and the initial letter or all of the second name is normative; and by 6 years of age and following, both boys and girls are expected to manage both first and last name.

By 5½ years, one can expect the "correct" use of small letters and capitals. And by 7, the child shows that he has come through in all sorts of ways, and is definitely on surer ground. Reversals and substitutions, so common especially at 5½, are no longer a problem to most. If they do occur, the child recognizes them, can erase them, and then can make them right.

The 7-year-old sees the relative values of capital and small letters even though he may struggle with their various usages until he is 10. But he no longer mixes them at random or executes the small letters as if they were capitals. He now feels comfortable with small letters.

SEVEN's control of his stroke is shown by the fact that his letters are now medium in size. He had tended, earlier, to make very large letters, as well as to execute his letters in an uneven fashion. Now he executes his letters more evenly (72% of girls, 54% of boys). By 7, too, there is good spacing between first and last names. However, a straight baseline is not normative in both sexes until 9 years of age.

The placement of the name on the page also tells something of age. Nearly one third or more of 5- and 5½-year-olds place their name in the lower half of the sheet of paper. By 6, this number tapers off. Six tends to place his name in the upper-left-hand corner of the page, and this position predominates from 6 on. A tendency to place the name at the top center of the page at both 7 and 8 years of age (16% ±) may be either an individual or an age response.

SEX DIFFERENCES

Any writing of name or letters in the preschool years is so minimal that few consistent sex differences are apparent, but at 5, when this ability is really coming in, girls are somewhat ahead of boys, with 70% of girls making first name or better, only 56% of boys. After 5, nearly all children of both sexes can print their first name or better.

However, so far as quality of printing or writing goes, girls in general

TABLE 10 *Writing Name and Letters*
(Percentage of Responses)

	2½ years		3 years		3½ years		4 years		4½ years		5 years		5½ years		6 years		7 years		8 years		9 years	
	G	B	G	B	G	B	G	B	G	B	G	B	G	B	G	B	G	B	G	B	G	B
No response	97	100	95	97	87	88	53	75	30	45	4	20	0	0	0	0	0	0	0	0	0	0
Random letters	3	0	5	3	10	12	30	23	30	30	26	24	4	2	0	0	0	0	0	0	0	0
First name only	0	0	0	0	3	0	17	2	30	23	44	36	42	46	10	10	2	2	0	2	0	0
First letter or letters of last name	0	0	0	0	0	0	0	0	8	2	10	12	10	30	20	16	0	0	0	0	0	2
First and last names	0	0	0	0	0	0	0	0	2	0	16	8	44	22	70	74	98	98	100	98	100	98

are somewhat more advanced than boys. Thus at 7 years of age, a time when both sexes are improving markedly, 82% of girls but only 56% of boys make medium-sized letters; and also at 7, 72% of girls but only 54% of boys make letters of a consistently even size. An even baseline is normative in girls at 7 years and again at 9, though not at 8; in boys an even baseline is not normative till 9 years of age.

ADDRESS

Though most are not ready to write their address at 7 years of age, they are asked at this age if they can write it. SEVEN may be fully capable of writing his whole name, but the addition of his address is definitely beyond most. The child of 7 may not even know the meaning of the word "address," or he may give his telephone number instead. But as soon as the examiner asks him where he lives, he can readily supply the answer. Maybe he will give only his street address initially, but he can usually be prodded to give his city and state. Many, however, are not interested in writing any part of it.

By 8 years of age, most are ready to tackle this task, even though it is not altogether easy for them; and most would prefer to write only their street address. They do not yet grasp the total concept of a name and address as it would be placed on a letter, but tend to string it out on one or two lines (60%). At 8 years of age, 54% of girls and 46% of boys can give their street and number, city and state, and nearly all can give these four items at age 9. However, errors, especially in punctuation, persist through 10 years.

NAME AND ADDRESS

It is not until 9 years of age that the child grasps the concept of placing his name and address on three or four lines (72% G, 66% B) as one does on an envelope. (See Table 11.) (It is no wonder that with his new-found ability, the 9-year-old begins to use the United States Postal Service, sending in box tops, asking for information.) Though cursive writing has been introduced in the school curriculum, many shift to printing their address after writing their name in a cursive style. NINE may still have trouble remembering that words should be capitalized. His spelling may not be the best, but he knows how to place his name and address on a sheet of paper or on an envelope, and can put this ability to use.

It is interesting to scrutinize NINE's method of writing because it is a definite mark of his age. First of all, it tends to be smaller than it was; the child of this age is coming into good precision. Secondly, his letters are well formed, with a tight but rounded stroke. This is no product of the Palmer method, but rather the result of the intricate organization of NINE's mind.

Nine is the age when the child enjoys the flow of cursive writing,

TABLE 11   *Address*
(Percentage of Responses)

	7 years		8 years		9 years		10 years	
	G	B	G	B	G	B	G	B
Part Correct								
Street number	14	6	86	76	100	100	100	100
Street	12	6	86	82	100	100	100	100
City	6	2	56	48	100	100	100	100
State	6	2	56	40	98	100	98	100
All four	6	2	54	46	98	100	98	100
Errors								
Shift from cursive to printing			14	16	6	12	0	4
Does not capitalize			32	32	14	28	8	8
Extra capitals			6	6	0	0	2	2
Wrong spelling			26	20	12	24	2	6
Wrong punctuation			32	50	74	78	70	60
Number of Lines Used (Name and Address)								
One line			22	30	10	10	4	18
Two lines			38	30	18	24	12	28
Three lines			24	14	58	50	66	42
Four lines			4	6	14	16	18	12
Three or four lines			28	20	72	66	84	54

when he wishes to master it. As we see him struggle with cursive writing at 8, with letters growing larger, lines drooping down, we might question the reason for instituting cursive writing in the third grade. Printing is still more congenial to the 8-year-old, whose desire for speed is hampered by cursive writing.

DATE

Correctly naming the date (which includes month, day of month, and year) may seem easy to the 8-year-old, but the history of this ability to name a moment in time is long and complicated.

The 2-year-old thinks of the day in its 24-hour span, dividing it into night and day, darkness and light. The 3-year-old gives the day its parts, thinking of it in terms of morning and afternoon. By 4, days are known to have names such as "Saturday when Daddy is home." By 5, the child knows all the days of the week, separately and in order.

The child has already, by 4 years of age, begun to grasp the concept of seasons, especially the extremes of summer and winter. By 5, these seasons can be broken up into months. FIVE begins to learn the names of months as earlier he learned the names of the days of the week, but he still needs to cling to happenings and special occasions, such as Halloween and Christmas. By 6 it is the month of his birthday that has specific meaning for him. It will be another year before he can give the day of his birth.

When a child knows his birthday date, he is ready to start thinking of time in relation to date. The calendar has interested him since he was 5. Initially it was the numbers that interested him most. By 7 most are ready to name though not necessarily to write the day's date.

Administration

As with address, the 7-year-old may best be asked to give the date without being asked to write it. SEVEN's laborious and time-consuming execution in writing needs to be kept at a minimum during the test situation. He reveals himself in so many other, more important ways.

But his knowledge of the date, when he is asked: "What day is it today?" gives a clue as to his orientation to the naming of time. If he gives the name of the day of the week, as Tuesday, he is then asked: "What month is it?"

If he cannot answer this, he may be asked if it is some specific month other than the correct one (such as December, when it is June). He is then asked the day of the month. If he cannot answer this, he may be asked if it is the beginning, middle, or end of the month. Finally he is asked what year it is. If he cannot answer, he is asked if it is some far-fetched year, such as 1492. (This type of questioning may also be needed for an older child in case he cannot give the date.)

By 8 years of age the child is asked to write the date without any preliminary questioning. He may need to be asked specific questions such as the above to encourage his writing. If he omits the year, he should be asked if he has completed the date. If this does not give him a clue, he should be asked what year it is. Any specific clues given should be recorded in parentheses, such as "(year)," indicating that the examiner had to give the child the idea.

Findings

The ability to write the date in its complete three-part form is well established by 8 years of age (82% to 92%). Our figures at 7 (30% ± success) show a beginning interest. As with some other behaviors, the half-year period of 7½ may show the beginning of a normative rating.

Most children are highly accurate about day, month, and year at 8 years and following. (See Table 12.)

When the date is asked directly after the writing of name and address, the child usually places it under his name and address, if it is organized in three or four lines, or he continues on the same line if name and address are placed on one or two lines. A few separate the date from name and address, especially to the upper right half of the paper or even the upper right corner.

TABLE 12   *Writing Date*
(Percentage)

	7 years		8 years		9 years		10 years	
	G	B	G	B	G	B	G	B
Succeeding								
Any date	32	34	92	86	98	98	100	100
Month	32	28	90	86	98	96	100	100
Day	26	20	90	86	98	96	100	100
Year	32	30	92	82	94	96	100	100
Errors in Punctuation								
Omits dot for abbreviation, or comma			6	6	4	16	8	14
Misuse of punctuation			2	0	0	0	2	2
Unnecessary dot where no abbreviation			4	4	6	6	2	14

Errors in writing the date are few from 8 years on. Errors in punctuation are also limited, but do point up difficulties which some children experience. Punctuation is more often omitted, but it also may be overused, as when a dot is unnecessarily placed after the unabbreviated name of the month.

NUMBERS

Administration

If the child has been able to write name or letters, the examiner then asks: "Can you write any numbers?" If there is no response, say: "Can you make a number 1?" Again, most 2½- and 3- and 3½-year-olds, and many 4-year-olds, cannot write any numbers, and thus the examiner should go on very quickly to the next task.

At 5 years of age a child's ability to write numbers tends still to be very spotty. He is asked to write what numbers he knows after he has completed printing the letters he knows. If he asks, as he often does, where he should put them on the paper, he is told to place them wherever he chooses.

After 5½ years, when the ability to write numbers has markedly improved, this task is delayed until after the three-dimensional forms have been tried. The child is then asked to write his numbers from 1 to 20, or as far as he can go. Part of the reason for this delay is to see how he will utilize the space left on the page and whether or not he will feel the need for starting a new page.

Writing of numbers is a good opportunity for the examiner to observe the child's pencil grasp, and to record any observations about this, along with the recording of the numbers written. The posture and behavior of the child's nondominant hand is as important as that of the dominant hand. Is it flat on the tabletop and held close to the dominant hand? Does it move as the dominant hand moves? Does the child shift the paper instead of moving his hands? Does the nondominant hand stabilize the paper? Is the nondominant hand placed inside the dominant hand and thus crossed over to the right side of the paper (if the child is right-handed)?

Findings

As Table 13 shows, it is close to 5 years of age before a substantial number of children can write their numbers up to 5; $5\frac{1}{2}$ years of age before they can write up to the number 6 or more. By 6 years, the ability to write to 20 is close to a normative level (42% G, 56% B). Since figures for success in writing up to 20 are almost at the 100th percentile at 7 years, we may conjecture that a substantial growth must have occurred at $6\frac{1}{2}$ years.

FIVES, especially, may omit numbers as they write a sequence. There may be some mixing up of order, but on the whole this is negligible. Or numbers may be confused with letters.

ORGANIZATION OF LINES

Of the few children under 5 who do make numbers, most place them at random. From $5\frac{1}{2}$ on, most make them in a horizontal line. To write all twenty numbers on one line demands planning of space, and also an ability to write small enough so that all numbers from 1 to 20 will fit on one line. This ability shows a peak at 8 years of age (38% G, 36% B). If a second line or more is needed, the succeeding numbers are usually placed under the original line in a left-to-right direction. However, especially at 6 and 7 years, the second line may be placed above the first one, or the numbers may be placed from right to left or up and down. Or the paper may be shifted to a horizontal position, perhaps to secure a better expanse of space for writing the numbers horizontally.

SIZE

The size of the numbers made gives a very good clue to age. At 5 and $5\frac{1}{2}$ years the predominant size is large ($\frac{1}{2}$ to 1 inch). Even very large numbers, 1 to 2 inches in height, show up in sizable percentages (22% to 32%) at these same ages. This very large size does not occur after 6 years of age.

Six appears to be a transition age so far as size of numbers goes. By 7 and after, medium-sized numbers ($\frac{1}{4}$ inch $\pm$) predominate. The large-

TABLE 13 Numbers Written from 1 to 20

	4 years		4½ years		5 years		5½ years		6 years		7 years	
	G	B	G	B	G	B	G	B	G	B	G	B
No record	75	90	57	57	16	18	2	4	2	2	0	0
Fails	15	10	20	25	0	0	0	0	0	0	0	0
1 to 5*	8	0	15	18	38	66	20	24	6	2	0	0
1 to 6 or more (up to 10)	2	0	8	0	30	6	40	36	14	14	2	0
1 to 11 (up to 20)	0	0	0	0	14	10	38	36	78	82	98	100
1 to 20	0	0	0	0	2	0	16	8	42	56	96	100
Omits numbers	3	0	15	8	18	22	6	12	6	2	0	0
Mixes or reverses sequences	2	0	15	8	4	0	2	4	4	2	0	0
Confuses letters, numbers	0	0	0	3	0	4	0	0	0	0	0	0
Placement												
At random	8	0	12	8	?	?	0	4	0	2	2	0
Horizontal line or lines	2	0	10	10	?	?	92	78	86	74	84	88
1–20 on one line†	0	0	0	0	0	0	0	0	10	20	22	28
Baseline												
Uneven					70	66	78	84	74	84	26	32
Even					0	2	16	10	22	12	74	68
Spacing												
Inadequate record					44	56	8	6	4	2	0	0
Poor spacing					18	30	12	34	4	8	2	0
Fair spacing					38	14	70	58	78	84	58	68
Good spacing					0	0	0	2	14	6	40	32

* At 4 and 4½ years, those in this category do not necessarily get up to 5; may in fact make only the 1.
† This item does not become normative during the first ten years.

sized numbers are almost nonexistent from 8 years on, but small numbers ($\frac{1}{8}$ inch $\pm$) increase at 8 years and reach their high point at 9 years (36% G, 46% B). (Letters, too, tend to be small at 9 years of age.)

The relative size of numbers is also significant. In the early ages—5 to 6 years—before a greater stabilization of evenness has occurred, one can almost feel the dynamics of energy exchange as one views the shifting size of a child's numbers. Some get larger as the child proceeds, others get smaller, or they may fluctuate. By 7 years of age, numbers are executed more evenly (68% G, 50% B), and this evenness increases steadily into 10 years of age.

BASELINE AND SPACING

Along with an evaluation of size, it is important to evaluate the baseline and also the spacing of the digits, especially digits in the teens. An uneven, often undulating baseline persists through 6 years of age. At 7 years, there is a sharp switchover into a predominantly even baseline, and this predominates thereafter. (See Table 13.) This again suggests that a marked area of growth has occurred at $6\frac{1}{2}$ years.

Correct spacing is more difficult to achieve. Spacing may well have something to do with rhythm. Jangly, poor spacing, especially in boys, shows up very clearly at 5 and $5\frac{1}{2}$ years. Good spacing does not become normative till 9 years of age.

A rhythmic shift in spacing is often noted in writing the teens. A fairly typical example of this shift is a short interval between one number and the next in the early double numbers (10 to 12), followed by a widening of the spacing in the mid-teens, and again a narrowing of the spacing at the end of the series (18 to 20). When an examiner has once noted this type of spacing, he can easily recognize it thereafter. This rhythmic spacing shows a marked increase in girls at 7 years (30%) and persists from 8 to 10 years at a fairly high level (14% to 22%).

The good spacing which begins at 6 years increases steadily until it reaches a normative level at 9 years (76% G, 56% B).

REVERSALS

Reversals show up mostly in the years 5 to 6. The numbers 1 and 8 cannot be reversed from right to left or vice versa, but they can be executed in reverse (from the bottom up). Similarly, the zero is often reversed by being drawn clockwise from the bottom up. We lack figures, but our impression is that the shift in direction occurs more often in boys, and mostly from 5 to 6 years of age.

The position of the parts of a double number may be reversed without reversing the numbers themselves. Thus 10 becomes 01, 20 becomes 02, and 14 becomes 41, though they may be formed correctly and, as in 14, the 1 may be written before the 4. It is interesting to note that reversals of

10 and 20 are likely to occur as isolated reversals, suggesting that the strain of these transition points may have produced the reversal. (The strain of the transitional points is also evident when a child is counting. He may be going along splendidly and then get stuck at 29 or 99.)

Rather than reversing the actual position of the double-number digits, the child may reverse them merely by writing the second digit first. Thus a 16 may be made by first writing the 6 and then placing the 1 in front of it. This occurs especially at 6 years of age (26% G, 30% B) and continues minimally through 8 years of age. It is still present in a few boys at 9 (8%). It can readily be understood that a boy who continues to execute his double numbers in this way cannot build up the rhythmic flow of spacing that one anticipates by 9 and 10 years of age.

This flow can also be broken into when the child stumbles on a number, even though he may then be able to correct himself. This stumbling occurs especially at 7 and 8 years (24%, 16% G; 24%, 28% B). A few boys still stumble on numbers as late as 9 years of age (20%).

The number of reversals made is sizable, especially at 5½ years (62% G, 60% B). There is a definite reduction at 6 years, when the normative subject does not reverse (52% G, 64% B). This absence of reversals increases definitely at 7 years (88%) and reversals are not expected from then on.

CHAPTER 5

COPY FORMS

|||||||||||||||||||||||||||||||||||||||||||||||||||||||||||||||||||||

Introduction

One of our basic and most effective ways of measuring child behavior is the Copy Forms test, in which the child is asked to copy the following six forms:

In his response to these forms the child seems to give evidence of recapitulating the history of the race. As we see him struggling from one stage to the next, we somehow come to know what mankind must have struggled through from its primitive beginnings to its modern stance of civilization, precarious as that sometimes appears.

Behavior growth in its orderly way, if we but know this order, demands that one stage follow another. Over the years, in our own study of infant and preschool behavior, we have been fascinated by the child's response to pencil and paper. At first it is the paper itself that intrigues the infant of, say, 7 months. He wants to get it in his hands and to crumple it. He likes the sound it makes and he loves to tear the paper and bring it to his mouth.

A big red crayon, which may be presented in place of a pencil up to 3 or 4 years of age, is an interesting object to this same 7-to-10-month-old or slightly older infant, but nothing more. He will pick it up in one hand, transfer it to the other, bring it to his mouth, chew on it, and bang it till it finally breaks.

It is not until around a year of age that the infant bangs the crayon

As an aid to evaluation of the Copy Forms product, we provide, through Programs for Education, 101 Park Avenue, Suite 1236, New York City, 10017, a set of *Copy Forms Playing Cards,* which illustrate typical responses at all age levels.

40

against the paper, making marks of which he is aware. By 15 months, his own back-and-forth arm movements against the tabletop suggest that he is getting ready to make a horizontal scribble.

Within a few months he will be able to make a more selective, isolated stroke. At 18 to 21 months he shows this new readiness as he goes on his daily walk. He selects any stick he can find, squats down, and strokes with it on sidewalk or earth. It is a vertical stroke that he makes, more often drawn toward him.

When confronted with a paper and crayon at this age, he will obligingly imitate a *vertical stroke*, but a *horizontal stroke* is beyond him until he is 27 months of age. To combine these two strokes takes considerably more time. By 30 months he will make two parallel strokes in imitation, but they do not cross. It is not until 3 years that the average child can successfully imitate a *cross*.

At the same time that the child is mastering the control of the vertical and horizontal stroke he is also struggling with the circular movement. The 15-monther can scribble back and forth in a continuous stroke, but to bend this stroke into a *circular scribble* will take another 6 to 9 months. This circular scribble may reverse itself at 2½ years. Finally, by 3 years of age or younger, the child is able to stop on the first circle around, making a *single circle*, but this does not complete the ability to make an effective and usable circle. Many stages will need to be traversed before this form becomes an integral and very important part of his handwriting.

The next stage after the cross in the use of vertical and horizontal is to put two of each of these strokes together in a square formation. At first the child sees the square more as a circle, or at least he draws it as such. In the years that precede the time when he can imitate a *square*, at 4 years of age, he has been preparing to take this step of expressing a square space in miniature. At first it is the sides of the square which he sees, wherefore he often makes two vertical lines and crosses them with two horizontal lines with very sloppy corners. He will gradually become better able to turn the corner with his pencil, as he makes a square. The multiple ways in which children copy the square formation will be discussed later on.

Following the mastery of the square comes the conquest of the *triangle*. It is only as we see a child of 6 or 7 years still having difficulty in executing an oblique stroke that we realize what an accomplishment the ability to copy a recognizable triangle at 5 really is. What is this oblique, other than a modification of both horizontal and vertical lines? This is a more complicated stroke, but like all complicated processes, once it is mastered it simplifies further development. Note how often the child who has trouble in the early school years and who has trouble in grasping reading may also have had trouble in mastering the use of the oblique stroke earlier.

The fifth form, the *divided rectangle*, as it is called, is a unique form in that it combines the preceding three forms in some way or other. From the vantage point of the study of development, this Copy Forms test is a gold mine. Even now, after years of experience with this test, we have in no way mined all its secrets. However, much has been revealed, even though there is still much to come.

Last but not least of the six forms to be copied is the *diamond*, in both horizontal and vertical orientation. How it captures the imagination of the child when he finally finds it within his grasp! He practices and practices so that he can reverse the oblique lines—so like a triangle and yet so different. Further discussion of behavior stages in response to this form will reveal how different!

The seriated use of these six forms is a manifestation of the genius of Arnold Gesell. He did not live to see the full impact of these forms' revelation of growth, but he firmly established the groundwork for this test.

And finally, for children from 5 years on who have responded well to the original six forms, we have added two three-dimensional objects: a 1.5-inch cylinder and a cube. The cylinder alone is presented at 5 and 5½ years. By 6 years, the cube can be presented, first in a face-on and then in a point-on position.

Administration

MATERIAL

Examiner: Test page 3

Copy Forms cards: Circle, Cross, Square, Triangle, Divided Rectangle, and Diamond in two positions

Extra sheets of green paper

Child: 8½-by-11-inch sheet of green paper and a sharp No. 2½ pencil

GENERAL DIRECTIONS

The green sheet of paper is placed in front of the child in a vertical position, with the pencil in the middle of the sheet, pointing away from the child. Further sheets of paper are provided if the child asks for them or whenever the examiner judges that the record is becoming unreadable.

The circle, cross, or square, but not the other forms, should be demonstrated by the examiner if the child's copy is clearly inadequate. If a child is unable to copy any form, do not present the next form. Center any demonstration needed at the top of the child's page, always starting on a new page.

PROCEDURE

Place the Copy Forms cards in a pile above the upper edge of the child's paper. Indicate the top card, which shows a circle. Say: "Make one like this on your paper."

As each form is completed by the child, remove the card so that the next form can be seen, and say: "Now make this one."

If the child is under 3½ or fails to copy the circle, give horizontal and vertical strokes as follows:

Horizontal and Vertical Strokes

Vertical Stroke: Secure the child's attention and, using a pencil, draw a straight vertical line the length of the paper, near the edge of the paper at the child's left. Say "Make it go down like this" (dramatic gesture and inflection).

Hand a pencil to the child and say: "Now *you* make one." If necessary, give the child three trials, demonstrating each time.

Horizontal Stroke: Secure the child's attention and, using a pencil, draw a horizontal line across the whole top of the paper, from left to right as viewed by the child. Say: "Over like this."

Hand a pencil to the child and say: "You make one." If necessary, give the child three trials.

Circle, Cross, and Square

If the child is unable to copy the circle, cross, or square from the model, the examiner should demonstrate these drawings immediately following the child's effort at each, and have the child imitate this demonstration on the same page.

Demonstration of Circular Stroke: Draw a continuous circular line, starting your circle at the top and saying: "Around like this."

Demonstration of Cross: Make the vertical line first, and say: "Down like this." Then make the horizontal cross line, going from left to right and saying: "And over like this."

Demonstration of Square: Make the two vertical lines first, starting with the one on the left. Say: "Down like this and down like this." Then make the two horizontal lines, starting with the top one and saying: "Over like this and over like this. Now you make one."

Demonstrations are made at the top of the child's page, but only one demonstration on a page. Demonstrations—only one for each form—should be fairly large—about 2 inches per line.

Three-Dimensional Forms

If the child has succeeded or has made a good attempt at copying all six forms, two three-dimensional objects, a 1.5-inch cylinder and cube are presented, and the child is asked to draw a picture of each on the paper, the examiner saying "Draw this the way it looks to you." The cylinder alone is presented at 5 and 5½ years. By 6 years, the cube can be presented, first in a face-on and then in a point-on position.

In the early stages of copying, at 5 to 6 years, when it is difficult to know what part of the three-dimensional form the child is drawing since he usually draws but one surface, it is wise to ask: "What part did you draw?" He may be able to respond with "Top," "Bottom," or "Whole thing." But if he cannot respond, he may be asked: "Did you draw the top, the bottom, or the whole thing?"

RECORDING

Record on test page 3 all comments made by the child as he works. Check in the appropriate space the child's dominant hand. Describe pencil grasp. Record direction of strokes with arrows and also indicate starting points and paper shifts.

Indicate need for additional questions with a / mark.

After the test is completed, transfer to the child's page directional arrowheads and number of strokes. Above any unrecognizable form draw a small replica of what the form is supposed to be.

COPY CIRCLE

Except for the vertical and horizontal lines, not usually given after 2½ years of age, the circle is the first form to be mastered. Though before 3 years of age some children can merely *imitate* this form, by 3 years and thereafter, copying a *recognizable* circle or better is normative in girls and boys.

An *acceptable* circle—that is, one which is well proportioned—comes later. It is normative in girls from 5½ years, in boys from 6 years. (See Table 14.) The roundness of this *acceptable* circle is confirmed by actual measurement of the relationship of the horizontal to the vertical diameter. By 6, there is a definite reduction in the oval circle (flat, vertical, or oblique), the wobbly circle, the lopsided circle, and the circle with over-lapping or open closure point.

These last four are all reminiscent of the preschool years, when the stroke may be wobbly in character and there may be real difficulty in closure, either in missing the mark or in overemphasizing the closure point. The lopsided circle is of special interest since it suggests the 3½-year-old's difficulty in the last half journey of his circle. He starts out so well with a nicely formed half circle, only to wobble back to the beginning point by truncating the form. The 5-to-6-year-old's lopsided circle does not show this extreme, but the return path of the last half may be difficult and often produces a wobbly and shortcut path.

Special aspects of the circle which the examiner will keep in mind are its decreasing size with age, and the changing starting point and direction of drawing.

During the earliest preschool years a child's circle, and other forms, may fill a whole page, so that he makes only one form to a page. But by 4, and increasingly by 4½, size is reduced so that all forms made may be crowded onto a single page.

The place of starting and direction of drawing are highly significant even though difficult to demonstrate normatively in the early years. In following individual children longitudinally, we have observed that at the earliest ages, 3 or 3½ years, many boys and girls start their circle at the top and draw it counterclockwise. Such circles tend to be large and wobbly, but the direction is that usually taken by a right-handed adult.

Some six months after such a circle is drawn, many shift both starting point and direction. They start at the bottom and draw in a clockwise direction. This manner of drawing continues until 5 or 5½, when the original method is resumed.

However, since the time of the earliest change is a highly individual matter—some have already shifted to bottom up and clockwise by 3 years of age—Table 14 does not clearly reveal these changes. It shows merely that a top start and counterclockwise direction is close to norma-

TABLE 14 *Copy Circle*
(Percentage of Occurrence)

	3 years		3½ years		4 years		4½ years		5 years		5½ years		6 years		7 years		8 years		9 years	
	G	B	G	B	G	B	G	B	G	B	G	B	G	B	G	B	G	B	G	B
Imitates recognizable circle or better	73	82	87	85	90	95	97	92	100	100	100	100	100	100	100	100	100	100	100	100
Copies recognizable circle	57	69	84	70	90	93	97	92	100	100	100	100	100	100	100	100	100	100	100	100
Copies acceptable circle	0	10	14	3	20	0	35	25	44	44	52	30	56	58	84	76	94	84	90	92
Starting point:																				
Bottom	23	21	30	33	47	28	38	35	18	48	14	26	4	20	0	4	0	2	0	4
Top	45	49	38	35	25	38	43	35	66	28	82	56	90	66	100	94	98	96	92	94
Right	13	10	5	18	10	13	3	8	4	8	2	8	6	10	0	2	2	0	6	2
Left	8	5	22	13	15	23	18	20	12	16	2	10	0	4	0	0	0	2	2	0
Other	11	15	5	1	3	0	0	2	0	0	0	0	0	0	0	0	0	0	0	0
Direction:																				
Clockwise	43	39	62	58	68	53	58	55	40	60	24	40	16	36	6	18	8	10	8	8
Counterclockwise	45	46	32	40	30	48	43	43	58	40	72	58	82	60	86	82	90	74	84	92
Other	12	15	5	3	3	0	0	3	2	0	4	2	2	4	8	0	2	16	8	0
Number of strokes:																				
1	88	85	95	97	97	100	100	97	98	100	96	98	98	96	92	100	98	84	92	100
2	0	0	0	0	3	0	0	0	2	0	4	2	2	4	8	0	2	14	8	0
Other	11	15	5	3	0	0	0	3	0	0	0	0	0	0	0	0	0	2	0	0

tive at 3 years of age and that the shift to bottom up and clockwise is increasing by 3½.

Later changes do become normative. Thus girls at 5 and both sexes at 5½ clearly are starting at the top and drawing counterclockwise. This tendency is even more prominent in the years that follow.

COPY CROSS

Imitating the examiner's demonstrated cross successfully—so that the product is recognizable as a cross—is normative at 3 years of age, and copying a recognizable cross from the printed model is normative by 3½ years. (See Table 15.) A perfectly proportioned cross comes in much later—normative in girls at 8 years, in boys at 9.

It may seem surprising that the crossing of a vertical line with a horizontal line could pose such problems for the preschooler. To the 4-year-old especially, it is almost as if the vertical line had bisected the horizontal line into two parts, one to the right and one to the left. (A similar but much less common response occurs when the horizontal stroke is left intact and the vertical line is bisected.)

When the horizontal line is made in two parts, each part is usually drawn out from the center or vertical stroke. The 4-year-old who shifts his pencil readily from one hand to another solves his problem by drawing the horizontal line at the right with his right hand and that at the left with his left hand. This phenomenon of split horizontal stroke occurs mostly in the preschool years and shows up only at the 5th percentile by 5½ years of age. Its presence, as with other splits, alerts us to a two-sidedness that has not yet taken the next integrative step.

The most common method used in copying the cross, well established by 5 years of age and often earlier, is the making of two lines, the vertical downward and the horizontal from left to right. Actually, this method predominates from 3 years on.

The vertical stroke up is made infrequently, its high point being 18% in boys at 5 years. The horizontal stroke made from right to left occurs mostly in left-handed boys and girls. Though this may be a reversal phenomenon at 5 and 6 years, it becomes the preferred method of drawing for left-handed children from 7 years on.

COPY SQUARE

Copying the square has long been considered a 4-year-old item, though 4-year-olds as a rule imitate rather than copy the form. Copying is thought to come in at 4½. Present data bear out our customary findings. At 4 years, 50% of girls, 55% of boys, can imitate a square and some of these can copy it. By 4½, copying a recognizable square becomes normative (65% G, 60% B). (See Table 16.)

However, a well-proportioned square has reached only around 40%

TABLE 15 *Copy Cross*
(Percentage of Occurrence)

	3 years		3½ years		4 years		4½ years		5 years		5½ years		6 years		7 years		8 years		9 years	
	G	B	G	B	G	B	G	B	G	B	G	B	G	B	G	B	G	B	G	B
Imitates recognizable cross or better	60	51	93	73	88	93	100	95	100	100	100	100	100	100	100	100	100	100	100	100
Copies recognizable cross or better	25	21	70	50	85	83	100	83	100	100	100	100	100	100	100	100	100	100	100	100
Perfectly proportioned cross	0	0	5	0	13	8	30	20	22	18	34	24	34	24	24	24	56	40	54	56
Number of lines:																				
4 or more	0	3	3	0	6	0	0	0	0	0	0	0	0	0	0	0	0	0	0	0
3	12	10	14	15	20	20	20	10	16	16	6	4	0	6	0	0	0	0	2	2
2	48	38	76	58	62	73	80	85	84	84	94	96	100	94	100	100	100	100	98	100

TABLE 16 *Copy Square*

	3 years		3½ years		4 years		4½ years	
	G	B	G	B	G	B	G	B
Imitates recognizable square or better	13	21	38	35	50	55	75	68
Copies recognizable square or better	5	3	19	20	35	35	65	60
Copies well-proportioned square	0	3	0	3	0	0	15	5

incidence even by 10 years of age. At 9, it is seen in only 34% of girls, 44% of boys. (See Table 17.)

Method of Copying

A method of drawing common in the preschool years is to make two parallel vertical strokes, which are then crossed top and bottom by two horizontal strokes. But already by 5, children show a variety of other ways of copying the square. With four sides to cope with, considerable variability is possible.

The too vertically shaped square so common at 4 is still conspicuous at 5 to 6 years of age, though it steadily decreases thereafter until it is negligible by 8 years and following. The horizontally shaped square, on the other hand, is minimal at 5 years and steadily increases until it predominates at 8 and 9 years, especially with girls (38% G, 42% B).

The outstanding method of copying the square at all ages from 5 years through 8 is in a counterclockwise (CCW) direction (see Table 17), most often with one continuous line, and most often starting with the left side down. This method or some near variation reaches normative proportions in both sexes by 5½ and 6 years (54% G, 50% B at 5½ years; 66% G, 64% B at 6 years), and gradually reduces in percentage from then on, though it is still the most common method of copying at 8 years of age (28% G, 32% B). The clockwise (CW) method of drawing is much less common, and most often starts with the right side down.

A method conspicuous at most ages may be described as a D formation.

With its variables, it ranges between 8% and 36%, showing a low point at 5½, 6, and 7 years. A form closely allied to the D form and called the broken D shows a definite rise from 8 years (up to around 14% at 9 years). Both the D and the broken D are among the more common adult methods of copying.

Starting the square with left side down may be compared with drawing the circle CCW and from the top down.

Another significant trend is that the continuous one-line stroke, which reaches a peak at 6 years (80% G, 72% B) and is still normative at 7 years (58% G, 66% B), breaks up into two, three, or even four strokes at 9 years. This breakup is still seen in the adult, in whom the D and the broken D forms are common. The shift of the bottom stroke of the broken D form, when it appears, suggests the strength of the drive to stroke from left to right.

A main difficulty in copying the square is to make good vertical and horizontal lines. One or more lines are often made at an oblique angle. This finding is quite persistent throughout, with a peak at 6 years (38% G, 36% B). Another error is the execution of lines with a wavy or circular stroke, but this does not assume any high proportion at any age. A single rounded corner, especially the last one drawn, occurs at 5 and $5\frac{1}{2}$ years, but only occasionally thereafter.

TABLE 17   *Copy Square: Number and Direction of Lines, Type of Structure*

	$4\frac{1}{2}$ years*		5 years		$5\frac{1}{2}$ years		6 years		7 years		8 years		9 years	
	G	B	G	B	G	B	G	B	G	B	G	B	G	B
Number of Lines Used														
1	24	32	56	44	70	72	80	68	58	64	52	40	28	32
2	16	18	34	30	18	20	14	22	22	28	26	42	26	32
3	12	8	2	4	6	6	2	4	18	6	16	8	26	12
4	38	32	6	20	4	2	4	6	2	2	6	10	20	24
Other	8	10	2	2	2	0	0	0	0	0	0	0	0	0
Type of Structure														
CCW	8	12	50	28	54	50	66	64	46	54	46	36	28	32
CW	16	20	10	24	24	32	14	8	12	12	4	4	2	0
All continuous	24	32	60	52	78	82	80	72	58	66	50	40	30	32
D formation	16	14	26	30	8	12	8	18	22	22	22	36	26	24
Broken D	12	2	2	6	6	0	8	2	8	6	14	14	16	20
All D	28	16	28	36	14	12	16	20	30	28	36	50	42	44
Variables	38	40	12	8	8	6	2	8	12	6	14	10	28	16
Parallel lines	8	12	0	4	0	0	2	0	0	0	0	0	0	8
Total	98	100	100	100	100	100	100	100	100	100	100	100	100	100
Well-proportioned	—	—	12	6	28	16	20	10	34	32	26	32	34	44

* *School Readiness* subjects. When data for 4½ are available for *School Readiness* subjects, they are used. Otherwise 4½ data are from our current preschool study.

TABLE 18 Copy Triangle

	3 years		3½ years		4 years		4½ years*		5 years		5½ years		6 years		7 years		8 years		9 years	
	G	B	G	B	G	B	G	B	G	B	G	B	G	B	G	B	G	B	G	B
Fails entirely or not given	100	100	97	84	77	90	28	56	20	10	2	0	2	0	0	0	0	0	0	0
Recognizable or better	0	0	3	13	20	5	72	44	80	90	98	100	100	100	100	100	100	100	100	100
Well-proportioned	0	0	0	3	3	0	18	14	14	20	38	42	36	50	56	68	78	62	66	64
Number of strokes:																				
1							8	14	26	20	36	30	40	38	30	30	20	32	12	18
2							26	26	46	36	34	52	40	32	52	48	30	26	26	26
3							50	40	28	44	30	18	20	30	18	22	50	42	62	56
Starting point:																				
Left side down									62	40	60	46	68	78	82	80	78	80	84	80
Left side up									14	16	14	10	14	8	6	6	8	8	14	12
Right side down									10	28	12	28	8	8	4	6	8	6	2	2
Right side up									2	4	4	4	4	0	6	2	4	2	0	0
Bottom L to R									6	8	10	12	6	6	2	6	2	2	0	6
Bottom R to L									6	4	0	0	0	0	0	0	0	2	0	0

* School Readiness subjects.

Closure points pose a problem, especially at 5 to 6 years. A line is apt to lap over, or two lines may cross (25% ±). Leaving an open space is less common (14% ±) and is not much of a problem after 5½ years. Some correct an open space by adding an extra separate line, and others adjust by turning an extra corner so they can contact the beginning line.

COPY TRIANGLE

The triangle presents a whole new problem both in the angled control of line required and in the conquest of the oblique stroke. It is not until 4½ years that the majority of girls can make a recognizable triangle. Boys do not make a recognizable triangle until 5 years of age. The figure does not attain good proportions until 6 years in boys, 7 in girls.

No single method of drawing reaches normative proportions, though a starting stroke of left side down is normative in girls from 5 years on, and in boys from 6 years. The leading single method at all ages (though even this ranges only from 22% to 34%) is a D formation, with left side down, a single second stroke made right side down, and a stroke across the bottom from left to right.

The number of strokes used, as Table 18 shows, is highly variable. When the triangle is first copied, there is a tendency for children to use three strokes. From 5½ through 7 years they are most likely to use only one or two; but at 8 years, three strokes are again coming into prominence and three strokes is the normative figure by 9 years of age.

DIVIDED RECTANGLE

The divided rectangle is an extremely challenging form, which tells us a great deal about the child. It is often viewed by the 4- and even the 4½-year-old as "too hard"; yet most from 4 on are willing to tackle it. There is little real success in the way of having the horizontal and angled lines cross the central vertical line until 5 years of age or later. Before that, assuming that the child goes beyond a mere scribble of lines, the so-called ladder formation—an outside square bisected by one vertical line with several short horizontal lines on each side but not crossing the center line—dominates.

Outside

During the preschool years, if this form is tried, the outside tends to be circular or square. Even as late as 5, some make a circular framework (8% G, 4% B), and a good many make a square (38% G, 42% B). However, the majority make some kind of rectangle. A vertical rectangle

TABLE 19 *Divided Rectangle*
(Percentage of Responses)

	4 years*		4½ years		5 years		5½ years		6 years		7 years		8 years		9 years	
	G	B	G	B	G	B	G	B	G	B	G	B	G	B	G	B
Pattern of the Outside																
No trial, no outside, or circular	80	97	34	34	8	4	0	0	0	0	0	0	0	0	0	0
Square	0	0	32	32	38	42	40	18	28	34	12	18	4	6	0	0
Vertical rectangle	0	0	20	14	16	14	4	20	8	4	2	4	0	2	0	0
Horizontal rectangle	20	3	14	20	38	40	56	62	64	62	86	78	96	92	100	100
Manner of Drawing Outside																
Continuous CW					16	20	18	36	18	26	24	12	10	8	6	2
Continuous CCW					30	18	44	44	56	44	36	56	28	34	12	24
All noncontinuous					54	62	38	20	26	30	40	32	62	58	82	74
Pattern of Inside																
Vague markings inside, or H line or lines			38	48	4	12	0	0	0	0	0	0	0	0	0	0
Central star patterns			14	16	12	6	8	6	4	8	0	4	2	0	0	0
Vertical cleavage, ladder design			34	10	38	32	36	28	22	24	20	26	6	20	8	4
Crossover patterns			6	18	46	50	56	66	74	68	80	70	92	80	92	96
Crossing of lines:																
3 cross at one point					2	8	16	10	20	24	16	18	34	28	40	32
4 cross at one point					6	0	0	0	14	2	14	12	24	14	28	32

* 4-year-old data from preschool; 4½ ff. from *School Readiness* subjects.

is made by 16% of girls and 14% of boys, but 38% of girls and 40% of boys make a horizontal rectangle.

As Table 19 shows, production of some kind of successful rectangular outside shape for the divided rectangle is normative at 5½ years and following. The method of making this rectangle varies widely. FIVE makes a noncontinuous rectangle, but a continuous CW or CCW line is normative in both sexes at 5½, 6, and 7 years. Some discontinuous method of drawing again prevails at 8 and 9 years.

Inside

Before 4 years of age, the divided rectangle is not given or is refused or failed by most children. At 4, though the majority fail, those who do attempt the form are likely to come up with rather a scramble of lines. At 4½, however, there is a tendency (34% G, 10% B) to make a so-called ladder design. This consists of a vertical line bisecting the outside form, with three or more (usually more) short vertical lines, *which do not cross the center,* on each side. This pattern continues in about one third of our subjects at 5 years of age, though at 5 some kind of crossover pattern is normative in boys, nearly normative in girls. At 5½ and following, crossover patterns are normative in both sexes.

Another pattern seen in a few children at 4 and 4½ years (from 6% to 16%) is the central star pattern—a central dot with radiating spokes.

Though at least some lines cross over the central vertical dividing line from 5 years in girls, 5½ in boys, as Table 19 shows, the crossing of all four lines at some single central spot is not normative in the present age range. Even by 9 years of age only 28% of girls, 32% of boys, achieve this perfection.

Contact Points Between Inner Lines and Frame

The spaces left between contact points in the divided rectangle are wider, the overlapping lines longer, than in any other form. Even so, it seems almost unbelievable that the contact with the frame could be missed by such a wide space as is left by many children, especially at 5 and 5½ years of age.

It seems that as the child concentrates on one aspect of the form, he cannot include all other aspects. Very wide spaces are uncommon after 5½ years of age. Missing the frame by a small space, however, is still strongly evident even at 7 years and though it definitely decreases, it is still present in a few children as late as 10 years.

The overlapping of inside lines over outside frame is even more in evidence and reaches a peak at 6 years of age (74%). Control of stroke slowly improves but is still a problem with a few as late as 10 years of age.

Corner Contacts

The success of corner contacts of the diagonals with the frame is in large part dependent upon whether the diagonal is started or ended in the corner in question. The chances of success are far greater for the start of a line than for the ending. The 5- or 6-year-old's line may wobble into a corner, but on the whole it has reached this corner only by great restabilizing efforts, or by chance. At 5 years the item "no correct corners" is so high that it is at near normative levels (46% G, 50% B).

A 5-year-old may have the full four lines crossing each other, but he has great trouble in controlling their angle. They may even land on top of each other. Corner contacts improve steadily with age. One or two are usually correct at 5½, 6, and 7 years, two or three at 8 and 9 years, and three or four at 10 years. When a child over 9 is still unable to contact one single corner, something may be seriously wrong with his perception and/or coordination.

COPY DIAMONDS

The diamond, the sixth and last of the Copy Forms, was an essential item included by Binet. He considered it to be a 7-year-old item, which it still turns out to be, with 76% of girls, 60% of boys, making it correctly at that age. (See Table 20.) But it has a long developmental history before and after the 7-year critical stage. Although Binet presented this form only in a vertical position, a conventional diamond position, we had it printed horizontally on our cards since it fitted better in this orientation.

Originally we shifted the card to present the diamond in a vertical position. Almost by accident, we stumbled onto letting the card remain in its original position, then presented it a second time in a vertical position. Frequently we noted that a child could copy the diamond in one position but not in the other. Responses to the horizontally and vertically presented diamond as shown in the accompanying table actually are very compatible, but there are some differences.

The need of the child to shift the horizontal diamond to a vertical position in order to draw it is four times as common as the opposite condition. Younger patterns are more persistent in response to the horizontal diamond, and when one form only is copied successfully, it is more often (three to four times) the vertical diamond in the period from 6 to 8 years, when there is a differential response to the two positions.

The 4-year-old initially views the diamond as being "hard," but still he is willing to tackle it. Even the younger, unsuccessful attempts do show some patterning, and reveal an edge of comprehending the form. These young patterns are seen most often at 5 and 5½ years. They vary from a primitive irregular blob, to a single line in either a vertical or a horizontal direction, to two lines, to a single open point, a point coming out of a shapeless mass, two points, three points, and finally a shape in which two side points jut out like ears. When closure is difficult, the form may even end with five sides. Another variable may be a horizontal or vertical rectangle, suggesting that the child recognizes the relative shape but cannot execute an oblique stroke.

On the whole, the three-sided form and the forms with ears are the most common of the younger patterns. They persist through 6 and even into 7 years of age. No younger patterns are used in reproducing the vertical (V) diamond, and virtually none in reproducing the horizontal (H) diamond, after 7 years.

Though the younger patterns predominate at 5 years of age, they rapidly reduce thereafter. Even by 5½ years the more patterned forms have reached a normative level. But the successful reproduction of both forms is not normative before 7 years of age. (See Table 20.)

The patterns of reproduction fall chiefly into the CCW and CW continuous forms, D and broken D patterns, and vertical and horizontal cleavage patterns. All continuous patterns combined reach normative values for the horizontal diamond at 7 years of age (54% G, 66% B) and for boys only (54%) for the vertical diamond at this same age. The CCW direction, mostly starting with left side down, definitely leads. The continuous method of drawing, however, decreases slowly from 7 years on.

The most common vertical cleavage pattern is made with two single side strokes,

as is also the two-line horizontal pattern.

The diamond may still be relatively successful, even with some quality flaws. The quality, however, becomes an important part of the final appraisal. Probably one good evidence of superiority is a relatively good diamond at 5½ or 6 years of age.

TABLE 20 Copy Diamonds
(Percentage of Occurrence)

	4 years*		4½ years		5 years		5½ years		6 years		7 years		8 years		9 years	
	G	B	G	B	G	B	G	B	G	B	G	B	G	B	G	B
Success in Copying the Diamond in Its Two Positions																
No trial or refusal	60	70	0	0	2	6	0	0	2	0	0	0	0	0	0	0
Neither acceptable	40	30	98	98	92	76	74	62	58	46	0	4	0	4	4	0
V alone acceptable	0	0	2	0	4	8	14	14	18	36	20	28	20	28	12	20
H alone acceptable	0	0	0	2	2	10	10	16	4	12	4	8	4	8	2	0
Both acceptable	0	0	0	0	0	0	2	8	18	6	76	60	76	60	82	80
Kinds of Errors																
Blob					6	2	0	0	0	0	0	0	0	0	0	0
Triangle with 3 points					30	34	20	18	6	10	0	0	0	0	0	0
Ears					24	10	24	24	30	16	20	2	0	0	0	0
Paper shifts to H, child draws V					0	0	0	2	0	0	8	4	2	10	10	4
H & V reversed					0	0	2	4	2	0	0	0	4	2	4	0
V drawn for both					4	8	6	8	6	4	2	6	4	4	2	0
Manner of Drawing ◇																
All CCW					2	2	20	20	22	26	24	40	20	34	18	16
All CW					6	20	14	8	12	16	30	26	8	12	4	22
All continuous					8	22	34	28	34	42	54	66	28	46	22	38
All noncontinuous					92	78	66	72	66	58	46	34	72	54	78	62
Manner of Drawing ◇																
All CCW					4	6	20	24	26	20	20	40	22	28	16	20
All CW					8	6	10	6	14	18	10	14	6	10	4	8
All continuous					12	12	30	30	40	38	30	54	28	38	20	28
All noncontinuous					88	88	70	70	60	62	70	46	72	62	80	72

* 4-year-old data from preschool data; 4½ ff. from *School Readiness*.

THREE-DIMENSIONAL FORMS

Cylinder

The 5-year-old is most likely merely to draw a circle in response to the request that he draw the cylinder (52% G, 60% B) and to report that he has drawn the bottom of the form, or the whole thing. A circle remains the preferred, though decreasing, method of copying through 6 years of age. However, at 6 most say that they have drawn the top of the cylinder. This single-circle method of copying is strong through 6 years and also in boys at 7, but uncommon after that.

Another fairly common method of copying, right through 8 years of age, is a front view drawn as a square or triangle. As a child begins to recognize surfaces, he may draw a square formation and then cut into it with a curved line at top and bottom. (See Table 21.) This response occurs, minimally, throughout the entire age range.

Another expression of the recognition of surfaces, which occurs in a few children, is to draw two ovals, one for the top and one for the bottom, either in vertical formation or one inside the other. A next step is to combine the two separate circles with vertical lines.

This response is coming in at 5½ and 6 years, is quite sizable by 7 years of age (22% G, 20% B), and still occurs conspicuously in boys at 9 years (24%). Children who make this response know the bottom of the cube exists and can't seem to eliminate it in their drawings even though they don't see it.

By 7 years of age many make a fair semblance of a cylinder, but the baseline is flat (24% G, 32% B). However, at 7 most use more or fewer than the expected four lines, suggesting a real struggle in the child's mind with surfaces and lines and their combination. By 8 years of age a curved baseline is coming in (22% G, 28% B).

Table 21 gives age changes in the response to Copy Cylinder.

Face-On Cube

Although the face-on cube is easier to copy as a single square surface through 7 years of age, the symmetry of the point-on cube becomes easier to master from 8 years on when the child has gone beyond the single-surface response.

With the face-on cube, the single square surface, which may relate to the bottom, the top, or the front surface, is normative from 5½ through 7 years. The next step is a response to the awareness of two surfaces, usually the top and the front. These two surfaces may be drawn in either

TABLE 21   *Copy Cylinder*
(Percentage of Responses)

	5 years		5½ years		6 years		7 years		8 years		9 years	
	G	B	G	B	G	B	G	B	G	B	G	B
No response	20	34	12	26	2	4	0	0	0	2	0	0
◯	**52**	**60**	44	48	34	46	12	26	8	0	4	2
8	0	0	6	4	20	12	22	20	14	8	6	24
⊟	0	0	2	2	6	14	24	32	26	24	34	32
⊟	0	0	0	0	0	0	8	0	22	28	36	38
Other	28	6	36	20	38	24	34	22	30	38	20	4
Total	100	100	100	100	100	100	100	100	100	100	100	100

TABLE 22   *Copy Face-On Cube*
(Percentage of Responses)

	5 years		5½ years		6 years		7 years		8 years		9 years	
	G	B	G	B	G	B	G	B	G	B	G	B
None	**78**	**72**	16	26	34	32	0	0	0	0	0	0
☐ (⊏⊐)	22	24	**82**	**72**	**56**	**60**	**78**	**56**	52	38	24	18
⊟	0	0	0	0	6	0	6	16	0	16	20	22
⊞	0	0	0	0	0	2	0	6	10	6	10	0
⊞	0	0	0	0	0	0	0	0	4	2	10	10
⊿	0	0	0	0	4	0	4	10	16	4	12	12
Other	0	4	2	2	0	6	12	12	18	34	24	38
Total	100	100	100	100	100	100	100	100	100	100	100	100

horizontal or vertical alignment. An awareness of and need to draw the bottom, as with the cylinder, occurs with some children.

An awareness of the side of the cube is beginning at 7 years, but doesn't come in strongly before 10. It is evidently difficult for the child to put the surfaces together. At times he draws both sides. A certain number at 9 years have learned the trick of a transparent drawing. Only a few, mainly boys, copy this form correctly even by 10 years of age (2% G, 20% B), though a few others are close to success as they make a good face-on cube but with a flat baseline (6% G, 10% B). (See Table 22.)

Point-On Cube

The point-on cube may not be attempted much before 7 years of age. SEVEN's capacity to draw a diamond shows up very nicely as he draws only the top surface of the point-on cube as a diamond shape (34% G, 44% B). This response remains fairly high at 8 years (22% G, 34% B). At the same time, a fair number are making a rather good reproduction of the cube, showing the two sides, but with a flat baseline to the figure. This type of response reaches a peak at 9 years of age (36% G, 32% B), but is superseded by a correct copy with angled baselines at 10 years of age in 34% of girls, 46% of boys. The success of the copy of this form is in marked contrast with that for the face-on cube, but for both forms the boys are definitely ahead of the girls. (See Table 23.)

TABLE 23   *Copy Point-On Cube*
(Percentage of Responses)

	5 years G	5 years B	5½ years G	5½ years B	6 years G	6 years B	7 years G	7 years B	8 years G	8 years B	9 years G	9 years B
None	82	74	84	66	44	62	12	0	4	0	0	0
▢ (▭)	12	10	6	8	14	8	8	10	2	2	2	2
◇	0	4	8	18	22	18	34	44	22	34	6	10
⬠	0	0	0	0	8	2	20	12	26	18	36	32
⬡	0	0	0	0	0	0	0	6	8	12	16	30
Other	6	12	2	8	12	10	26	28	38	34	40	26
Total	100	100	100	100	100	100	100	100	100	100	100	100

COPY FORMS: ORGANIZATION ON PAPER

Quite as telling as the way the individual forms are copied is the organization of all forms on the page. Rather clear age changes are evident in this respect, the range being from the very large one-form-to-a-page of the young preschooler to the single horizontal row or several horizontal rows taking up half a page or even less at the later ages.

SPACE USED

Children under 4 tend to require one whole page for each form imitated or copied. Even at 4 and 4½, the majority use more than one page for all the forms.

Improvement sets in at 5 years, when 72% of girls, 68% of boys, need only one half to one page for all forms. From 5½ years, substantial numbers of both sexes require even less than half a page.

Figures 1 to 5 illustrate typical changes which may be expected, and Table 24 presents the data in tabular form.

PLACE ON PAPER

The overall age trend is for figures to become increasingly small and less and less of the page to be used with increasing age. As Table 24 shows, 5-year-olds tend to use the whole page, more or less. From 5½, the largest number of subjects place forms in horizontal rows, though this does not become normative in girls until 7 years, in boys until 10.

From 5 through 7 years, substantial numbers of children place forms in more or less shapeless bunches (17% to 24%). An increasing number arrange figures in neatly boxed squares in one of the four quadrants of the page, though percentages are always small.

FIVES, when not using the whole page, may work initially in the lower half of it. By 6, most are able to orient toward the top of the page, more often to the left. This orientation suggests that the child is establishing a left to right direction.

If he orients initially in the center of the top of the page, he may work either from L to R or R to L, indicating that a single direction has not been established. Some who work in one quadrant of the page only can nevertheless maintain their L to R direction. When a shift in direction occurs as the child works, this suggests that other reversal patterns may also be present, as with reversal of letters or numbers so customary at 5½.

There are some children who need to make multiple starts. This is more common at 5 years. And there is the child who shifts his paper repeatedly so that he may execute each stroke as a vertical stroke toward himself, or away from himself: this suggests difficulty in orienting to a given position. The only way such a child can solve his problem is to shift

TABLE 24   *Copy Forms: Organization on Page*

	4 years G	4 years B	4½ years* G	4½ years* B	5 years G	5 years B	5½ years G	5½ years B	6 years G	6 years B	7 years G	7 years B	8 years G	8 years B	9 years G	9 years B
Amount of Space Used																
More than 1 page	65	72	52	68	6	10	8	4	4	2	2	4	2	6	12	4
½ to 1 page	32	25	38	27	72	68	50	56	60	50	60	40	50	60	74	60
Less than ½ page	3	3	10	5	22	22	42	40	36	48	38	56	48	34	14	36
Arrangement on Paper																
Random			52	32	26	32	26	30	22	18	16	18	12	18	10	20
Circular			20	46	42	42	28	16	26	16	18	16	22	24	12	12
Vertical			10	10	2	12	8	6	10	14	10	14	16	8	24	18
Horizontal			14	12	28	12	32	38	36	44	52	48	50	42	52	42
H & V mixed			4	0	2	2	6	10	6	8	4	4	0	8	2	8
Relative Size of Individual Forms																
Variable			70	56	42	54	40	46	38	30	24	34	32	32	30	34
Getting larger			8	16	6	14	14	24	20	30	22	18	10	20	14	14
Getting smaller			20	28	24	20	20	8	12	22	6	20	10	20	6	16
Even			2	0	28	12	26	22	30	18	48	28	48	28	50	36

* 4½-year-old data are from preschool data; the rest from *School Readiness*.

the environment, in this case the paper. These children often need an environment which will adjust to them until they have acquired the ability to adjust to their environment.

ARRANGEMENT OF FORMS ON PAGE

Table 24 gives a comprehensive idea of how organization develops in the years from 4½ to 9. Through 6 years of age there is considerable variation in performance from child to child. At 4½, placement is either at random (52% G) or somewhat circular (46% B). At 5 years of age, the largest number arrange forms in some sort of crude circular formation, either in or out of order. Conspicuous numbers, however (one quarter of subjects or more), still have merely random placement. Almost an equal number are already placing forms horizontally, in correct order.

By 5½ years, the largest number of subjects, though still only about one third, have horizontal placement. Horizontal placement predominates from here on, and becomes normative in girls at 7 years, in boys not until 10 years of age.

Figure 1. Sample Copy Forms pages at 3½ years

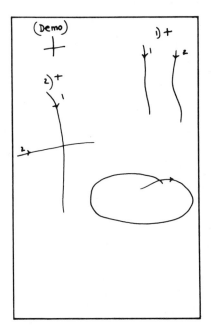

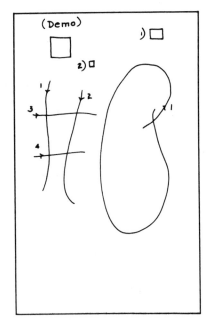

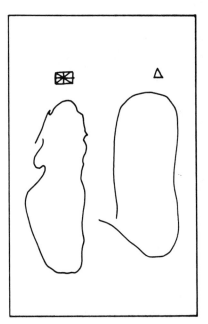

GIRL 3⁶

3½-YEAR HALLMARKS

1. Most characteristic is that the child needs to use several sheets of paper to complete the forms.
2. Succeeds at circle but even for cross cannot copy without demonstration.
3. Asked to copy the square, makes circular figure only and even with demonstration cannot achieve a "good" square.
4. Triangle and divided rectangle are quite beyond her, yet she is willing to attempt them. Forms now become blobs.
5. Note especially very large size of forms, the square, triangle, and divided rectangle each taking up nearly half of an 8½-by-11-inch sheet of paper.

Figure 2. Sample Copy Forms pages at 4 and 4½ years

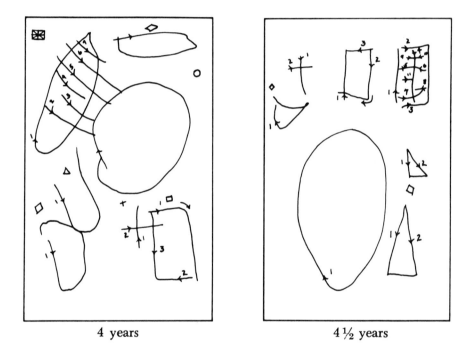

4 years   4½ years

BOY 4¹

4-YEAR HALLMARKS

1. Note the big improvement since 3½ years. Now child can reproduce more forms and in a more recognizable manner.
2. This 4-year-old is, characteristically, making his circle from the bottom up and clockwise.

3. Unlike his just-earlier self, he can now copy a square and usually does not need demonstration.
4. Triangle is beyond him. Copy of divided rectangle shows awareness that there are many lines, but he does not know what to do with them.
5. There is a tendency to return to blobs when forms become difficult.

BOY 4[6]

4½-YEAR HALLMARKS
1. Child now uses even less than a full page for his forms. He starts out with a large circle and then shows some awareness that other forms must be smaller, in order to fit on the page. (However, some still need more than one page.)
2. Note good cross with vertical line drawn top to bottom and horizontal line from left to right. Horizontal line slightly above midline.
3. Square is rectangular and triangle represents a very good try.
4. Divided rectangle is a typical 4½-year-old product, with center vertical line bisecting his outer figure and then ladderlike horizontal lines, some crossing and some not crossing center dividing line. Rectangle is made in a horizontal rather than in a vertical position.
5. Child is willing to tackle diamond in both orientations, though is still far from being able to make a "good" diamond.
6. As often during the preschool years, successive forms more or less circle around the initial circle instead of being placed in horizontal orientation as they will be later. (Order may be correct or at random.)

GIRL 5[3]

5-YEAR HALLMARKS
1. Circle is placed quite centrally on page; executed top down CCW, with some difficulty on last lap.
2. Cross has extra line added to equalize sides of H line on either side of V line.
3. One side of triangle is extended to match other side; baseline is at oblique angle.
4. Divided rectangle shows attempt to angle two lines from a central point; other two oblique lines are drawn H.
5. V and H diamonds show their position and general outline.
6. Forms vary in size, lines are at times wobbly, and organization is spotty.

GOOD QUALITY
1. Square is drawn CCW with continuous stroke.
2. Triangle has two good obliques.
3. Rectangle has one crossover line (H); two upper obliques are paired and lower ones are drawn in same direction.
4. Careful closure points.

LETTERS AND NUMBERS
At Age
Child writes only a few letters and numbers, placed in middle of page.
Quality

Figure 3. Sample Copy Forms pages at 5 and 5½ years

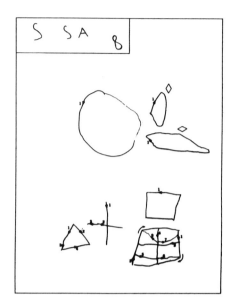

GIRL 5³

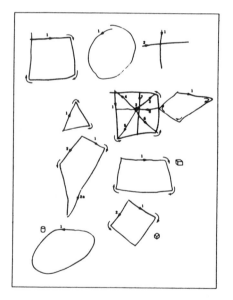

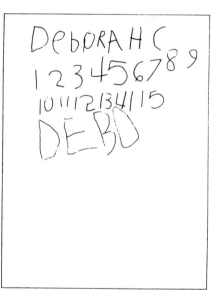

GIRL 5¹⁰

66

Execution is excellent. Figures are of relatively small size, and there is an excellent attempt to make an "8" in advanced pattern.

GIRL 5¹⁰

5½-YEAR HALLMARKS
1. Surety of stroke.
2. Beginning of organization with many shifts—circle is placed at top of page, cross and square on either side of it; H organization L to R on next line, then V organization.
3. One form runs into another.
4. Good centralizing of divided rectangle with a dot; central H line is from R to L.
5. Trouble with closure points—either has wide space, as with circle; or overshoots, as with square.

GOOD QUALITY
1. Fair consistency in size.
2. Good obliques in triangle.
3. Excellent H diamond.
4. Child is able to tackle point-on cube; draws top in diamond shape.
5. Closure points steadily improve.

LETTERS (WITH RIGHT AND LEFT HAND) AND NUMBERS
At Age
1. Child is able to write whole first name.
2. Small letters size of capitals—child prefers capitals; wavy baseline.
3. Child writes to 15; reverses 14 to 41; numbers vary in size; wavy baseline.

GOOD QUALITY
1. No individual letter or number reversals.
2. Organizes well on a line.

GIRL 6⁰

6-YEAR HALLMARKS
1. Divided rectangle drawn with crossover pattern; outside is a square; H central line from R to L.
2. V but not H diamond is correct.

GOOD QUALITY
1. Divided rectangle nicely executed, with central meeting point of all four lines.
2. Cylinder shows two parts.
3. Good closure points.

QUESTIONABLE QUALITY
1. Only one oblique to triangle.
2. Organization of forms around a central circle.

NUMBERS
At Age
1. Child writes numbers to 20.

Figure 4. Sample Copy Forms pages at 6 and 7 years

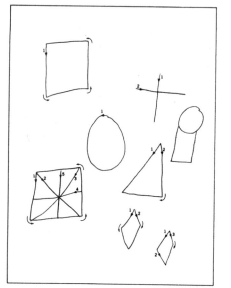

GIRL 6⁰

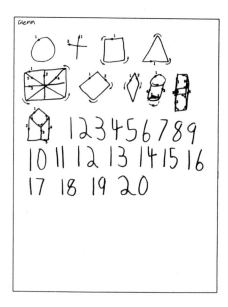

BOY 7⁸

2. Numbers are of variable size but tend to be big; no spacing; wavy baseline.
3. Child executes "9" in two parts.

At Age
1. Child writes full name (last name written but not shown).
2. Letters are medium to large.
3. Baseline tends to go down.
Quality
1. Child handles small letters well but still uses them as capitals (not shown).
2. Name placed third of way down paper (5½ years).

BOY 7[8]

AT AGE
1. Forms are relatively small, fairly even in size.
2. H-organization is consistent.
3. Divided rectangle has rectangular shape, crossover pattern; central H-line is from L to R.
4. Child draws relatively good V-diamond; fair H-diamond.
5. Child draws base of cylinder, but then erases.

QUALITY
1. Good placement on the page.
2. Good crossover pattern on divided rectangle.
3. Good point-on cube.

NAME AND NUMBERS
1. Excellent small printing of name (last name not shown), placed high in L corner.
2. Numbers nicely formed with spacing of teens (8 years), but large size (6 to 6½ years).

GIRL 8[4]

NAME (WITH RIGHT AND LEFT HAND), ADDRESS, AND DATE
1. Child writes cursively.
2. Child writes address on same line with name, plus second line. (Street not shown.)
3. Good date, with abbreviation and correct punctuation.

COPY FORMS
1. Organized horizontally, three on a line.
2. Fair size consistency.
3. Good quality: Central crossing of divided rectangle; rounded baseline of cylinder; good attempts at two cube positions.
4. Less good quality: Child uses continuous stroke for square, triangle, and diamonds. Triangle is vertical with oblique base. H-diamond has a curved line and points are off center.

NUMBERS
Small and moderately well executed. Separation of teens by spacing, but child still uses commas to separate numbers.

Figure 5. Sample Copy Forms pages at 8 and 9 years

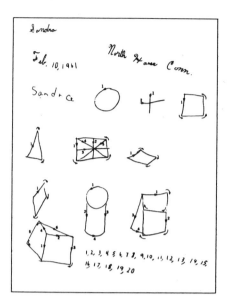

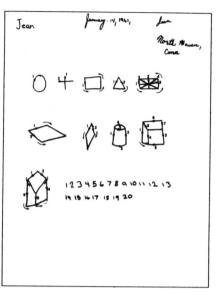

GIRL 8⁴   GIRL 9⁸

GIRL 9⁸

NAME (WITH LEFT AND RIGHT HAND), ADDRESS, AND DATE
1. Child organizes name and address nicely on four lines (fourth line not shown).
2. Typical, carefully formed 9-year-old cursive handwriting.
3. Date shows overuse of punctuation, with period after month.

COPY FORMS
1. Small, four or five on a H-line.
2. Nice breakup of lines of triangle and diamonds.
3. Oval top to cylinder, rounded baseline.
4. Partial angulation of lines of cubes—good quality.

NUMBERS
1. Adequately formed.
2. Some irregularity in size, spacing, and angle of stroke.

RELATIVE SIZE OF INDIVIDUAL FORMS

The individual forms are quite variable in size, especially at 4½ and 5½ years. There is a slight tendency for succeeding forms to get larger, especially at 6 and 7 years or when the execution of a certain form is difficult for the child. (The opposite trend, of forms getting smaller, is sometimes seen.) By 7 and 8 years, the girls are showing a marked tendency to draw their forms more even in size. This increases steadily until even size is normative in girls at 9, though in boys only 46% make even forms as late as 10 years.

When a marked and irregular shift in size from very small to very large in the several forms made by any one child occurs after 7 years, the presence of some instability in the child should be suspected. However, when the shift is orderly and well patterned, as with a sudden shift with the three-dimensional forms to very small or very large forms in contrast to an even size of the Copy Forms, it may be considered that it is merely the harder demands of the more difficult task which have brought about this shift in size.

There is also marked variability in performance from child to child. The circle, which shows the greatest variation of all forms, especially at 5 years, may range from .6 cm. to 10 cm., with considerable difference in the vertical and horizontal diameters. But by 10 years the variation from child to child stabilizes to between 1.5 cm. and 4.5 cm., with only around 3% of children above or below these limits.

QUALITY OF STROKE

The quality of the stroke is one further aspect of the response which should be considered. There is the querulous stroke, the heavy stroke, the slashing stroke, the faint stroke—all possibly telling something of the personality of their maker. At times the type of stroke seems to have an age relationship. The 3½-year-old makes the querulous, wobbly, light stroke. He is anxious and unsure of himself. But not so six months later, when as a 4-year-old he becomes forthright, ready to step out into the world and to make dashing, gross motor strokes as he copies the forms.

The stroke may have heavy pressure in this 4-to-6-year-old period, but by 7, modulation and inhibition are coming in, along with a lighter stroke on the paper.

In general, there is fairly steady improvement in that children, with increasing age, use less of the page in copying forms, and improve from random order to the use of one, two, or three horizontal rows, and from large, uneven figures to medium-sized, even figures.

TABLE 25 *Extent to Which Directionality Contrary to the Usual Is the Work of Left-Handed Subjects*
(Percentage)

A = Percentage of this kind of response made by left-handers
B = Percentage of left-handers who respond otherwise–i.e., more conventionally

		5 years		5½ years		6 years		7 years		8 years		9 years		10 years	
		G	B	G	B	G	B	G	B	G	B	G	B	G	B
(circle CW)	A	30	7	33	30	63	22	100	55	100	100	75	25	100	100
	B	25	80	43	33	44	55	63	29	43	57	50	83	14	66
(R to L)	A	55	50	85	60	55	62	100	87	100	100	71	80	85	100
	B	50	50	14	33	55	55	12	33	0	30	11	83	14	66
(square CW)	A	69	17	100	16	100	100	100	80	100	100	100	0	80	100
	B	75	80	14	77	33	66	50	43	57	30	83	100	43	77
(square CW)	A	69	66	100	50	50	50	75	50	50	75	100	77	50	100
	B	75	80	86	77	77	88	62	86	86	70	66	66	86	77

A	100	100	50	50	100	100	100	100	100	100				
B	87	80	85	88	77	100	57	73	71	86				

CW △

A	80	14	83	36	100	75	100	66	100	100	100	0	100	100
B	50	80	28	44	55	66	62	70	71	70	83	100	71	88

CW ◁

A	25	16	100	28	100	50	100	100	100	0	100	0	100
B	87	90	71	77	55	77	75	57	43	100	83	100	100

CW ⊠

R to L ⊠

Inside Lines Mostly from R to L

A	33	11	50	28	71	50	66	33	71	77
B	66	88	50	71	28	50	33	44	28	22

HANDEDNESS

A question arises as to whether it is always a sign of immaturity when children, in copying forms, draw lines opposite to the expected direction. Could it sometimes merely be a matter of handedness?

Responses to Copy Circle give at least a partial answer to this question. Preschoolers tend to copy a circle in a CW direction, but copying in a CCW direction becomes normative at 5½ years and following. However, at all ages some children continue to draw CW.

Table 25 (line A) shows what percentage of the children who draw CW are left-handers. Through 5½ years in girls and through 6 years in boys, only a small percentage of those drawing the circle CW are left-handed. However, from 7 years on, with some exceptions, most children who draw a circle CW are left-handed.

Thus we may fairly consider any drawing of a circle in a CW direction by a right-handed child beyond the age of 6 years an immaturity.

Next, the question arises: Do the majority of left-handed children continue to draw a circle CW up into the older ages? Table 25 (line B) answers this question by giving the percentage of left-handers who after 5 years draw CW—that is, counter to the usual manner. In the age range from 5 to 10 years, at two of the ages in girls and at five in boys, drawing CW is normative in left-handed children.

Table 25 also presents figures for drawing the horizontal line of the cross from R to L, the first line of the square down the right side or across the bottom, the first line of the triangle up or down the right side, the outside of the divided rectangle starting down the right side and continuing CW, or the inside lines of the divided rectangle mostly from R to L.

Nearly all these patterns of drawing, which are contrary to the normative methods, occur mostly in left-handed children, and the percentage of left-handers so drawing tends to increase with age.

In spite of this, many left-handed subjects do draw in the generally normative direction and manner for nearly all the different forms.

Thus for most forms used in the Copy Forms test we can expect children, both right- and left-handed, to follow the usual normative progressions with age. But when a child does draw in a direction opposite to that which is usually chosen, chances are high, as Table 25 shows, that he will be a left-hander.

Therefore, with left-handed children, care should be taken in judging adversely a reversal in the usual direction of drawing.

CHAPTER 6

INCOMPLETE MAN

|||||||||||||||||||||||||||||||||||||||||||||||||||||||||||||||||||

Introduction

Of all parts of the examination, this is often the child's favorite. The missing parts are fairly obvious and stimulate the child to get right down to work to make things correct, to complete this unfinished figure. Each of the missing parts, with the exception of the eyes, has a model already drawn to guide the child.

The line, angle, and length of each part, especially the arm, leg, and tie, allow for many stages of perception and therefore of execution. Thus the fact that a part is added is only the beginning of an evaluation of the child's response. It is the way the child completes the parts, the quality of his performance, that is especially significant.

A leg, then, must be considered from the point of view not merely of whether or not it is added, but also whether it is too near or too far from the printed leg, whether it is of good length or too long or too short, whether it is angled correctly, parallel to the good leg, too straight, or too widespread. The possible combinations of these several factors are almost infinite.

Also, the added foot may be of good length or poor, pointed to the right or to the left, angled correctly or incorrectly. Again the possibilities are multiple.

And so with other parts to be added. It takes much skill and considerable maturity before any child is able to complete the man in an adequate manner. And for the examiner, counting parts added is easy, but it requires considerable experience to make a qualitative evaluation of any given child's response.*

* As an aid to evaluation of the Incomplete Man, supplementing information given in this chapter, we provide, through Programs for Education, 101 Park Ave., New York, N.Y. 10017, a set of *Incomplete Man Playing Cards,* which illustrate typical responses at all age levels.

Figure 6. Incomplete Man

In general, the overlong arm, leg, hair, fingers, and foot, so character-istic of the preschool response, gradually become shorter. And the contact points of parts with body become more accurate. At first arm, leg, hair, may slash right through the man's body line. Gradually they meet more neatly.

Fortunately, perhaps, the eyes have no model. Therefore the child fashions them spontaneously. And in spite of wide individual differences, even here good, rather clear age trends are seen.

Administration

MATERIAL
Examiner: Test page 4
Child: Test page 5 and a sharp No. 2½ pencil

PROCEDURE
Place the green sheet of paper on which the Incomplete Man form is printed before the child. Ask: "What does this look like to you?"
If the child responds, say: "You finish him." If he does not respond, say: "You finish him and *then* you can tell me."
After the man has been completed, the examiner asks the following questions:
"How does he look?"
"How does he feel inside?" If the child responds either "Happy" or "Sad," examiner may skip the next question.
"Is he happy or sad?"
"How can you tell?"
For 7-year-olds on, these questions are preceded with: "What is his facial expression?" and "How can you tell?" If the child can answer these, the other questions need not be given.

GENERAL DIRECTIONS
If the child lags in his completion of the salient parts, he may be encouraged with either a suggested or a direct clue.
The suggested clue is: "Is there anything else missing?"
The direct clue is: "Is there anything else missing *here?*"—pointing with a pencil to the general area of the missing part.

RECORDING
Record the child's responses verbatim at the bottom of test page 4 in the space under the heading: "Incomplete Man."
Suggested clues given, such as asking: "Is there anything else?" are recorded by a broken line preceding the response, as: ___ ___ hair.
Direct clues, such as pointing to the general area of a missing part and asking: "Is there anything else missing *here?*" are recorded by a solid line preceding the response, as: _____ ear.
As the child adds parts, record vertically on the left side at the bottom of the examiner's recording sheet. Responses to the inquiry questions are recorded in the space at the

lower-right-hand side of the page, under the heading: "When completed ask . . ."
Abbreviations which may be used:

bl = body line
nl = neck line
ll = looks like
idk = I don't know
hl = How does he look?
fi = How does he feel inside?
hs = Is he happy or sad?
ht = How can you tell?

(Plus any other abbreviations the individual examiner wishes to use.)

When testing has been completed, transfer to the child's own paper his responses to the inquiry questions using the abbreviations above.

Findings

As indicated above, there are three levels of response to this test: the child's spontaneous response; his response after examiner asks: "Anything else?"; and his response after examiner points specifically to some area of the body. In testing preschoolers, after the years when our 5-to-9-year-olds were tested, the examiners scrupulously followed this elaborate method, which was *not* always followed in testing the older children.

A complication in analyzing data is that responses of very young children are sometimes a bit difficult to evaluate since some of their scribbles may or may not actually have been an arm, leg, ear, or whatever part of the body they somewhat resemble.

NAMING

Asking the child: "What does this look like to you?" is a comfortable way to begin this test, and even at 3 years of age the majority of children are able to name the figure.

Through 4½ years of age, a substantial number give some such response as "snowman" or "scarecrow." Any continuation of such response after 4½ years of age is a strong sign of immaturity. Girls at 3 years of age give such responses predominantly. Boys at 3 most often call the figure a boy. "Boy" continues to lead in boys at 4, but otherwise "man" is the leading response at every age.

At older ages, the child is likely to say, more discriminatingly: "Part of a man [boy]" or "Half a man" or "A man with only one arm, one leg, etc." "Person" also comes in more often at 7 years and following.

Except for boys at 4½, 5, and 5½ the figure is seen as female only by girls, though most girls at every age see it as of the masculine gender.

Typical verbal responses at every age are tabulated in Table 26.

TABLE 26 *Naming the Incomplete Man*
(Percentage of Responses)

	3 years G	3 years B	3½ years G	3½ years B	4 years G	4 years B	4½ years* G	4½ years* B	5 years G	5 years B	5½ years G	5½ years B	6 years G	6 years B	7 years G	7 years B	8 years G	8 years B	9 years G	9 years B
Some naming	67	75	73	70	100	87	84	76	98	92	98	98	98	96	98	100	90	92	100	100
No naming	33	25	27	30	0	13	16	24	2	8	2	2	2	4	2	0	10	8	0	0
Man	20	20	30	30	30	27	34	32	44	58	42	52	60	40	42	44	34	32	42	24
Part (½) man	0	0	0	0	0	0	2	2	4	4	4	10	8	16	24	14	16	18	18	32
Little boy	0	0	0	0	5	0	6	0	10	2	2	2	0	0	0	0	0	0	2	2
Boy	5	34	10	10	20	30	14	14	14	14	28	20	16	22	20	10	6	8	6	6
Part (½) boy	0	0	0	0	0	0	2	0	0	0	10	8	4	2	2	8	12	6	4	2
Person (People)	0	0	12	10	13	2	0	4	4	6	6	2	4	6	2	14	10	14	16	12
Part of person	0	0	0	0	0	0	2	0	0	0	0	0	2	4	6	6	4	10	10	22
Girl (or Lady)	7	0	3	0	2	0	0	4	12	2	2	2	0	0	2	0	0	0	0	0
Some animal	7	10	5	7	8	2	2	0	4	0	0	0	0	0	0	0	2	0	0	0
Snowman	15	0	3	7	8	15	12	6	2	4	2	2	2	2	0	0	0	2	2	0
Scarecrow (Dummy)	3	0	5	3	2	2	8	8	2	0	0	0	0	0	0	0	0	2	0	0
Other	10	10	5	3	12	8	2	6	2	2	2	0	2	4	0	4	6	0	0	0

* *School Readiness* subjects.

COMPLETION OF PARTS

Though the preschooler's initial attack may be on the leg and then on the arm, some kind of eyes are also normative even at 3 years of age. An ear, perhaps surprisingly, is (barely) normative as early as $3\frac{1}{2}$ years of age. Hair is normative in girls at 4 and in boys at $4\frac{1}{2}$; some treatment of the neck area is normative in girls at 4 years, and in boys at $4\frac{1}{2}$.

Table 27 indicates the age at which each part becomes normative. But, as will be detailed in the rest of this chapter, there is a vast difference between adding a part and adding it correctly. Also, obviously, not every child adds all those parts which are normative for the group.

As an examiner will soon recognize, the preschool stroke is often wobbly and uncertain, though by 4 years of age it often assumes the dashing, out-of-bounds character so typical of 4 and $4\frac{1}{2}$. Thus the $4\frac{1}{2}$-year-old's Incomplete Man may take on a wild look, with long hair, long arm and leg, long fingers, and long foot.

The imaginative preschooler is likely to supply a belly button, though this is seldom seen after 5 years of age. A very few preschoolers may also add genitals and breasts. (Older children may clothe the man with hat, gun, pockets, belt, and any other equipment their minds may dictate.) Some at $3\frac{1}{2}$ and 4 draw over the lines already there, or reproduce the figure at one side of the paper. Or they may draw around the entire figure.

Coming up into the 5-to-9-year-old range, less help is needed either to get the child started or to help him in completing all the parts. Boys may attack the arm and leg region first, girls the head region. Some proceed in a very orderly manner from hair to ear, to eyes, neck, arm, and leg. Others start with the area of greatest interest to them. Age may in part determine the response. SEVEN's interest in the tie area may be so strong that he will attack this first.

HAIR

The addition of hair is not normative till 4 years of age in girls, $4\frac{1}{2}$ in boys. Right through 9 years of age most children add too few hairs, and through $5\frac{1}{2}$, at least, hair tends to be too long. (See Table 28.)

These too few, too long hairs tend, right through 7 years, to cover too much of the head area. Especially at $4\frac{1}{2}$ they may come down over the ear and even approach the chin, giving the finished man a characteristically wild appearance.

It takes an extremely precise child to count the exact number of hairs on the printed figure and to reproduce them accurately. Even by 10 years of age, only 6% of girls, 12% of boys, reproduce the number correctly.

Though in the child's attempt to control the length of his stroke he is

TABLE **27**   *Age at Which Parts Are Added by*
50% or More of Subjects

	Girls	Boys
Hair		
Adds	4	$4\frac{1}{2}$
Good placement	9	9
Good length	7	7
Eyes		
Adds	3	3
Good placement	6	6
Matching types	5	5
Any pupils	—	9
Ear		
Adds	$3\frac{1}{2}$	$3\frac{1}{2}$
Good placement	9	8
Good size	9	9
Neck treatment		
Body line	$4\frac{1}{2}$	5
Neck	$5\frac{1}{2}$	6
Bow	$5\frac{1}{2}$	6
All 3 parts	7	7
Neck and bow only	—	—
Arm and fingers		
Adds arm	3	3
Upper third body line	$5\frac{1}{2}$	5
Good direction	$5\frac{1}{2}$	5
Good length	—	—
Fingers good	8	8
Leg and foot		
Adds leg	3	3
Placed correctly	7	8
Good direction	—	—
Good length	9	—
Foot good length	—	—
Naming		
Names	3	3
Names "man"	6	5

also trying to hit the head line precisely, in the early years he is more likely to overshoot and cross this line than to contact it accurately.

With the better control of stroke by 7, the majority achieve good length of hair (56% G, 60% B), but it is not until the precision of 9 years of age that the majority place the hair accurately (58% G, 52% B).

EYES

The eyes, perhaps more than any other part, provide the potential drama of this test. Because there is no model, the child is able to express

TABLE 28 *Hair*
(Percentage at Each Age)

	3 years		3½ years		4 years		4½ years*		5 years		5½ years		6 years		7 years		8 years		9 years	
	G	B	G	B	G	B	G	B	G	B	G	B	G	B	G	B	G	B	G	B
Makes any	22	22	27	32	73	45	88	76	86	76	98	90	96	96	100	100	98	92	100	98
Number																				
Too few	15	17	15	25	47	32	62	60	62	56	70	74	80	88	72	84	76	82	86	80
Too many	5	3	5	7	13	10	18	10	22	12	18	12	12	0	20	10	12	4	4	6
Nearly right	2	3	7	0	13	3	8	0	0	2	2	0	0	0	8	0	0	0	0	2
Correct	0	0	0	0	0	0	8	6	2	6	10	4	4	8	8	6	8	6	10	10
Placement†																				
None					21	55	12	24	14	24	2	10	4	4	0	0	2	8	0	2
Too far around					30	20	38	30	48	26	48	38	54	38	46	34	46	26	30	30
Too little space					20	14	30	22	20	34	22	26	10	20	14	22	8	20	12	16
± correct					30	10	20	24	18	16	28	26	32	38	40	44	44	46	58	52
Length																				
Too long	15	12	10	20	30	30	40	54	50	42	60	52	30	46	30	16	6	24	10	6
Too short	5	7	12	10	20	5	30	4	26	20	6	18	26	4	12	24	32	26	28	30
± correct	2	3	5	2	22	10	18	18	10	14	32	20	40	46	56	60	60	42	62	62
Correct	0	0	0	0	0	0	0	0	2	0	2	2	0	0	0	0	0	0	2	2

* *School Readiness* subjects.
† Place is difficult to determine at 3 and 3½ years because many children scribble.

himself spontaneously. In spite of this fact, fairly predictable age changes do occur.

Eyes are a delight to the researcher—they present so many possibilities. We ourselves have been analyzing them for more than thirty years now and still need to know more about them than we do.

For the examiner, however, they may be less than a delight because they present so many different aspects which must be evaluated. To begin with, there is the matter of placement: are they too high, too low, or just right? This covers vertical placement, but there is also a question of horizontal placement: are they too near the nose, too far from the nose, or correctly placed? Or is one correct and the other incorrect, since placement of the two eyes is sometimes unequal.

Then there is the matter of size: do they match in size and is their size reasonable in relation to the size of the face? And of course, the question of shape is paramount. Individual differences are very great, but there is a tendency for eyes when first added to be roundish scribbles. Gradually they then become either filled-in dots or open circles. Eventually they are oval in shape, though this is not normative till well past our present age range. (See Table 29.)

The real drama of the eye is when it becomes a seeing eye, indicated by the presence of a pupil. Even as early as 5½ years of age nearly one quarter of subjects make a pupil, and it is virtually normative by 9 years of age. Eyebrows, though not normative in this age range, do appear conspicuously at 8 and 9 years of age, but pupils, lashes, and brows (all three together) seldom are seen in the first nine years of life.

EAR

Though some kind of ear is normative as early as 3½ years of age, size, shape, and placement all present real problems not only to the preschooler but to the 5- and 6-year-old as well.

Placement is the problem most easily solved, and reasonably good placement is normative in 8-year-old boys, in both sexes at 9 years of age. Earlier the ear is not only placed incorrectly as to height, but also may be separate from the head line or may overlap it.

Good size comes in next, though not till 9 years of age is good size normative. Shape continues to present a tremendous problem right through 9 years of age. Even by age 9, only 36% of girls, 24% of boys, achieve an adequate shape. However, by 5½ years of age, as Table 30 shows, nearly one quarter of our subjects show an awareness of shape by making some kind of indentation in their added ear.

NECK AREA

This part of the test is very demanding of most children, especially as some do not even know what it is that they are to complete. (Some think the given tie is the man's hand, for instance.)

TABLE 29 *Eyes*
(Percentage of Responses)

	3 years		3½ years		4 years		4½ years		5 years		5½ years		6 years		7 years		8 years		9 years	
	G	B	G	B	G	B	G	B	G	B	G	B	G	B	G	B	G	B	G	B
Makes any	55	67	80	62	85	75	98	82	96	90	98	98	98	100	100	100	100	100	100	100
Placement																				
None or 1 only	45	37	20	38	15	25	2	18	4	10	2	2	2	0	0	0	0	2	0	0
Too low	20	32	38	25	47	53	44	60	48	62	34	32	14	18	24	14	6	24	32	24
Too high	20	15	17	17	23	12	22	6	34	12	32	26	32	16	24	18	12	18	10	16
Correct	15	20	25	20	15	10	32	16	14	16	32	40	52	66	52	68	82	58	58	60
Uneven	40	60	50	57	60	72	48	48	26	34	28	30	22	14	18	14	8	10	8	10
Even	15	7	30	5	25	3	50	34	70	56	70	68	76	86	82	86	92	88	92	90
Different types or sizes	30	20	53	50	50	60	48	70	30	0	26	22	16	20	16	22	12	8	10	18
Match	25	47	27	12	35	15	50	12	66	90	72	76	82	80	84	78	88	92	90	82
Types																				
Knot, scribble, or H or V line	20	20	20	15	7	17	8	8	6	44	0	2	8	6	0	0	6	0	2	4
Open circles	25	39	40	36	55	35	68	70	32	46	22	34	24	44	24	24	20	28	24	30
Filled circles	0	0	10	3	5	3	10	6	34	14	44	38	34	24	26	20	16	16	8	6
Dot	10	0	3	0	7	7	12	0	12	6	6	4	6	10	16	10	6	8	10	4
Pupils in round	0	10	7	7	10	7	26	12	10	24	20	22	20	16	22	22	18	28	22	28
Oval no pupil	0	0	0	0	0	0	0	0	0	0	0	0	2	0	2	2	2	4	12	6
Oval with pupil	0	0	0	0	0	0	0	0	0	0	6	0	4	0	10	12	22	16	26	22
Any pupil	0	10	7	7	10	7	26	12	10	24	20	22	24	16	32	34	40	42	48	50
Eyebrows	0	12	0	5	2	2	12	10	2	6	8	6	16	18	12	10	34	20	36	28
Eyelashes	0	0	2	2	0	0	2	4	2	2	4	0	6	4	2	2	6	4	8	6
Pupils, brows, lashes	0	0	0	0	0	0	2	0	0	0	0	0	2	0	2	2	6	2	6	6

TABLE 30 *Ear*
(Percentage at Each Age)

	3 years		3½ years		4 years		4½ years*		5 years		5½ years		6 years		7 years		8 years		9 years	
	G	B	G	B	G	B	G	B	G	B	G	B	G	B	G	B	G	B	G	B
Makes any	**30**	15	**52**	**50**	**70**	40	**70**	**78**	**88**	**86**	**96**	**92**	**92**	**96**	**100**	**100**	**94**	**96**	**100**	**100**
None	**70**	**85**	48	**50**	30	**60**	30	22	12	14	4	8	8	4	0	0	6	4	0	0
Placement																				
Too low	10	0	15	22	40	25	34	46	42	40	**52**	44	**58**	30	**52**	38	44	32	32	36
Too high	8	10	17	10	15	10	10	18	18	18	18	16	8	18	8	16	6	14	10	10
Correct	12	5	20	18	15	5	26	14	28	28	26	32	26	48	40	46	44	**50**	**58**	**54**
Size																				
Too big	17	10	17	32	18	30	42	24	28	38	34	24	24	42	32	32	14	34	16	20
Too small	5	5	27	10	40	8	18	38	42	30	32	**50**	34	24	28	24	36	30	24	22
Correct	8	0	8	8	12	2	10	16	18	18	30	18	34	30	40	44	44	32	**60**	**58**
Shape																				
Poor	27	14	39	38	**52**	25	44	**58**	**84**	**74**	**68**	**74**	**48**	40	38	**52**	26	28	10	20
Separate from head	0	0	0	0	0	0	8	8	0	2	2	0	4	0	0	0	0	0	0	0
Correct but no indent	3	0	10	10	18	12	8	4	2	4	10	4	10	12	22	16	28	18	22	18
Some indent but not correct	0	0	3	2	0	3	8	8	4	6	18	14	24	44	28	20	20	36	32	38
Correct	0	0	0	0	0	0	2	0	0	0	0	0	0	0	12	12	20	14	36	24
Good ear	0	0	0	0	0	0	0	0	0	0	0	0	0	0	0	0	4	2	10	8

* *School Readiness* subjects.

Individual differences here are great. For instance, 8% of 3½-year-old boys actually add a bow, a very advanced response. In general, though, the average child responds somewhat as follows:

The first part of the neck area usually added is a simple completion of the body line—that is, body line is extended to meet the given knot of the tie. Though this response is not normative in girls until 4½ years and in boys till 5 years of age, even at 3 years one third of girls do make this body line. At first, in most, the body line merely continues the given body line to meet the knot in the tie. However, a few preschoolers curve their added body line so that instead of going over to meet the knot in the tie, it goes up to meet the head line, near what might be considered the man's chin.

At 4½ and 5 years, many (just over one third) add a neck as well as a body line. In these cases, most often the body line, as earlier, continues along to meet the knot in the tie, and the neck line comes down and hits it at right angles.

Body line only is the predominant response through 5½ years; but body line and neck (together) are a strong second response at 4½ and 5 years of age. Though a few preschoolers *do* make a bow, a bow added to the earlier body line and neck is not normative till 7 years of age. Many 5½- and 6-year-olds do struggle to add this bow, and the way it is made, in many, shows the difficulty of the struggle.

Thus the neck tends to cross the bow, instead of correctly stopping short at its upper edge, well through 5½ and 6. And many at these ages make a double knot to the bow. Or the body line may go through the bow. This struggle with the arrangement of the three neck parts is perhaps most highly characteristic of 6 years of age.

By 7, things are smoothing out, though in many the bow is too small. And many children are 9 years of age before the neck area takes on a smooth and easy look.

Table 31 indicates major trends here, but it is almost impossible to include in tabular form all aspects of the combination of body line, neck, and bow which an experienced examiner will wish to consider. For instance, the neck when first added tends to be close to the given neck line, and it is only with increased age (7 years or older) that the added neck line is far enough to the right to give the neck a reasonable width.

ARM

The arm and the leg are the two parts of the man added earliest and most often. Even at 3 years of age, 70% of girls and 55% of boys are already adding an arm. Thus the important thing for an examiner to evaluate is not whether or not an arm is added. It is the quality of that arm that matters. The three main things to be noted are the placement of the arm on the body, the direction in which it is pointed (down, straight out, or upward), and its length.

TABLE 31 Neck Area
(Percentage of Responses)

	3 years G	3 years B	3½ years G	3½ years B	4 years G	4 years B	4½ years* G	4½ years* B	5 years G	5 years B	5½ years G	5½ years B	6 years G	6 years B	7 years G	7 years B	8 years G	8 years B	9 years G	9 years B
Makes any	**37**	**15**	**45**	**41**	**62**	**45**	**94**	**82**	**92**	**90**	**98**	**98**	**100**	**100**	**100**	**100**	**100**	**100**	**100**	**100**
Body line	33	17	42	10	48	16	**67**	40	**72**	76	**78**	**84**	**84**	76	**78**	**82**	**72**	**84**	**62**	**68**
Neck	5	3	5	20	20	10	36	28	38	34	66	44	**80**	70	**80**	**76**	**98**	**88**	**92**	**88**
Bow	3	0	0	8	5	3	28	14	20	10	52	38	**74**	62	**92**	**86**	**98**	**78**	**100**	**94**
Body line only	30	13	39	18	38	33	48	38	44	50	18	32	6	10	0	4	0	2	0	2
Neck only	5	0	3	13	15	5	0	0	12	6	6	4	2	2	0	0	0	0	0	0
Bow only	0	0	0	3	0	0	4	4	0	4	2	0	0	0	2	2	0	0	4	2
Body line and neck only	0	3	3	3	5	5	18	24	14	24	22	22	18	28	8	10	2	20	0	6
Body line and bow only	3	0	0	0	5	3	6	6	6	2	14	14	14	6	12	18	2	10	4	8
Body line, neck, and bow	0	0	0	0	0	0	10	2	8	0	24	16	46	32	**54**	50	**68**	**52**	**58**	**60**
Bow and neck only	0	0	0	5	0	0	8	2	2	4	10	2	14	8	26	16	28	16	34	22
Inadequate center							14	2	7	2	12	10	16	12	4	12	12	12	4	2
Neck crosses bow					0	0	0	0	2	2	8	2	10	16	18	20	8	26	12	20
Good 3 parts	0	0	0	0	0	0	0	0	0	0	0	0	0	0	6	2	8	8	6	0
Good 2 parts	0	0	0	0	0	0	0	0	0	0	0	0	0	0	4	0	10	8	12	4

* 4½ years ff. from *School Readiness*.

Though, as Table 32 shows, a substantial number of children place the arm in the upper third of the body line even in the preschool years, the number who so place it increases with age. At the earliest ages there is a tendency to place the arm very low or in the middle section of the body line. As Figure 8 shows, when individual children are followed longitudinally, it is sometimes seen that an arm which was originally placed too low moves upward as the child grows older.

Direction changes, too. An arm which points upward is not normative until 5 years in boys, $5\frac{1}{2}$ years in girls. At the earliest ages a sizable number point their arm downward, and somewhat later, straight out.

The downward direction, when it occurs, especially if the arm starts very low on the body, gives the impression that the arm is a continuation of the printed arm. A straight-out arm, starting from the middle of the body line, is most characteristic of the 4-, $4\frac{1}{2}$-, and 5-year-old age zone.

A third consideration is the length of the arm. With small exceptions, a too long arm is strong through 6 years. It becomes shorter with age and by 8 years a good-length arm is nearly normative.

Thus it will be seen that as the individual child grows older, three things may be taking place in the arm added to the man: the arm moves upward on the body line; it shifts from pointing in a downward direction, through a time when it may point straight out from the body, to the time when it points upward; and gradually it decreases in length.

Though there are many individual exceptions, these shifts, when they do occur, give striking evidence of the orderliness and predictability of the changes in behavior which growth brings about.

Fingers, too, have their story to tell. Adding some kind of fingers is normative at 4 years of age, but fingers have a long way to go before they match the fingers on the printed hand. As Table 32 shows, reasonably correct fingers are not normative until 8 years of age.

Earlier they are, to begin with, often just an extension of the arm. Then by 4 and $4\frac{1}{2}$ years of age, many add what we call a "rake" hand, a vertical line with three or more spokes extending at right angles. Then comes a set of fingers which are made simply by placing a line across the end of the arm. Then come two angled lines, one at each side of the end of the arm. It is not until 8 years of age that correct fingers—that is, fingers which match the printed form—become normative.

And at first fingers, like other additions, are too long. They gradually shorten in length. The number of fingers made may range from one (a mere addition to the arm) or two to six. Four often makes four fingers. Five may prefer five.

LEG

Next to the arm, a leg is one of the most sure-fire additions. Even by 3 years of age, 75% of girls, 62% of boys, add a leg. As with the arm,

TABLE 32 *Arm*
(Percentage at Each Age)

	3 years		3½ years		4 years		4½ years*		5 years		5½ years		6 years		7 years		8 years		9 years	
	G	B	G	B	G	B	G	B	G	B	G	B	G	B	G	B	G	B	G	B
Any arm	70	55	65	52	85	87	96	96	96	98	98	100	100	100	98	100	98	100	100	96
Placement																				
None	30	45	35	48	15	13	4	4	4	2	2	0	0	0	2	0	2	0	0	4
Lower third	2	7	7	7	0	17	18	8	36	12	10	10	6	4	0	2	8	4	2	0
Middle	7	17	13	20	32	15	36	50	22	22	22	30	22	12	10	20	10	16	14	10
Upper third	60	30	45	24	52	55	42	38	38	64	66	60	72	84	88	78	80	80	84	86
Just right	20	5	13	7	10	15	—	—	6	10	22	12	20	12	20	22	24	38	36	46
Direction																				
Down	15	15	25	12	22	30	22	16	16	14	2	8	10	0	2	2	4	4	4	2
Straight	22	20	17	17	32	30	40	44	52	34	30	16	16	8	2	12	6	4	2	2
Up	32	20	22	22	30	27	34	36	28	50	66	76	74	92	94	86	88	92	94	92
Length																				
Long	40	20	27	27	47	55	54	54	36	64	34	46	38	54	32	38	2	26	22	24
Short	22	25	27	20	25	27	28	14	34	16	44	28	26	22	36	34	50	32	32	34
Correct	7	10	10	5	12	5	14	28	26	18	20	26	36	24	30	28	46	42	46	38
Fingers																				
Any	18	23	48	23	73	65	98	90	92	96	98	98	100	100	98	100	100	100	100	100
2 fingers	5	5	5	0	10	10	4	10	8	32	4	10	4	4	6	0	4	2	2	0
More than 3	3	0	10	5	15	15	12	16	16	24	8	4	8	8	2	4	4	4	2	8
+	0	2	2	7	10	7	4	4	20	16	16	4	4	16	10	12	2	0	0	2
Varied	11	14	16	5	6	15	48	34	34	4	8	8	4	12	12	18	2	0	2	2
3, too long	0	2	15	7	32	18	14	18	8	18	50	42	48	38	36	34	28	32	22	22
Correct	0	0	0	0	0	0	16	8	6	2	12	30	32	22	32	32	62	62	72	64
All O.K.	0	0	0	0	0	0	0	0	0	0	0	0	0	2	2	2	8	10	10	12

* *School Readiness* subjects.

TABLE 33 *Leg*
(Percentage at Each Age)

	3 years		3½ years		4 years		4½ years*		5 years		5½ years		6 years		7 years		8 years		9 years	
	G	B	G	B	G	B	G	B	G	B	G	B	G	B	G	B	G	B	G	B
Makes any	75	62	82	87	95	97	100	96	96	100	100	100	100	100	100	100	100	100	100	100
Placement																				
None	25	28	18	13	5	3	0	4	4	0	0	0	0	0	0	0	0	0	0	0
Too far	17	5	38	30	27	37	54	54	40	64	48	70	42	52	28	50	44	32	36	40
Too near	43	42	30	32	40	35	16	12	30	14	26	8	16	8	14	14	6	14	12	18
Correct	15	15	13	25	27	25	30	30	26	22	26	22	42	40	58	36	50	54	52	42
Direction																				
± parallels other	25	10	7	10	5	12	6	2	8	0	4	4	0	0	2	0	4	2	2	4
Too widespread	12	10	10	12	10	23	14	6	20	34	22	48	8	36	10	2	4	8	4	6
Too straight	20	35	45	37	60	48	62	58	56	52	52	32	62	30	46	64	58	54	64	50
Correct	20	27	20	27	20	14	18	30	12	14	22	16	30	34	42	34	34	36	30	40
Length																				
Too long	48	43	54	63	62	55	54	66	42	24	32	40	26	20	24	28	16	24	32	28
Too short	20	17	20	17	12	35	28	10	44	50	32	38	52	42	40	42	42	28	14	36
Correct	7	2	7	7	20	7	18	20	10	26	36	22	22	38	36	30	42	48	54	36
Foot																				
None	63	70	33	40	20	15	0	10	4	0	0	0	0	0	0	0	0	0	0	0
Too long	20	15	27	40	37	45	48	42	44	50	42	32	32	36	24	32	14	22	22	18
Too short	12	15	23	7	25	22	32	20	34	34	16	28	28	34	48	24	48	34	32	36
Good length	5	0	17	10	17	17	20	28	18	16	42	40	40	30	28	44	38	44	46	46
Double	0	0	0	0	0	0	4	10	10	0	0	0	0	0	0	2	0	4	4	0
Up too much	5	0	0	3	0	0	10	6	2	16	16	32	12	46	28	32	60	26	50	46
Pointed wrong†	18	12	28	35	28	45	24	38	26	32	26	26	28	16	12	10	2	4	2	2
Pointed right	20	12	35	17	47	30	76	52	70	68	74	74	72	84	88	90	98	98	96	96
Good leg and foot	0	0	0	0	0	0	0	0	0	0	2	0	2	2	6	2	6	6	6	6

* School Readiness subjects.
† Some feet point neither way, being merely scribbles.

however, it is not the mere addition of the leg that is significant, as it is what *kind* of leg is added.

Three things are important in evaluating a leg response: the placement of the leg, the length of the leg, and its angle or direction. (To say nothing of the kind of foot added.)

As early and consistently as the leg appears, it is one of the last additions to settle into good form. It sometimes seems that the older the child grows and the harder he or she tries to make a "good" leg, the more inaccurate the leg becomes.

The most observable thing about any leg is its length, and right through 4½ years the typical leg is much too long. Even by 9 years of age only girls (not boys) normatively make a leg of the correct length. (See Table 33.)

Placement, too, has its problems. An added leg may of course be too near or too far from the given leg, as well as, eventually, accurately placed. As Table 33 shows, a correctly placed leg is not normative in girls till 7 years of age, in boys till 8.

In direction, the leg may parallel the given leg, be too widespread, too straight, or be correctly angled. In our subjects, a too straight leg predominates at most ages.

In general, what seems to be happening to the leg with age is that it shortens in length, moves from being too near the given leg to farther from it, and its angle becomes slightly improved.

And then there is the foot, which brings its own problems. Some kind of foot is normative by 3½ years and following. At first, if added, the foot is definitely too long and very likely to be pointed in the wrong direction—that is, toward the left.

By 4½ years, the foot is normatively pointed in the right direction, and by 5½, a foot of a reasonably good length is nearly normative. However, the angle of the foot has not been brought under control even by 9 years of age.

Illustrations on pages 99–100 give some notion of the complexities and many different possibilities of leg and foot construction. A "good" leg and foot are nowhere near normative even by 9 years of age. It should be especially noted that the leg more than any other part added often becomes less accurate as the child grows older. In many, the greater effort which accompanies added awareness results in diminished accuracy.

EXTENT TO WHICH ARM AND LEG MEET, CROSS, OR FALL SHORT OF BODY LINE

At the very earliest ages, either or both arm and leg tend to be added as a long, careless slash. This slash very often crosses the body line. As Table 34 shows clearly, an arm which correctly meets the body line (neither falling short nor crossing it) is normative in girls at 4½ years of age, in boys at 5.

TABLE 34 *Extent to Which Arm and Leg Meet, Cross, or Fall Short of Body Line*
(Percentages)

	3 years G	3 years B	3½ years G	3½ years B	4 years G	4 years B	4½ years G	4½ years B	5 years G	5 years B	5½ years G	5½ years B	6 years G	6 years B	7 years G	7 years B	8 years G	8 years B	9 years G	9 years B
Arm																				
None	25	38	9	24	8	10	0	6	4	2	2	0	0	0	2	0	2	0	0	4
Crosses	31	37	33	48	64	25	26	31	16	20	14	12	10	14	24	10	8	10	8	12
Falls short	17	15	14	14	7	20	12	19	24	14	16	22	24	26	8	6	12	10	14	8
Correct	27	10	44	14	21	45	62	44	56	64	68	66	66	60	66	84	78	80	78	76
Leg																				
None	10	13	12	14	0	0	0	0	4	0	0	0	0	0	0	0	0	0	0	0
Crosses	52	32	38	55	65	25	37	50	26	26	14	24	22	14	12	8	4	6	6	6
Falls short	21	30	12	14	7	15	12	6	14	22	20	10	16	12	4	12	8	8	4	2
Correct	17	25	38	17	28	60	50	44	56	52	66	66	62	74	84	80	88	86	90	92

* All data here from *School Readiness* subjects.

A leg which correctly meets the body line is normative in girls at 4½ years. Perhaps surprisingly (certainly inconsistently), such a leg is normative in boys at 4 years and from 5 years, but not at 4½.

NUMBER OF PARTS AND EXTRA PARTS AND MARKS

Predictably, with few exceptions, the number of parts added increases with increasing age from, in general, three parts added at 3 years of age to a mean of eleven and a median of ten at 9 years. In the early years, girls tend to add more parts than do boys. (See Table 35.)

Some "extra" parts are added by some children at all ages. As one might expect, this number is largest from 3 through 4½ years of age, and diminishes as the child grows older. With the exception of boys at 3, adding some extra parts is normative through 4½ years in girls, through 5 years in boys.

The extra part most often added is the belly button, which is seen very frequently through 4½ years of age. A belly button at 5½ years or after is considered a sign of immaturity. From 5 years on, some children start what may have started as a belly button, and cover up this inclination by adding more dots or circles and saying: "That's buttons on his coat." As will be seen, nipples or genitals are very rare.

At all ages a few children mark over the given nose or mouth. An extra arm or leg or extra fingers occur to some extent in the preschool years, very little thereafter.

FACIAL EXPRESSION

Many examiners prefer to terminate the Incomplete Man situation after the child has added a final part, by merely remarking: "That was fine" or "He looks better now, doesn't he?"

However, some find it useful to pursue the situation further by including inquiries as to the man's facial expression or his emotions. Perhaps the most informative part of this inquiry is the question: "What is his facial expression?" Though children are not, normatively, able to respond to this question until they are 8 years of age, enough can answer at 7 to warrant asking this question of children that age.

Before 7 years, if one wishes to inquire about the man's feelings, the three following questions may be asked, in this order:

"How does he look?"; "How does he feel inside?"; and "Is he happy or sad?"

During the preschool years the majority, if they do answer the first of these questions—"How does he look?"—usually say "Good," perhaps meaning that they have done a good job. Others may say "Fine" or "OK."

The second question—"How does he feel?"—makes a greater demand of the child, and quite a few who can answer the first and third questions fail to respond to this. "Is he happy or sad?" is most often

TABLE 35 *Number of Parts and Extra Parts and Marks**

	3 years G	3 years B	3½ years G	3½ years B	4 years G	4 years B	4½ years G	4½ years B	5 years G	5 years B	5½ years G	5½ years B	6 years G	6 years B	7 years G	7 years B	8 years G	8 years B	9 years G	9 years B
Number of Parts Added																				
Mean number	3	2	4	3	6	3	7	5	8	8	8	7	9	9	10	10	11	10	11	11
Median number	3	3	4	3	6	3	8	5	8	8	9	8	9	9	10	10	10	10	10	10
Percentage of Extra Marks and Parts																				
% adding extras	62	43	75	78	57	55	50	27	40	50	27	40	11	22	12	24	16	22	30	30
Belly button	17	22	15	22	30	7	22	7	10	25	2	7	7	7	0	0	0	0	0	0
Buttons	0	2	0	0	0	2	7	2	0	2	17	17	7	2	2	8	6	2	10	8
Clothes	0	0	0	0	0	0	0	0	2	2	0	0	2	2	4	2	2	2	0	4
Filling in	0	0	0	0	0	0	0	0	7	0	2	0	0	0	0	0	0	0	0	0
Nipples or genitals	5	5	2	0	2	2	0	0	0	2	0	2	0	0	0	0	0	0	0	0
Scribbling over all or part	35	22	7	15	0	7	7	0	0	0	0	0	0	0	0	0	0	0	0	0
Marks on:																				
Nose or face	10	7	17	22	7	12	0	12	10	2	2	4	8	0	2	6	4	4	8	4
Mouth	12	7	17	2	20	2	5	10	12	4	10	7	8	5	4	12	4	12	16	14
Other	55	25	32	30	7	22	0	0	0	17	0	10	0	0	0	2	0	8	0	0

* Data through first 6 years from Walker et al.[51]

TABLE 36 *Facial Expression*
(Percentage of Responses)

	3½ years		4 years		4½ years		5 years		5½ years		6 years		7 years		8 years		9 years	
	G	B	G	B	G	B	G	B	G	B	G	B	G	B	G	B	G	B
Some answer about emotion	75	65	80	82	95	92	94	86	92	84	98	76	96	98	94	90	98	94
Facial expression																		
Answers	0	0	0	0	0	0	4	0	6	0	14	0	18	18	56	36	80	86
Fails to answer	100	100	100	100	100	100	96	100	94	100	86	100	82	82	44	64	20	14
How looks	42	42	57	67	57	67	48	46	18	36	68	48	26	10	22	38	4	4
How feels	32	37	47	55	32	27	36	34	78	36	14	28	44	62	2	4	12	12
Happy or sad	72	62	62	75	92	87												
Smiling, happy, O.K.	12	12	25	15	32	27	28	28	18	8	18	20	22	32	20	20	28	18
Fine, good, nice	50	32	32	37	37	45	22	20	4	20	8	12	6	4	0	2	0	2
Sad, unhappy, mad	57	47	37	40	20	62	22	26	22	30	52	36	56	50	36	36	32	28
Plain, normal, in between	0	0	0	0	0	0	0	0	0	0	0	2	2	4	12	4	10	18
Fine/sad or happy/sad (a double answer)	3	0	0	0	0	0	2	0	4	6	6	2	0	6	6	6	8	6
Looks good, feels sad (not a double answer)	0	0	0	0	0	0	18	6	40	18	0	4	0	0	0	0	0	0
Some positive emotion only	25	12	37	37	40	25	50	48	22	28	26	34	30	40	32	26	28	38
Some negative emotion only	10	18	20	26	20	30	24	32	26	32	60	35	60	52	50	58	38	50
Both in some way	40	35	20	20	32	37	20	6	44	24	6	6	0	6	6	6	8	6
How tell:																		
Some meaningful reply	15	13	25	8	46	42	32	26	46	56	52	50	84	88	40	64	68	66
Mouth or smile	3	3	15	3	32	20	20	14	30	42	42	34	62	62	36	46	54	50
Face or eyes	7	7	7	0	7	17	12	12	16	14	10	16	12	10	4	22	14	16
Other	5	3	3	5	7	5	4	6	8	10	0	10	12	16	0	12	2	6

responded to with "Sad." Whether this means that the child actually thinks the man is sad, or merely says "Sad" because that is the second of two offered alternatives, is not certain. That the choice may be made simply on the basis of the fact that "sad" is mentioned last is suggested by the fact that many children who say that the man looks "Happy" or "Good" also say, to the third question, that he is "Sad."

The actual value of these responses is somewhat questionable, though the child who says that the man is "Sad," "Unhappy," "Mad," may very likely be projecting a different kind of feeling from the one who says "Happy," "Smiling," "Fine," "Good," or "Nice."

A final question which many examiners like to ask, after the child has indicated some kind of emotional feeling or facial expression, is: "How can you tell?" Since a meaningful reply to this question is not normative till 5½ years of age in girls, 6 in boys, it may well be omitted at the earlier ages, or at least not pursued at any length. Even when the child does answer this question, the reply is likely to be, as Table 36* shows, "Mouth" or "Smile."

AGE SUMMARIES†

2½ YEARS

Most add an arm or a leg, long and slashlike; and may scribble over part or all of the printed figure.

3 YEARS

Most add three parts: a too long arm, a too long leg, and possibly eyes. May make marks on or outside the figure or may scribble on the form.

3½ YEARS

Most add three or four parts: arm, leg, eyes, and possibly one other part, as fingers or ear. At this age, especially in girls, there is little scribbling on the form, but extra marks may encircle the head, body, or total figure. Or child may make marks outside the figure.

4 YEARS

There is a marked sex difference here, even more than at most ages. Girls on the average add six parts, whereas boys still add, on the average, only three. Conspicuous in girls is a belly button. Arm is now shorter and may extend straight out from the body, halfway up the body line. Though not yet normative, a body line at the neck area is made by 48% of girls. Fingers are normative.

4½ YEARS

Girls on the average now add seven parts, boys five. It is at this age that many make what we term a "wild" man, with hair in some circling the entire head, including

---

*Figures in this table may not be entirely consistent, since not all examiners asked all ages all three of the questions.

†As with other descriptive data, this summary does not differentiate between parts added spontaneously and those hinted at or pointed out by examiner.

under the chin. Girls still add a belly button. Arm and leg continue to be overlong.
A continuation of the body line is now normative in girls and is made by many boys.

5 YEARS
Girls on the average now add eight parts to the man, boys add six. Instead of a simple
extension of the body line, as earlier, some now make a slanted combination of neck
and body line. Arm and leg are becoming shorter in some. This is the last age when
a good many add extra parts or marks.

5½ YEARS
Now girls add eight parts on the average, boys seven. Arm and leg are becoming shorter;
arms are moving upward and point upward. Neck area tends to consist of a two-part
straight neck and body line. Eyes are becoming smaller (may be open) and are better
placed. Hair and/or ear are usually included.

6 YEARS
The average child now adds nine parts: arm and hand, leg and foot, hair, ear, eyes, and
at least two parts at the neckline. Leg is of good length, and in girls, the arm as well.
Many are now struggling with the tie. Eyes tend to match in size and vertical placement, though horizontal placement may not as yet be accurate.

7 YEARS
Now both girls and boys add, on the average, ten parts: hair, ear, eyes, a three-part neck
area, arm and hand, leg and foot. Arm may be quite well placed now and of a good
length. Fingers are improved, leg is reasonably well placed. Neck may cross bow, but
there is less of a struggle with the neck area than at 6.

8 YEARS
Ten or eleven parts are now added, with the three neck parts and an occasional pupil
accounting for the increase. In fact, the "seeing eye," even though not yet quite normative, is highly characteristic of the 8-year-old performance. All parts are coming into
better shape.

9 YEARS
Now the mean number of parts for both sexes is eleven, including a three-part neck and,
in many, a seeing eye (with pupil). Though the delicate stroke of the 10-year-old is
not yet seen, many now give a very creditable performance. Even the hair, in some,
is beginning to be of graduated length.

Special Things to Look for at Different Ages

The Incomplete Man is a highly sensitive test and its possibilities
seem almost endless. The longer one works with it, the more it has to
offer. Each examiner will in the long run develop his or her own special
ways of using it and of deciding what to look for.

Any examiner will start out by counting parts added and then, even
without too much technical training, will move on to comparing the looks
or quality of the parts the child adds with those provided on the model.

More than this, there are certain special things to look for at different
ages. Thus for 2½- and 3-year-olds, an examiner will especially note

whether the child merely scribbles or marks on the form, or actually adds two or three parts.

From 3½ to 4½, an examiner will wish to note whether or not the long single-stroke arm and leg are becoming shorter and are taking on shape with the addition of fingers and feet.

From 4 to 5½, an examiner will be especially interested in the upward movement of the arm and the fact that in many the arm meets the body line rather than ruthlessly crossing over it.

And for many, the ages of 4 through 6 emphasize the gradual improvement of the neck area: first the extension of the body line to meet the knot in the given bow, then the addition of the neck, and then the struggle with the bow. At this time, when some arm and fingers, leg and foot, hair, ear, and eyes can be pretty well taken for granted, how the child handles the neck area can be an examiner's best clue as to how far that child has developed.

At 7 and after, when often body line, neck, and bow have all combined with reasonable smoothness, the examiner's special interest may shift to shape and placement of the ear, increasing accuracy of the hair, and most of all, to what is happening with the eyes.

Even though pupils are not normative till 9 years of age, by 7, one third of our subjects do add a pupil. By 8, 40% add this pupil, which gives the eyes their "seeing" look. This, combined with the oval shape (achieved by nearly one quarter of the children at 8 years of age) and the addition of eyebrows (again made by approximately one quarter of subjects at 8 years of age), gives the response in many a very human and individual appearance.

Illustrations

Figure 7 shows plainly outstanding and typical age changes which take place in response to the Incomplete Man figure from ages 2 through 9. An initial mere scribble response is followed, by 2½ to 3 years of age, with a long slash of arm and leg. As the child grows older it will be seen that the arm in general tends to move upward on the body line, turn up, and become shorter, with fingers coming into increasingly good form.

The leg becomes shorter and is increasingly well placed and angled. Hair varies from too much and too far around at some ages to too little at others, but finally settles down. The ear becomes increasingly well placed and of improved shape.

Eyes, which are at first large open circles, gradually acquire pupils and finally take on an oval shape. The neck is most difficult for many children. Around 4 years of age, many add a simple body line. The neck is added by 6, the tie comes in around 6 or 7. By 9 or 10 years, some are able to add just the neck and bow without the body line.

2 YRS.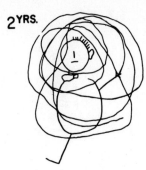

2½ YRS.

3 YRS.

3½ YRS.

4 YRS.

4½ YRS.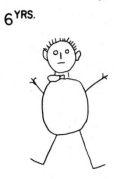

5 YRS.

5½ YRS.

6 YRS.

7 YRS.

8 YRS.

9 YRS.

Figure 7. Typical responses, at successive age levels, shown to the Incomplete Man test

D.B. 5 YRS.   5⁶   6⁵

S.F. 5⁷   6¹⁰   7⁸

D.M. 6⁸   7⁶   8⁵

M.H. 7²   8⁴   9⁵

Figure 8. Samples from among selected individual cases showing characteristic age changes as they take place from one year to the next

100

Figure 8 shows characteristic age changes which take place in the Incomplete Man completions of four individual children at three successive age levels. Anyone who is planning to make serious use of this test is encouraged to keep his or her own longitudinal records, as one's clearest notion of the way responses to the man change comes from checking these responses in any one individual child from year to year.

CHAPTER 7

RIGHT AND LEFT

||||||||||||||||||||||||||||||||||||||||||||||||||||||||||||||||||||||||||||||||||||||||

Introduction

In examining children over the years, we have been especially interested in their orientation to right and left, as related not only to their own bodies, but also to the bodies of others. We have observed a great deal of confusion about sidedness especially in children between the ages of 4 and 7 years.

The more confused children seemed to have other confusion patterns as well, particularly as to the orientation of letters. Even single letters posed a problem for them, for they knew not which way these letters were supposed to go. No sooner had they worked out a correct orientation than, flip-flop, the letter turned in their minds in the opposite direction. Sometimes, as at 5½ years, we found children who became fixed in an inaccurate direction and named right as left and left as right with utter certainty and consistency.

This orientation difficulty extended considerably beyond the mere naming of right and left. Thus a child might be able to name his right hand and left hand, but when asked to name his left ear, would become bewildered. A request might have to be spelled out: "If this is your left hand"—pointing to left hand—"then what is this ear?"—pointing to left ear. Usually this clue was enough, but it did not necessarily mean that over a period of six alternating requests the child could maintain an accurate orientation.

Some years ago we came upon the work of Dr. J. Robert Jacobson[33, 34] in relation to an adult test of right and left orientation. We were intrigued by the comprehensiveness of his testing, his use of many parts of the body, his idea of timing the individual's ability to carry out certain commands, including orientation to pictures of opposing hands in which certain fingers were touching each other. These pictured hand postures were to be reproduced by the subject being examined, either verbally or motorwise.

Before 5 years of age we ask the child merely to identify left hand and right hand. FIVE can name his thumb, little, and middle fingers, giving them his own special names; but the index finger and ring finger were not only difficult to name but also hard to find after they had been named. Any requests involving index and ring fingers were therefore omitted in testing the 5-year-old.

The concept of right and left begins to intrigue, and confuse, a child of 3 or 4 years. At 3 or even younger, the child has grasped the concept of top and bottom, right side up or upside down. By 4, he is grappling with front and back, and may still put his shirt on backward. The step of mastering sidedness and of distinguishing right from left is far harder to take. At one point a child may seem to have figured it out, has supposedly learned it, and suddenly a switch-around occurs and one side becomes its opposite in his mind. Right becomes left and left becomes right.

The ten single and ten double commands in the third and fourth sections of this test appear fairly simple at first glance, but the task of recording stopwatch readings in seconds, and simultaneously fathoming and ironing out the child's misconceptions and errors, presents the examiner with many hazards.

If the examiner himself has trouble with concepts of right and left, he may be ready to give up this test before he has had enough practice with it to become proficient. A beginning examiner should not become discouraged; he needs time to become more comfortable with the test. He will develop skill in orienting the child, in manipulating the stopwatch, and in recording his timing and his observations of the child's process of carrying out the commands.

Initially, if he is unsure of his timing and recording, he may rely most heavily on his general impression of the child's response. This test is not so important in the final analysis of an individual's record as to demand great precision, but it is a test that can tell us much about the child's way of orienting. When a child, especially one of 5 or 6 years, orients easily and scores well on this test, the evidence points to a well-integrated and effectively operating organism.

After the examiner has mastered the easy manipulation and reading of a good stopwatch with a quiet mechanism (a noisy stopwatch that startles the child every time it is clicked on and off is very disturbing), he is well advised to learn by doing. If he learns on the 5-year-old, he will have mastered the most difficult task first, because the 5-year-old needs expert handling and many allowances.

Because the right-left examination is more difficult with a 5-year-old than with an older child, the demands of the test are clipped down to what the child should be able to do. Any questioning or directions about index or ring fingers, as mentioned above, are omitted. Also the time demanded for sustaining is cut down to what the 5-year-old can manage. Thus the ten single commands are cut down to six, and the ten double commands are cut down to two.

Materials and Parts of Test

Materials for this test are a scoring sheet on which directions for the various parts of the test are printed, with adequate space to record the timing and behavior, and a stopwatch. The scoring is determined by averaging the time it takes for carrying out the various commands. As suggested above, both for the examiner's convenience and in an effort not to disturb the child, a silent, easily manipulated stopwatch should be chosen.

The different parts of the test as we use it are as follows:

1. Naming parts of (examiner's) body
2. Naming right and left, own and examiner's
3. Single commands
4. Double commands

Detailed instructions for the separate parts of the test as we use it are presented below. All of these are given from 5 to 9 years, except for Naming Right and Left, which begins at 3 years.

Administration and Findings

1. NAMING PARTS OF THE BODY (5–9 YEARS)*

First we wanted to see if and how the child named parts of the body.

* Below 5½ years, omit index and ring fingers.

We also wanted to make sure that he knew the names of the parts of the body that he would be asked to orient to in later sections of the test.

In administering this section, the examiner points to some parts of his own body, telling the child: "I'm going to point to some parts of my body and I want you to tell me what I am pointing to."

He then points, in turn, to his own eye, eyebrow, palm, elbow, thumb, index finger, middle finger, ring finger, and little finger.

Eye. The naming of the eye poses no problem even for the child 4 years old or younger. (See Table 37.) A certain number, around 10% from 6 years on, may refer to the eye in the plural as "eyes." On the other hand, the child with the almost too precise mind may respond with "corner of the eye" or "upper [lower] eyelid," or he may refer to the right or left eye, whichever the examiner is pointing to, naming it correctly or otherwise.

TABLE 37   *Naming Parts of the Body—Eye, Eyebrow, Palm, and Elbow*
(Percentage of Responses)

	5 years	5½ years	6 years	7 years	8 years	9 years
		Naming Eye				
Fails	5	0	0	0	0	1
Eyes or the Eyes	4	3	10	11	9	5
Some other, with help	10	9	0	0	3	4
Eye	**81**	**88**	**90**	**89**	**88**	**90**
		Naming Eyebrow				
Eyebrow	50		46	**71**	**82**	**91**
Eyebrows	18		34	11	4	4
Success, 2nd trial	10		4	5	10	2
Variations:						
Eyelash	4		8	0	2	1
Eyelashes	2		8	12	0	2
Other	16		0	1	2	0
		Naming Palm				
"I don't know"	0	14	14	0	0	1
Hand	**74**	**62**	**42**	**52**	20	10
Middle	15	0	14	0	3	0
Other	0	4	1	0	0	2
Palm	11	20	29	48	**77**	**87**
		Naming Elbow				
"I don't know"	5	10	14	1	0	1
Incorrect	4	2	0	5	1	1
Correct	**91**	**88**	**86**	**94**	**99**	**98**

Eyebrow.   Eyebrow is not quite so easy, though even by 5, 50% of subjects were able to name it. (See Table 37.) A few, thinking in more general terms, may call it "head." Others restrict their scope slightly and call it "forehead." With this type of naming, the examiner usually needs to give the clue: "What is this hair up here called?" This usually enables the child to name correctly.

There are still a few, however, who may need to be helped further with the name itself: "Point to your eyebrow." When they have done this, the examiner again points to his own eyebrow and asks: "Then what is this?" "Eyelash" is a fairly common substitute for eyebrow. If this is given, the examiner will point to his own eyelashes, saying: "This is the eyelash, but this"—again pointing to the eyebrow—"is the eye . . . ?" Usually the child is then able to respond correctly.

Palm.   The palm is more usually named "hand" by the 5- and 5½-year-old. If pressed for a more specific name ("What else do they call it?"), a child in the 5½-to-6-year-old age range may say "middle." If pressed still further, he may say "skin," wrist," "vein," "wrinkles," "fist," or "bottom."

At an earlier age, as 4 years, he may refer to the palm as the "place where you hold things" or "place where you carry things."

If it becomes obvious that the child cannot give the name "palm," the examiner, as with eyebrow, asks him to point to his own palm. If this is successful, as it usually is by 5 years, the child is then asked: "If that is *your* palm, what is this on me?"

If with all this coaching the child still returns to his former response, persisting with "middle" or whatever he has first called it, then there is very real evidence of a stuck mechanism which may impede learning. "Palm," however, is a difficult word and is not usually mastered before 7 or 8 years. (See Table 37.)

Elbow. As a rule, the elbow is as easy or easier to name than the eye. Most 5-year-olds (91%) can name it. (See Table 37.) A few persist in the more global or general response "arm" or "bone." Some have trouble in saying the word clearly or understandably. A very few confuse elbow with knee.

Thumb. Some form of the word "thumb" is well known to the 4-year-old (80%). He is perhaps more apt to give the response "thumkin," which he has been taught in finger-play songs, especially if he has attended nursery school. By 5, the child is moving out of this younger realm. "Thumb" then becomes the name of choice. (See Table 38.)

*Index finger.** Though the index finger is included in finger-play exercises in nursery school and is often called "pointer," it is neither easily named nor easily located (apart from the finger-play songs with demonstration) before the child is 5½ or 6 years of age (82% at 5½ years).

The index may be called simply "finger." To give it a more specific name is not easy for the 5- or 6-year-old. If the examiner helps by pointing and asking the child at 5½ to 6 years what he (the examiner) is doing, the child may quickly be able to answer "pointing" (82% at 5½ years to 92% at 6 years). (See Table 38.) Or he may say "tapping." The examiner can then translate this into calling the finger "pointer finger." Because of the difficulty both of naming and of locating the index finger, it is best not to include it in the test battery before 5½ years of age.

Middle finger. The middle finger (often called "big finger" or "tall man" by the young child) can be picked out readily because of its size. The child also feels comfortable in moving it separately from the other fingers.

Some will name it spontaneously with one of its possible names or when given the clue "What size is it?" If the child of 5 or 5½ cannot name it, he may be given a choice as to whether he wishes to call it "big finger" or "tall man." His choice is important since his own naming is used when specific commands come in.

---

* Start only at 5½ years.

TABLE 38 *Naming Thumb and Fingers*
(Percentage of Responses)

	5 years	5½ years	6 years	7 years	8 years	9 years
			Naming Thumb			
"I don't know" or other failure	0	2	6	0	0	0
Variations on thumb	4	6	0	2	0	3
Thumb	**93**	**92**	**94**	**98**	**100**	**97**
Thumb, 2nd trial	3	0	0	2	0	3
			Naming Index Finger			
"I don't know"	—	10	8	3	0	0
First finger, fore-finger, other	—	8	0	8	9	10
Pointer finger After demonstration	—	**82**	**92**	50	37	31
Without demonstration	—	0	0	32	28	35
Index	—	0	0	7	26	24
			Naming Middle Finger			
"I don't know"	5	0	0	0	0	0
Finger	0	10	0	0	0	0
Second or third	29	5	0	0	0	0
Big	13	9	0	4	0	1
Tall man, tall finger	14	27	**50**	18	8	8
Middle	15	18	14	30	37	37
Other	14	14	0	4	1	3
Second trial	10	5	0	0	0	0
Examiner demonstrates (2 & 2)	0	12	36	44	**54**	**51**
			Naming Ring Finger			
"I don't know" or other failure	—	13	30	1	0	0
(Wear?) Ring	—	40	24	20	16	18
Ring man	—	30	6	8	1	3
Ring	—	14	30	**63**	**81**	**77**
Other	—	3	10	8	2	2
			Naming Little Finger			
"I don't know"	6	8	0	0	0	0
Pinkie	17	25	44	32	21	12
Tiny, small, smallest	7	0	10	8	8	12
End man, last one	6	6	10	0	1	3
Baby	23	20	6	31	25	32
Little	40	33	30	28	45	40
Other	1	8	0	1	0	1

By 6 years, 50% still call the middle finger "tall man," but an increasing number have given up this preschool naming. They are often at a loss, however, because they have not yet learned the more advanced name "middle." As soon as they are helped by the examiner's demonstrating on his own hand with "Two on this side and two on this side, and it's in the . . ." they are usually able to respond "middle."

By 6 years of age, even though they have named this finger "tall man" or "big finger," they are told that it also has a different name. Then they are taught "middle" by means of the above demonstration. The name "middle" is purposely used from 6 years on, both because they are ready for it and also to contrast the sound of "middle" to "little." (See Table 38.)

*Ring finger.** The ring finger, even though it may be used in preschool finger play, when it is usually called "ring man," is as difficult to remember or to locate as is the index finger. Therefore it, too, is omitted from the battery of tests before 5½ years of age. It is not named spontaneously before 7 years. (See Table 38.) Prior to this age, the help of "What do you wear on it?"—examiner pointing to a ring on his own finger or to the area where it would be worn—usually brings forth the correct answer.

Little finger. The little finger is as well known to the preschooler as is his thumb. Both are on the outside of the hand and thus are easily located. They may even be confused with each other at 4 years of age. The very young child does not refer to this finger as "little," but more often calls it "pinkie," "baby finger," or "small finger." "Little" is actually not normative even through 10 years of age. "Baby finger" is used almost as frequently as "little" even at 10 years. "Pinkie" steadily drops from a high of 44% at 6 years to a low of 12% at 9 years. (See Table 38.)

Though the little finger may be named variously (pinkie, small, baby), the examiner steers the child into the use of "little" after 6 years of age. If the child has not called it this, the examiner will suggest: "Another name for this finger is 'little.' I'm going to call it 'little' when I ask you to do various things." The sound of "little" is used to contrast with "middle" to determine whether or not there is difficulty in auditory discrimination.

2. NAMING RIGHT AND LEFT (3–9 YEARS)

In this part of the test, the examiner asks as he points to the child's right hand: "What is the name of this hand on you?" (Or: "Show me your right hand.") He then asks about the child's left hand, and his own right hand.

Naming right hand. As suggested above, the examiner points to the child's right hand and asks: "What's the name of this hand on you?"

---

* Start only at 5½ years.

If the child names some specific part that the examiner is pointing to (back of hand, knuckle, thumb, little finger), having just named parts of his body—or does not understand what the examiner means—the examiner clarifies the question.

Thus she helps the child by saying: "Show me your right hand." With this much help, a bare majority of 5-year-olds know their right hand (60% of girls, 48% of boys). It is not until 7 years (or possibly 6½) that the child can correctly name his hand without this help (82% of girls, 68% of boys, at 7 years). (See Table 39.)

Telling how he knows which hand.   Once the child has responded, he is then asked how he knows. Answers are highly variable. Some come right out and confess that they don't know. Others give a cocky or cocksure response in a 4-year-old manner: "Just know"; " 'Cause"; "Just thought"; or "Just guessed."

Those who give the source of their knowledge as "Mummy showed me" are responding in a characteristic 5- or 6-year-old way, relating themselves both to an experience and to a person. Their knowledge of right and left does not yet stand on its own.

Their own action may also be the basis of their knowledge, as when they report that they eat with, write with, or pledge allegiance with the hand in question. The experience at school as reflected in the pledge of allegiance is indeed becoming a part of the process of learning. A few will relate a side to some physical clues such as a scratch or a wart. This is helpful as long as the clue lasts.

Some have a vivid memory of being taught at the piano or the table, or as they were putting on their shoes. At the opposite extreme, an 8-year-old who says, "Right because it's on the right side," is thinking like an adult and gives a suggestion of having built up a fluid use of right and left in his thinking process.

Naming left hand.   When the right hand has been named correctly or incorrectly and the reason given, the left hand is then pointed to, as the question is asked: "And what is the name of this hand?"

Most FIVES, having just had the experience of naming their right hand, will be able to name the left hand correctly. In fact, correct naming of the left hand is normative in girls at 4 and 4½ years, though not in boys. Some 5½-year-olds are so obliging, as well as possibly thinking of both sides of the body together, that as soon as they have named the right hand they will immediately refer to the left hand, saying: "And this is my left hand."

If the child has named his right hand as its opposite (left), or has shown his left hand as his right, and is consistent in naming the right hand as left, the examiner will need to decide whether he will allow the child to settle for the opposite. The consistent use of the opposite is most characteristic of the 5½-year-old.

TABLE 39   *Shows or Names Right Hand*
(Percentage of Responses)

	3 years		3½ years		4 years		4½ years		5 years		5½ years		6 years		7 years	
	G	B	G	B	G	B	G	B	G	B	G	B	G	B	G	B
Names																
Fails	**94**	**97**	**78**	**83**	**73**	**64**	**55**	**62**	**74**	**66**	**78**	**76**	**62**	**56**	14	16
Correct	3	3	11	10	17	18	21	19	18	20	12	22	34	34	**82**	**76**
Opposite	3	0	11	7	10	18	24	19	8	14	10	2	4	10	4	8
Shows																
Fails	43	37	30	31	18	13	7	12	8	4	2	0	2	2	0	0
Correct	40	23	26	29	38	24	18	28	42	28	**66**	**60**	36*	34*	10	10
Opposite	11	37	22	23	17	27	31	22	22	34	10	16	24	20	4	6
Shows or names correctly	43	26	37	39	55	42	38	47	**60**	48	**78**	**88**	**70**	**68**	**92**	**78**

Reason Why Child Knows Right and Left

	5 years		5½ years		6 years		7 years	
	G	B	G	B	G	B	G	B
No answer	6	10	2	4	14	12	6	2
I don't know	24	2	16	16	6	10	4	14
Mummy (or someone) told me	26	18	18	14	20	12	12	12
Just know, thought, or guessed, or Because	20	34	26	36	10	22	18	4
Confused, or some other answer not listed here	10	14	12	4	12	20	0	12
Facing this way or on this side	6	0	10	8	8	6	14	16
Write, eat, pledge allegiance	8	12	16	18	30	18	26	18

* These numbers are smaller at older ages since if subject succeeds in *naming*, he is not asked to *show*.

Table 39 includes data for telling how children know right and left.

Identifying examiner's right hand. Having established his knowledge of his own right and left sides at 6 years, it is next important for the child to adjust to an opposing person face on. This takes a new capacity of adaptation, a new ability to manipulate sides in space.

The examiner, facing the child, holds up his right hand and asks: "What's the name of this hand on me?"

The hand was named correctly at 6 years by 64% of subjects and a correct response was established in nearly all subjects by 8 years (95%). Reasons for knowing the examiner's right hand are given in Table 40.

3. SINGLE COMMANDS (TIMED IN SECONDS)

The ten single commands are as follows (only six of these commands are given at 5 years):

1. Touch your eye.
2. Show me your pointer finger. (Not asked at 5 years.)
3. Show me your ring finger. (Not asked at 5 years.)
4. Show me your middle finger. (Not asked at 5 years.)
5. Close your eyes and bend your head.
6. Bend your head and tap the floor with your heel.
7. Raise your head and open your mouth. (Not asked at 5 years.)
8. Touch your right ear.

TABLE 40   *Naming Right and Left: Identifying Examiner's Right Hand*
(Percentage of Responses)

		Years		
	6	7	8	9
No response	0	0	3	2
Opposite	36	26	2	2
Correct	**64**	**74**	**95**	**96**
Reasons for Giving Answer				
No answer	14	0	4	2
"I don't know"	12	6	8	1
Some individual response	32	16	15	4
Response related to fact that they write with right hand	0	10	10	0
"I just know"	2	0	3	1
"Opposite my left hand"	2	6	5	5
"Facing different way" or "My right opposite yours"	24	38	31	72
"Because if I turned around . . ." and those who turn around	14	24	24	15

9. Show me your right thumb.
10. Show me your left index finger. (Left middle substituted at 5, using the child's own naming of "big finger" or "tall man.")

(The recording of timing, demanded in the last four parts of the test, may seem very difficult to a beginning examiner. The timing is taken from the moment the examiner has completed his command to the moment that the child finally carries out the instructions. The word "finally" is used since there may be many steps in the child's process of carrying out a command. As the examiner becomes more proficient, timing a child's response is like second nature. It becomes automatic.)

As we analyze responses to these commands, we find that the request to "show" is easily understood by the child. "Touch" is equally understood, though the very literal child may actually touch his eyeball when asked to touch his eye. Closing the eyes is understood, though a few 5-year-olds and a fair proportion of 4-year-olds may refuse to obey this command. "Bending," however, can pose a very real problem. The child may ask "Which way?" referring to back, forward, or to one side or the other. If he does ask, he is told he may choose whichever way he wishes.

"Raise your head" poses the problem of not knowing what "raise" means. That is why this command is omitted at 5. Even at 6 and 7, some children do not know what "raise" means, or they are unsure as to whether they should bend their head back or stretch it straight up. They can be told to lift it up, or the examiner can demonstrate for them. "Tap" poses a problem for the 5-year-old because he usually relates tapping to a hand movement. Thus he often brings his hand to the floor in carrying out the command in which the heel is supposed to tap.

The only part of the body referred to here that has not up till now been named or pointed to in the initial requests is the heel. The child may need to be taught "heel" before he can carry out the command. Often the clue "the heel of your shoe" is all that he needs to locate it quickly.

For this part of the test the scoring results (Table 41)) show that FIVE is responding nicely to the single commands within the two-second (2.1 to 2.5 seconds) realm, with the exception of "Bend your head and tap the floor with your heel" (5.4 seconds) and "Show me your big finger" (3.7 seconds).

FIVE reveals himself most clearly by the way he responds to "Bend your head and tap the floor with your heel." To begin with, his whole body is involved. If he doesn't know "heel," this has to be taught. Though he has just responded to "Close your eyes and bend your head," this command was confined to the head region. Now bending the head becomes to him something different. He tends to bend his head way over onto the table if he remains seated, or into his lap if he pushes his chair back, or even down to the floor, especially if he chooses to stand. Along

TABLE 41   *Right and Left Single Commands*
(Average Time in Seconds)

	5	5½	6	Years 7	8	9	10	Adult
Touch your eye	2.1	1.8	1.1	1.2	1.2	1.0	.8	.9
Show index		1.9	3.5	2.4	2.0	1.0	1.1	.6
Show ring		6.2	3.3	2.8	2.4	1.6	1.5	1.1
Show middle		2.0	1.7	1.6	1.1	.6	.7	.7
Close eyes, bend head	2.2	1.2	.9	1.4	2.4	1.1	1.0	.5
Bend head, tap floor with heel	5.4	5.8	3.4	3.8	3.3	1.8	1.8	2.1
Raise head, open mouth		3.0	2.4	2.0	1.4	1.2	1.0	.6
Touch right ear	2.5	2.6	1.9	1.7	1.8	1.3	1.2	.7
Show right thumb	2.4	2.0	1.8	1.5	1.3	.9	.8	.7
Show left index	3.7	3.6	2.8	2.5	2.1	1.2	1.1	.6
Average in seconds per command	3.0	2.8	2.3	2.1	1.8	1.2	1.1	.85
Range, time in seconds	.4–30.0	.3–25.0	.3–20.0	.2–15.0	.2–10.0	.2–7.0	.2–6.0	

with this excessive bending, he is apt to bring his hand to his foot, to his heel, or to the floor. The examiner may have to repeat the command, emphasizing: "Tap the floor with your *heel.*" No wonder it can take him as long as 20 to 25 seconds to carry out this command.

The next single command that the 5-year-old has some trouble with is to locate the middle or big finger on his left hand. To locate it in the first place is difficult. He is most likely to look at all his fingers held tightly together and to choose the biggest one. Choosing the correct left hand is still a fair matter of chance, which makes the scoring difficult in this 5-to-6-year-old period.

The examiner needs not only to record the time it takes to respond to the command (and by this is meant the time it takes to respond correctly even though with help), but also to record as far as possible the way the child carried out the request. If he responds to the command of "Touch your eye" with right hand to right eye, "R to R" should record this move. If, however, he points to his right eye with his left hand, the recording should show "L to R." This significant "crossover" pattern we relate to a younger age. Other younger patterns may also be present in the child who shows a crossover pattern.

If the child bends his head back or to the side, these movements should be recorded. Bending the head back is an extensor pattern more expected of a 4-year-old. If this occurs, other extensor patterns are watched for, such as a sharp extensor release of the pencil. Along with extension or quick release patterns, the sustaining capacity of the child is often found to be below par.

Bending the head to the side doesn't occur very often and may be thought of as possibly atypical. However, it occurs frequently enough at 9 years of age (15%) to make us wonder whether it is not an expression of some age pattern at 9.

FIVE is known to have "stuck" patterns. Part of this is related to the fact that he so often completes himself through another person. This is why he often cannot act until he is given permission, as when his teacher replies to his request: "Yes, you may go and get some paper." In a similar way, after he has responded to "Close your eyes and bend your head," he may remain stuck in this position until the examiner releases him either with the next command or by telling him: "You may come up now" (50%–60% at 5–6 years). Even this may not be enough, because the examiner told him only to "Come up" but did not mention opening his eyes. Therefore the examiner may need to add: "And you may open your eyes." If a child tends to overhold, this can be recorded with the letters "O.H."

By 5½, most children can take the full battery of Right and Left tests, both single and double commands. If it becomes apparent that the full set of commands is beyond a child, the examiner should restrict the test to the 5-year-old battery.

The greater fluidity of the 5½-year-old's characteristic response is soon apparent. He studies his fingers as he chooses them. They pop up as he locates them. He may talk to his fingers, saying, "Hey, you," when they don't do quite what he wants them to. He may still confuse thumb and little finger or toe and heel (15% at 5 years, 9% at 5½).

By 6 (or even 5½), there is no question but that the child is ready for the full battery of commands. He often starts at once before the examiner has completed his request, or he may repeat the command out loud before he executes it. Sometimes the child repeats the request as a question, thus needing further help from the examiner. Often his response to a command is very rapid. SIX, by nature, responds with speed and completes with speed.

By 7, though the child may still repeat some of the commands, he is more likely to repeat them in a whisper. He often reveals his process of thought as he inhibits an initial response, such as the choice of the opposite hand, or of a wrong adjacent finger, before he responds correctly. This inhibited response should be recorded if possible (e.g., "inh. opp"; "inh. adj. ring").

Single-command scoring shows, on the whole, a steady improvement from age to age (see Table 41). The request "Bend your head and tap the floor with your heel" remains the hardest of the ten single commands throughout these years from 5 to 10 and even into adult life. (It is interesting to note that the 10-year-old on the average is faster to execute this command than the adult—2.1 seconds for the adult in contrast to 1.8 seconds for the 10-year-old.) The average time it takes to respond to these ten single commands shows a steady decrease from 3.0 seconds at 5 years to 1.1 seconds at 10 years. These figures prove that there are definite growth patterns that have occurred in these years. The growth of more advanced neurological contacts has undoubtedly enabled the organism to respond with increasing speed.

It is also interesting to consider the *range* of time of the responses which can occur in a standardization group of 100 subjects. As shown in Table 41, the range is fairly wide at 5 years but decreases from an outer limit of 30 seconds at 5 years to 6 seconds at 10 years. The very fast responses of .2 to .4 seconds are found in some from an early age.

There can be a markedly fluctuating timing for a single child in the 5-to-7-year realm especially, but on the whole the timing tends to settle down by 9 years of age and no longer shows wide variation from one command to another.

4. DOUBLE COMMANDS (5–10 YEARS) (TIMED IN SECONDS)

The ten double commands are as follows:

1. Touch your right thumb with your right little finger.
2. Place your left hand on your left knee.
3. Put your left ring finger to your right eyebrow.
4. Put your right elbow in the palm of your left hand.
5. Put your right middle finger on your left cheek.
6. Place your left thumb against your right thumb.
7. Place your right middle finger against your left little finger.
8. Place your right little finger against your left ring finger.
9. Place your left middle finger against your right index finger.
10. Place your left thumb against your right ring finger.

These are all straightforward requests. The one stumbling block may be "cheek," since the child has not been checked on this. A few confuse cheek and chin. The examiner needs to be careful to give the word used by the child for his index finger. Very few use "index" or "forefinger." The majority speak of the index as "pointer" and respond best to its being called this.

*1. Touch your right thumb with your right little finger.** This first double command is one of the two exacted of the 5-year-old. It usually taxes his ability to its limit, but at the same time reveals much about him.

---

* An example sheet (Figure 9) will be given at the end of this chapter to familiarize the examiner with abbreviations and ways of recording responses.

We can trace the origins of his difficulties as we examine the 4-year-old's response. To begin, FOUR needs to locate his right hand, then the thumb and little finger of that hand. As he looks at his outspread hand, he often says, "I can't."

When urged to try, he will try to push the thumb and little finger together just above the knuckle area. This is almost impossible to do without breaking a finger. The examiner, sensing his dilemma, then demonstrates that fingers can come together over the palm area rather than over the back of the hand. Even such a gesture may be difficult for the 4-year-old since his fingers tend to remain in extension, or one finger may flex but the other extend. The child will then need to push them together with his free hand.

There is one delightful response of the superior ingenious 4-year-old who, sensing his dilemma with his extended thumb and little finger on his right hand, closes the gap by placing his left thumb and little finger against his right thumb and little finger. You can't argue with him, for he has by this circuitous route touched his right thumb with his right little finger.

Both 5- and 6-year-old still tend to flex thumb and little finger over the back of the other fingers, but they effect closure just above the nail area or first joint. On occasion the fingers are physically not long enough to be able to touch each other.

This first double command persists in being one of the most difficult commands to carry out even at later ages. It is not until 7 years that the majority (63%) are able to execute it correctly on first trial. (See Table 42.)

TABLE 42   *Double Commands: Percentage of Children Responding Correctly on First Trial*

	5	5½	6	Years 7	8	9	10
Right thumb, right little	60	42	46	63	69	91	91
Left hand, left knee		51	72	76	83	86	83
Left ring, right eyebrow		24	44	44	58	78	80
Right elbow, palm left hand		60	64	75	92	98	96
Right middle, left cheek		38	24	54	64	87	78
Left thumb, right thumb		95	100	100	100	100	100
Right middle, left little	45	58	58	52	76	92	89
Right little, left ring		45	54	54	71	96	87
Left middle, right index		30	36	61	73	92	87
Left thumb, right ring		35	28	79	78	98	98

Besides the above-described difficulties, a good proportion at 5½ to 6 years (60% at 5½, 54% at 6) cross over to the other hand, placing their right thumb against their left little finger or vice versa.

The examiner repeats the request as often as an error persists. If repetition is not enough, the examiner will need to give help in a step-by-step fashion (21% at 5½, 24% at 6 years). He will say: "Show me your right thumb." When this is located, examiner holds the child's right thumb so he won't lose his choice. Then examiner continues: "Now show me your right little finger." When this is finally located, the child is told: "Now put them together." This need to be helped in a one-by-one fashion indicates a lack of good combining ability. It is as if the child can handle only one request at a time. This is an example of the focalization on a single idea or item so characteristic of FIVE.

2. *Place your left hand on your left knee.* The majority of subjects at 5½ (51%) can respond correctly to this request on first trial. Enacting the opposite of the command (that is, right hand on right knee) is the most common error (46% at 5½), but this decreases rapidly from then on. A probably significant error is a crossover pattern of placing the left hand on the right knee. The very literal child will need to expose the knee. Another variable is to lift the knee to the hand, a move which may demand swinging the knee out from under the table and thus consuming more time.

3. *Put your left ring finger to your right eyebrow.* This is a surprisingly difficult command to execute. It is consistently one of the commands taking the most time throughout the years it is given (from 5½ to 10), though the average time scores show steady and significant improvement. (See Table 43.)

Not only is finding the ring finger difficult, but also finding specifically the left ring finger. Added to these problems is the universal difficulty of isolating and extending the ring finger by itself so that it can be used to touch the right eyebrow.

The commonest error in finding the ring finger is to choose an adjacent finger, usually the middle finger, or to confuse ring and index fingers. Another common error is to choose the same-side eyebrow rather than the requested opposite eyebrow. The perplexity this command produces is often expressed by the child who says, "I'm all confused." Some need to be helped out of their confusion, especially at 5½ to 6 years, with step-by-step help.

4. *Put your right elbow in the palm of your left hand.* This is a relatively easy command even for the 5½-year-old (60%). There is the usual error of choosing the opposite. Occasionally a 5½-to-6-year-old will think he has been asked to place his right elbow in his right hand and flatly and correctly denies that this is possible.

5. *Put your right middle finger on your left cheek.* Not until 7 years of age can the average subject comply correctly with this command on first trial. There is a slight tendency to choose an adjacent finger in error; a greater tendency, especially at 6 years, to choose the little finger for the

middle finger. Some children become quite indignant, saying: "But you said 'little'" or "I thought you said 'little.'" The choice of the wrong hand is fairly common through 6 years. Chin is confused with cheek especially at 6 years (18%). And the choice of the same-side, or right, cheek is quite common (36% at 6 years). Errors persist fairly strongly with this command through 8 years of age. There may be need for step-by-step help at 5½ and 6 years.

6. *Place your left thumb against your right thumb.* This becomes a delightful moment of relaxation for the child after some of the harder commands. At 5½ years of age, 95% of subjects can obey this command correctly on first trial. In some, however, there is an unusually long delay in touching the two thumbs. This may be due to a literal interpretation that the left thumb must be sought first, so that it can touch the right thumb.

7. *Place your right middle finger against your left little finger.* The four double commands 7 to 10 should be considered together since they all involve a finger of one hand touching a finger of the other hand. The sequence of timing (Table 43) shows the clearly increased speed of response which comes with increased age.

This is the second of the two double commands asked of the 5-year-old, and may not be easy for him (6% refuse). One of the commonest errors is to choose both fingers on the same hand (22%). This may be influenced by the previous double command (1) given the 5-year-old. This error persists through 9 years. Quite often (17%) the child needs to be helped out of his difficulties by a step-by-step process.

By 5½ years the majority (58%) can execute this command on the first trial, but there is not a good margin before 8 years of age. (See Table 42.) There are the usual opposite and adjacent errors. Thumb may be confused with little finger through 5½ years. A common response which may show later significance is to match either both little fingers or both middle fingers.

8. *Place your right little finger against your left ring finger.* By 6 years, the majority (54%) are able to carry out this command on the first trial. (See Table 42.) There are the usual errors of opposite side, adjacent finger, middle for little, index for ring, choice of same side, or a tendency to match the same finger of the opposite hand. The thumb may still be chosen in place of the little finger through 6 years of age (4%). Step-by-step help may still be needed through 6 years of age (6%). It may be difficult to pry the ring finger up so that it can be used to point to the little finger.

9. *Place your left middle finger against your right index finger.* This command doesn't achieve majority rating of success on the first trial until 7 years of age (61%). (See Table 42.) The choice of opposite (incorrect) fingers is still quite marked at 5½ to 6 years (40%–50%).

TABLE 43 *Right and Left Double Commands*
(Average Time in Seconds)

			Years			
	5	5½	6	7	8	9
Right thumb, right little	14.6	12.1	11.6	6.8	6.0	4.3
Left hand, left knee		3.8	4.1	3.8	2.3	1.6
Left ring, right eyebrow		11.8	10.0	9.2	7.3	4.2
Right elbow, palm left hand		4.6	4.0	4.3	2.5	1.1
Right middle, left cheek		9.1	7.6	6.9	4.9	3.1
Left thumb, right thumb		2.7	2.3	2.1	1.5	1.2
Right middle, left little	12.1	9.6	6.3	8.2	4.8	3.0
Right little, left ring		8.0	8.0	6.8	5.2	2.0
Left middle, right index		12.6	9.8	9.7	6.0	3.0
Left thumb, right ring		9.8	7.2	5.7	4.2	2.3
Average time per command	13.3	8.4	7.1	6.4	4.5	2.6
Range	1.2–55.0	.6–40.0	.3–40.0	.3–40.0	.3–35.0	.2–20.0

Right and Left

Name **Boy**

Age **6¹¹**

Naming parts of body

1. Eye
2. ˙Eyebrow
3. Palm **hand (what else) (show)**
4. Elbow

Naming fingers () 5 yr. items

(1) Thumb
2 Index (pter)
(3) Middle (2-2) **ring, tallman**
         (2-2) center (or)
4 Ring (wear)
(5) Little **pinkie**

Naming R & L

    R hand (point to child's R hand)

    Show me your R hand (if can't name R hand)

    How do you know?

    L hand (point to child's L hand)

    Ex-er's R hand (show)

    How do you know? **If I turned over that way**
                          it would be my R. hd.

Single Commands () 5 yr. items

		Seconds	Method
(1)	Eye	1.4 R to R	
2	Index	10.1 mid (r) ring(r) L to R	
3	Ring	2.9 R to L	
4	Middle	1.0 R to L	
(5)	Cl. eyes, bend head	1.4 c.u.	
(6)	Bend head, tap fl. with heel	3.9 b.back	
7	Raise head, open mouth	5.4	
(8)	R ear	2.4	
(9)	R thumb	1.4 L to R	
(10)	L index (5 yrs-L big)	2.1 inh. mid, R to L	
	Total	32.0 Av. 3.2 (7 years 2.1)	

Double Command () 5 yr. items

		Seconds	Method
(1)	R thumb-R little	3.1	on top
2	L hand-L knee	1.6	
3	L ring-R eyebrow	7.2	L e.b.(r)
4	R elbow-palm L hand	5.4	L fist (r)
5	R middle-L cheek	3.0	
6	L thumb-R thumb	4.0	inh. R lit.
(7)	R middle-L little	1.8	
8	R little-L ring	4.8	ring pulled up
9	L middle-R index	17.2	R ring(r) R mid(r)
10	L thumb-R ring	18.1	R index(r); L hand on top of R hand
	Total	66.2	Av. 6.6 (7yrs.6.4)

Summary Comments:

    Scoring better than quality shows. Bends head back;
    confuses thumb and little; adj. errors.
    Deficit on double commands 7 to 10.

Figure 9. Sample record, Boy 6¹¹, of Right and Left tests

This may partially be due to fatigue. As with the above two commands (7 and 8), the errors include an adjacent choice, mixing little for middle or ring for index, and matching the same finger on the opposite hand. Considerable confusion is engendered during the carrying out of this command and also considerable help through a step-by-step method (10% at 5½ and 6 years) may be needed.

10. *Place your left thumb against your right ring finger.*   As with the above command (9), the majority do not succeed on first trial before 7 years of age (79%). (See Table 42.) As above, the choice of opposite fingers is strong at 5½ and 6 years (50%). The confusion of ring and index, considerable at 5½ to 6 years (23% at 5½, 20% at 6 years), as well as adjacent errors (10% at 5½ years, 16% at 6 years), indicate that it is difficult to localize an individual finger, especially if it is the ring finger. Only a few match with the same finger on the opposite hand or choose both fingers on the same hand. Some step-by-step help may be needed.

As with the single commands, very definite improvement with age is apparent in the double commands in relation to the scoring time. (See Table 43.) The harder commands persist in their higher time scoring and the easier commands persist in their lower time scoring. Steady but real improvement is evident from year to year. Substantial gains are evident at 8 years, with definite consolidation of these gains by 9 years.

CHAPTER *8*

MONROE VISUAL TESTS

||||||||||||||||||||||||||||||||||||||||||||||||||||||||||||||||||||||||||||

VISUAL ONE

In our early exploration of ways and means to test the young child's mind in its readiness for school, we glimpsed his pleasure in matching forms. Visual One, a matching test from Marion Monroe's Reading Readiness test, suited our purposes ideally. We found it to be a task that demanded understanding of direction, carrying out of orders, and the ability to sustain and to find one's place repeatedly. This was no small demand even of the 5-year-old, yet it is what he needs to have at his command before he can accept the demands and enjoy the delights of a kindergarten situation. Visual One, we soon came to realize, had only a rather short longitudinal life of usefulness as a test, but what it tells us makes it well worth including in our test battery.

Administration

MATERIAL

The Visual One work sheet (see Figure 10) neatly assembles twelve double forms (one of each pair being the same as the model presented on the test card) in twelve squares, three across and four down, thus nicely orienting the child to the vertical page. In each square the correct form, which matches the one on the card, may be either at the top or at the bottom. (The correct forms are checked in Figure 10.)

Examiner: Test page 7
Child: Test page 8; a sharp No. 2½ pencil; twelve Visual One cards

PROCEDURE

Place test page 8, and the pencil, on the table in front of the child. Just beyond the upper edge of the child's page place the pile of twelve Visual One cards.

Say: "This is a matching game. We're going to work across like this." Gesture L to R, line by line across the page.

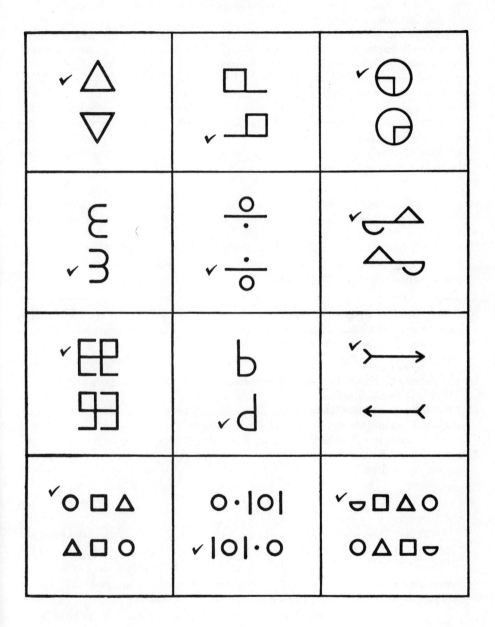

Score............

Figure 10.   Visual Test I

Say: "We're going to start here." Point to the first box. Then say: "One of these is just like this one," and point to the top card. Then say: "I want you to put a circle around the one that looks just like this one."

If no response, gesture with finger and say: "The one that goes in the same direction." If the child circles the wrong choice, say: "Which one has the point going up?" Demonstrate by indicating the point on the triangle.

If the child encircles both, say: "Just one." If the circle is placed beside or inside the form, say: "Make the circle go around." Demonstrate by gesturing.

If directions need to be clarified on the second card, gesture over the horizontal baseline of the form on the card from R to L and say: "Which one goes this way?" but give no further instruction.

From then on merely present the cards in order. Give no further help except to assist the child in finding his place.

RECORDING

At the top of test page 7, use the circles to record the direction of the child's strokes. Place arrowheads on each circle to indicate where the child starts his stroke and the direction of the stroke.

Place an X inside the circle if the child needs help to find his place. Next to the circle make a minus sign (−) if the child circles the incorrect choice. Record any comments made by the child as he works.

SCORING

After the testing is completed, transfer minus signs (−) and X's to the child's page. In the lower-right-hand corner, record on the line provided the number of correct choices over the number given, as 10/12, or 6/6.

GENERAL DIRECTIONS

Directions may be clarified on the first two cards only. From then on, the child is given help only to locate his place.

If the child is unable to circle a choice (as with most 3-to-3½-year-olds), allow him to point. If he is unable to understand the task—that is, continues to need help with directions after the third or fourth card is presented—then terminate the test.

If the child has difficulty sustaining his efforts (as with many 3-to-3½-year-olds), present the first six cards only.

Findings

Visual One is FIVE and FIVE-AND-A-HALF's test. (Even the 4½-year-old, as Table 44 shows, is not really up to it and some FIVES find it too difficult. The 5½-year-old really seems to enjoy it. SIX, too, may enjoy it very much, but his ease and nonchalance sometimes suggest that he thinks the examiner hasn't chosen too well.

The actual scoring results show how well this test is suited to both 5- and 5½-year-olds. FIVES are just over the 50% hump of getting ten or more out of the twelve correct, whereas FIVE-AND-A-HALVES fall in the 90th percentile of getting ten or more correct, twelve correct being normative at this age. A marked improvement has occurred from the 14% of girls and 8% of boys giving all twelve correct at 5 years of age, to 76% of girls and 66% of boys at 5½. Most SIXES and SEVENS get all correct.

Even though a test, so far as actual scoring goes, may become too easy, the quality of the response can still reveal much. The quality is especially important at 5 and 5½ years. In the first place, FIVE often has difficulty in understanding what he is to do. He usually can be made to understand and can carry out the instructions, even though he is apt to lose his discriminative powers on the last half of the test and is likely to encircle each top form, without matching. The child is thus becoming perseverative in his 5-year-old way, but he is still complying, for he wishes most to do what is right, and to please.

Often he has trouble in locating the next square, especially when he has to shift to a new line. Each transition becomes a new task not related to the last task. So having finished one task, his eyes dart over the page trying to locate the next square, seemingly so easily in his reach. Over and over again the examiner may need to help locate him in the right square. Then he happily goes about the business of matching, but orienting him once does not necessarily help him to locate the succeeding square, even though he has been told he is to move across the page from left to right.

Achieving the ability to locate the next square occurs strikingly at 5½. One comes to know that a real growth step has been taken when the child can go easily from one point to the next in an orderly fashion. It is the 5½- and especially the 6-year-old who is heard to say, "Don't tell me," as he searches for his place. FIVE-AND-A-HALF's main difficulty is shifting to the next line.

The quality of the child's method of encircling with respect to the starting point, direction, and closure also tells us something about his sustained functioning. Though girls can copy a single circle from the top CCW at 5 years of age, the method of starting at the top is not likely to be sustained for the majority of the Visual One forms before 6 years of age (60% G, 64% B). (See Table 44.) The CCW direction, however, tends to be established by 5½ years, when 66% of girls, 50% of boys, draw over half the forms CCW.

FIVE is most likely to start from the bottom in this test. He may maintain a CW direction. As he comes into 5½, however, he tends to shift a good deal, starting at top, bottom, or at either side—going CW at one time, CCW the next. (This variability characterizes much behavior at 5½.) Closure is hard to judge, but it is at least *fairly* well accomplished by 6 years (68% G, 56% B).

Table 44 gives data on Visual One for the number of responses made correctly, type of closure, starting point, and direction of drawing.

Apart from his scoring, the individual child tells a good deal about himself by the way he encircles. There is the child who encircles the

TABLE 44   *Visual One*
(Percentage)

	4½ Years		5 years		5½ years		6 years		7 years	
	G	B	G	B	G	B	G	B	G	B
Number Correct										
10 correct	12	11	26	14	4	10	6	2	0	4
11 correct	9	3	18	30	12	20	6	6	16	0
12 correct	9	3	14	8	76	66	86	90	84	96
10 or more	29	17	58	52	92	96	98	98	100	100
Tracing	0	0	4	4	2	0	0	0	0	0
Closure										
No record			4	4	0	0	0	0	0	0
Poor			30	34	42	44	6	30	4	0
Fair			50	46	52	46	68	56	56	60
Good			16	16	6	10	26	14	40	40
Starting Point										
Bottom, all forms			8	18	12	18	16	16	0	8
Top, all forms			8	8	22	16	38	34	48	32
Bottom, more than ½			46	60	32	48	26	26	32	44
Top, more than ½			36	22	42	36	60	64	68	54
Direction										
CW, all			8	42	14	26	22	18	28	12
CCW, all			24	6	32	30	42	46	36	48
CW, more than ½			56	78	30	46	34	38	36	28
CCW, more than ½			40	22	66	50	66	62	64	72

forms with a rapid, heavy, sloppy, gross motor stroke. These are the active, gross motor children. Or there are those who can't stop and who keep encircling with a circular scribble. This is the type of child who needs limits or he becomes disruptive in the classroom. In the early grades such a child may need to be put on reduced attendance. Then there are those who produce wobbly circles with very poor closure points, suggesting that their fine motor control hasn't as yet come into good form. Some of these children need extra stimulation and help in the fine motor field. When a child produces clean-cut, well-formed, well-closed-in circles, consistently starting from the top in a CCW direction, there is every evidence that his is a well-constituted organism.

VISUAL THREE

Along with Visual One from Marion Monroe's Reading Readiness test, we include Visual Three, a Memory-for-Designs test which tells us much about the growing child's power of recall. This test, unlike Visual

One, has a longitudinal potential. We have found that it still has some-thing to tell us even in the teens, and also in old-age research. It was one of the most discerning tests to help determine whether an older person still held on to those threads of learning potential that were in the equip-ment of a 5-year-old or older child.

Here again, as with Visual One, Monroe showed a unique capacity to assemble a variety of shapes and forms without inherent meaning that demand great accuracy of perception as the subject responds. The ✕

and the ⊤ are the only obvious letters, and even these can readily be

seen as other than letters because of the addition of the dots.

The form ❘•❘ , which is often seen as an eleven, is for many trans-formed into something quite different by the presence of the dot. The apparent difficulty of all these forms made it of interest to explore the way in which children saw the forms and the way they would project into them.

Material and Comment

On each of four 8½-by-11-inch cards there are four figures placed in horizontal alignment. (See Figure 11.) The forms are in black and lines are ⅛ inch wide. It may be because the line is this wide that some children draw it as a double line and may even blacken in the first space between these double lines. One form on each of the first three cards is half blacked in. On each of the first three cards there is also a form with a separate but related dot. On the fourth card there is a form in which the dot is an integral part of the pattern. ⊤

How the child reproduces these forms gives us an idea of how he is seeing them. The examiner will find it helpful to know the forms so well that he can readily produce them from memory. Then as the child is being tested he can more readily judge what has meaning to this special child. Does the child choose all the filled-in forms, or all the dot forms? Does he select the first forms, or the last forms? Does he select the first and last forms, that is, the outside forms, in the way in which a 7-year-old often sees only the first and last letters of a word. SEVEN knows how a word begins and how it ends, but he has trouble in the middle.

The examiner soon comes to realize that a child's scoring is only one way in which he should be judged. The how and why of the response to the material is quite as important as the ability to recall.

In addition to the four white cards with their black figures, there is a pink work sheet (pink only for convenience in locating the sheet in a child's record) on which is a boxed-in form with four horizontal spaces—one space for the response to each card. (See Appendix A.)

Top 1 — Visual Test 3
(Expose 10 seconds)

Top 2 — Visual Test 3
(Expose 10 seconds)

Top 3 — Visual Test 3
(Expose 10 seconds)

Top 4 — Visual Test 3
(Expose 10 seconds)

Figure 11.   Visual Three forms

Administration and Scoring

The work sheet and a pencil are placed before the child. The examiner exposes the first card momentarily, telling the child that he will be allowed to look at this card for a while (actual exposure 10 seconds by stopwatch) and then it will be taken away.

The child is then told that he is to write down as many of the designs or forms as he can remember in the first horizontal space on the pink sheet. (Examiner points out the place.) The card is then placed on the table above his work sheet.

FIVE may have trouble in understanding, and may need a repetition of the instructions, or may wish to copy the forms while the card is being exposed. He is told that he is to wait until the card is removed. If this is still hard for him to understand, the examiner says he will help him to remember by holding his pencil until it is time.

(With some FIVES and even with some SIXES, the method of administration may have to be altered slightly. Many FIVES want to start drawing either at once, or after only a 2- or 3-second exposure. The examiner then shifts the procedure by asking the child to tell when he is ready, and recording the length of time the card was exposed. If the child seems bewildered by the multiplicity of the forms on the card, the examiner may suggest that he choose just one form to look at and to remember.)

After these initial instructions with the first card, no further suggestion is made as to where on the paper the child should place his forms. He may wish to place the forms outside the lined-in area. He may place them all from all four cards in the top space. He is allowed to place them where he chooses.

There is one special exception, most often necessary at 6 years. The child may reproduce the first card by placing the forms vertically, one in each space (or as many as he remembers). This is allowed, but then the examiner gives him a second pink work sheet and asks him to place the forms horizontally in the spaces, for the other cards. The child usually accepts this directive with ease, but at the same time he has revealed a choice of vertical orientation, which may have significance in that his method of organization is quite different from the model.

One other variable is allowed when a child wants more than the allotted 10 seconds before he is ready to start drawing. This demand is most frequent with the 7-year-old, who characteristically has trouble both in letting go and in finishing. He often wishes to take as much as 15 to 20 seconds before he is ready. Unfortunately, the longer he takes, seemingly the less he recalls. If this exception is permitted, it must of course be recorded.

The score for this test is determined by giving each correctly reproduced form a score of one point. If the form reproduced is recognizable but partially incorrect, it is given half a point. At times one may need to stretch one's imagination to classify the reproduction as recognizable. In such a case it might best be scored as questionable (?), without giving any point score. This difficulty is rare after 5 years of age.

A second type of score which should be obtained is the percentage of figures tried which are reproduced absolutely correctly. Thus if eight figures are tried but four are completely incorrect or only half correct, that leaves 50% reproduced correctly.

Findings

In Table 45, the scores of boys and girls were averaged together, since differences were very slight. The progression from age to age is

TABLE 45   *Mean Number Correct on Visual Three*

Age	Score	Deviation of Score from Age	Percentage of Tried Figures Made Correctly
5 years	3.5	−1.5	37
5½ years	4.5	−1.0	54
6 years	5.7	− .3	52
6½ years	6.8 (Weston)	+ .2	
7 years	7.6	+ .6	60
8 years	8.8	+ .8	68
9 years	10.4	+1.4	73
10 years	11.2	+1.2	74

clear. Since there was such a gap (almost 2 points) from 6 to 7 years, the Weston figure of 6.8 correct at 6½ years has been inserted.

It is interesting to note that this figure (6.8) is closest to the age it is scoring. At one time we thought there was a convenient relationship between the age of the child and the expected score, but this turns out to penalize the child below 6½ and to favor him after 6½. However, though slightly inaccurate, this notion may help some examiners to remember expected scores without consulting their scoring tables. The examiner needs to remember that these scoring figures indicate that 50% or more of the children examined received the score reported.

Table 45 also includes figures for percentage of all tried which are completely correct. As this table shows, by 5½ years we expect half the figures tried to be reproduced correctly.

Table 46 indicates the age at which each form is mastered by 50% or more of subjects. It will be seen that, in general, subjects do better on the first card than for subsequent cards, and that the first form of any given card is the one that is most likely to be correctly reproduced.

TABLE 46 *Visual Three: Age at Which 50% or More Respond Correctly (Sexes Combined)*

		Years
Card I		
Form One	△	$5\frac{1}{2}$
Form Two	◑	7
Form Three	⌐.	9
Form Four	⋁	9
Card II		
Form One	⊃—	7
Form Two	|•|	7
Form Three	◧	10
Form Four	⌂	9
Card III		
Form One	•✕	6
Form Two	◪	
Form Three	—⊦	10
Form Four	⊖	10
Card IV		
Form One	△	8
Form Two	⊓⊔	
Form Three	⊤	
Form Four	⊓⊔	

The fluctuation of the scoring from card to card reveals as much as the final numerical score itself. At 5, children score approximately the same on each card (.5 to 1.0 on each). By 6 years, there is a fuller grasp of the forms on a card, which may yield a 4 to 3.5 score on the first card, especially since SIX is good at beginnings. But the scores on subsequent cards may steadily decline to 2, 1, and finally .5. This we call a deficit pattern, so characteristic of SIX, who needs either to be given a change, or to be picked up or salvaged.

The more up-and-down scoring by SEVEN (2.5, 1.5, 2.0, 1.5, for example) suggests that he is not at the mercy of loss, and can pick himself up in part at least. EIGHT not only picks himself up, but may even improve as he proceeds. This may be classed as a "bounce-back" (2.5, 1.0, 2.0, 3.0 on successive cards).

An interesting kind of response, more related to personality than to age, is a very high score on the first two cards (2.0, 3.5) followed by a marked slump on the last two cards (1.0, .5). Thus the scores of the first two cards together might be 5.5 and the last two only 1.5. Children who respond in this way, we feel, can't hold up on a full assignment (the four cards), but they do quite nicely on half an assignment (two cards). (Teachers should be willing to recognize this inability. If a child like this is pushed in school to do the whole assignment, he's likely to end in doing nothing.)

Sometimes a child can't remember a single thing on some one card. It seems as though everything has flown right out of his mind. This phenomenon we call a "blackout." It occurs most in the early years, to the following extent: at 5 years of age, 31% of children experience a blackout on some one card; at $5\frac{1}{2}$ years, 17%; at 6 years, 15%; at 7 years, 1%; at 8 years, 5%; at 9 and 10 years, none. Though this occurs most at 5 years, awareness of such a blackout may be more marked at 6 years, when the child may say, "I don't know where they all went."

NUMBER OF FORMS ATTEMPTED, AND NUMBER REPRODUCED CORRECTLY AND INCORRECTLY

Tables 47–50 indicate, for each of the four cards separately, how many children at each age attempt or do not attempt each form; and for those who do attempt the forms, how many make the forms correctly and how many incorrectly.

Number attempted. As these tables show, the majority of 5-year-olds attempt Form One on Cards I, II, and III, with decreasing numbers trying the remaining forms. FIVE-AND-A-HALVES do little more.

Six-year-olds try the first two forms on the first two cards, and Form One on Cards III and IV. Seven-year-olds try all forms on Card I, the first three on II, and the first one on III and IV.

Eight-year-olds try all forms on the first two cards, Forms One and Four on Card III, and Forms One and Four on Card IV. Nine-year-olds

TABLE 47   *Visual Three: Responses to Card I*
(Percentage)

	5 years		5½ years		6 years		7 years		8 years		9 years		10 years	
	G	B	G	B	G	B	G	B	G	B	G	B	G	B
Form One △														
Not attempted	28	38	28	26	16	10	8	8	12	8	8	10	4	0
Attempted	66	54	80	74	84	90	92	92	88	92	92	90	96	100
Correct	28	30	50	60	62	64	82	76	78	80	84	82	88	94
Incorrect	38	24	30	14	22	26	10	16	10	12	8	8	8	6
Unscorable	6	8	2	0	0	0	0	0	0	0	0	0	0	0
Form Two ◖														
Not attempted	44	56	40	60	36	36	16	14	10	16	4	10	2	0
Attempted	50	36	58	40	64	64	84	86	90	84	96	90	98	100
Correct	16	8	36	16	24	20	52	60	70	74	88	86	82	96
Incorrect	34	28	22	24	40	44	32	26	20	10	8	4	16	4
Unscorable	6	8	2	0	0	0	0	0	0	0	0	0	0	0
Form Three ⌐•														
Not attempted	74	64	74	80	60	62	34	26	28	14	18	6	6	12
Attempted	20	28	24	20	40	38	66	74	72	86	82	94	94	88
Correct	2	4	8	6	12	16	30	40	34	48	48	60	48	60
Incorrect	18	24	16	14	28	22	36	34	38	38	34	34	46	28
Unscorable	6	8	2	0	0	0	0	0	0	0	0	0	0	0
Form Four V														
Not attempted	68	72	76	80	54	62	44	42	30	38	24	16	16	12
Attempted	26	20	22	20	46	38	56	58	70	62	76	84	84	88
Correct	8	4	16	12	20	34	34	38	50	48	58	52	58	62
Incorrect	18	16	6	8	26	4	22	20	20	14	18	32	26	26
Unscorable	6	8	2	0	0	0	0	0	0	0	0	0	0	0

try all on I and II, Forms One and Four on Card III, and all except Form Three on Card IV. Ten-year-olds at least try all forms.

Number responding correctly. No form is reproduced correctly by as many as 50% of 5-year-olds. However, 5½-year-olds succeed (50% or more of children) on Form One, Card I. By 6 years of age, the normative child can reproduce correctly Form One, Card I, and Form One, Card III. The 7- and 8-year-old reproduces correctly Forms One and Two, Cards I and II, and Form One, Card III. The 8-year-old also reproduces Form One, Card IV.

The 9-year-old succeeds on all forms, Card I; Forms One, Two, and Four, Card II; Form One, Cards III and IV. The 10-year-old succeeds on

TABLE 48   *Visual Three: Responses to Card II*
(Percentage)

	5 years		5½ years		6 years		7 years		8 years		9 years		10 years	
	G	B	G	B	G	B	G	B	G	B	G	B	G	B

Form One ⌐

	5 years		5½ years		6 years		7 years		8 years		9 years		10 years	
Not attempted	38	54	22	42	26	16	18	12	16	12	4	8	2	6
Attempted	56	38	76	58	74	84	82	88	84	88	96	92	98	94
Correct	24	10	46	22	40	50	58	64	62	60	70	68	72	76
Incorrect	32	28	30	36	34	34	24	24	22	28	26	24	26	18
Unscorable	6	8	2	0	0	0	0	0	0	0	0	0	0	0

Form Two |•|

	5 years		5½ years		6 years		7 years		8 years		9 years		10 years	
Not attempted	52	58	42	46	42	40	24	14	22	12	8	12	10	16
Attempted	42	34	56	54	58	60	76	86	78	88	92	88	90	84
Correct	28	22	38	40	38	42	54	64	58	82	80	78	76	72
Incorrect	14	12	18	14	20	18	22	22	20	6	12	10	14	12
Unscorable	6	8	2	0	0	0	0	0	0	0	0	0	0	0

Form Three ■□

	5 years		5½ years		6 years		7 years		8 years		9 years		10 years	
Not attempted	80	78	70	78	66	56	34	50	38	32	24	16	6	20
Attempted	14	14	28	22	34	44	66	50	62	68	76	84	94	80
Correct	4	0	10	4	10	12	16	20	24	38	48	46	60	56
Incorrect	10	14	18	18	24	32	50	30	38	30	28	38	34	24
Unscorable	6	8	2	0	0	0	0	0	0	0	0	0	0	0

Form Four ⬆

	5 years		5½ years		6 years		7 years		8 years		9 years		10 years	
Not attempted	76	76	72	82	54	86	60	58	42	38	22	44	20	28
Attempted	18	16	26	18	46	14	40	42	58	62	78	56	80	72
Correct	4	6	12	14	22	6	34	32	48	46	60	50	68	54
Incorrect	14	10	14	4	24	8	6	10	10	16	18	6	12	18
Unscorable	6	8	2	0	0	0	0	0	0	0	0	0	0	0

all forms, Cards I and II; Forms One and Three, Card III; and Form One, Card IV.

Thus it is not until 9 years that the majority of children can reproduce all four forms of Card I correctly. At 10 years, both Cards I and II are reproduced correctly, but only one to three forms on Cards III and IV. It is not until the teens that the majority can master Card IV.

PLACEMENT OF FORMS AND NUMBER OF LINES USED

In the instructions, the child is told to write down as many forms as he can remember from the first card onto the first line or space on the work sheet. The examiner indicates the place so that there will be no

TABLE 49 *Visual Three: Responses to Card III*
(Percentage)

	5 years		5½ years		6 years		7 years		8 years		9 years		10 years	
	G	B	G	B	G	B	G	B	G	B	G	B	G	B
Form One														
Not attempted	34	26	16	22	6	6	12	6	8	12	8	4	2	0
Attempted	60	66	82	78	94	94	88	94	92	88	92	96	98	100
Correct	16	18	42	30	56	60	46	78	66	70	82	88	84	88
Incorrect	44	48	40	48	38	34	42	16	26	18	10	8	14	12
Form Two														
Not attempted	76	70	68	70	62	56	78	54	56	62	52	46	36	42
Attempted	18	22	30	30	38	44	22	46	44	38	48	54	64	58
Correct	0	8	6	10	6	2	0	12	20	18	28	32	30	40
Incorrect	18	14	24	20	32	42	22	34	24	20	20	22	34	18
Form Three														
Not attempted	80	80	80	88	74	88	60	80	50	64	48	64	42	40
Attempted	14	12	18	12	26	12	40	20	50	36	52	36	58	60
Correct	8	10	10	10	18	10	32	18	46	28	46	32	52	52
Incorrect	6	2	8	2	8	2	8	2	4	8	6	4	6	8
Form Four														
Not attempted	74	72	74	84	76	68	64	62	44	44	34	40	38	24
Attempted	20	20	24	16	24	32	36	38	56	56	66	60	62	76
Correct	8	8	18	14	8	16	16	18	32	30	48	36	42	62
Incorrect	12	12	6	2	16	16	20	20	24	26	18	24	20	14

doubt. The majority of 5-year-olds (51%) place forms from one card after another all on the top line, never questioning that it should be otherwise. If the child runs out of space on the top line, especially at 5½ or 6 years, he may backtrack on the second line from right to left. It is not before 6 or 6½ that the child asks where he should place responses to the second card, as he points to the first space or the second one. He is told to choose whichever one he wishes. He tends to choose the second line for the second card and the third and fourth lines for the third and fourth cards.

There are a number of variables. Some use only two or three lines in all. Sometimes wide spaces may be left between forms on the top line, which are filled in later with forms from subsequent cards. This is more commonly seen at 5½.

The vertical placement of the forms on the first card has already

TABLE 50   *Visual Three: Responses to Card IV*
(Percentage)

	5 years G	B	5½ years G	B	6 years G	B	7 years G	B	8 years G	B	9 years G	B	10 years G	B
Form One ⌃⌐														
Not attempted	52	48	34	50	26	32	32	30	36	32	24	18	22	10
Attempted	42	44	64	50	74	68	68	70	64	68	76	82	78	90
Correct	22	24	36	26	44	54	44	42	52	52	70	68	70	82
Incorrect	20	20	28	24	30	14	24	28	12	16	6	14	8	8
Form Two ⊓⊔														
Not attempted	68	68	76	78	66	76	66	66	58	46	42	44	34	46
Attempted	26	24	22	22	34	24	34	34	42	54	58	56	66	54
Correct	12	6	14	10	24	16	24	24	34	36	44	52	50	26
Incorrect	14	18	8	12	10	8	10	10	8	18	14	4	16	28
Form Three ⊤														
Not attempted	78	70	68	80	76	88	68	74	48	60	58	64	42	48
Attempted	26	22	30	20	24	12	32	26	52	40	42	36	58	52
Correct	22	6	20	16	10	4	24	18	30	34	40	32	50	46
Incorrect	4	16	10	4	14	8	8	8	22	6	2	4	8	6
Form Four ⌐⌐														
Not attempted	90	92	92	90	80	82	48	52	50	34	30	20	6	24
Attempted	4	0	6	10	20	18	52	48	50	66	70	80	94	76
Correct	0	0	2	2	2	4	4	8	12	4	8	18	20	12
Incorrect	4	0	4	8	18	14	48	40	38	62	62	62	74	64

been mentioned. This is more likely to occur at 5½ years (5%). Another variable is placing the forms outside the allotted lined-in space.

Though SEVEN is able to take in the whole range of the four forms, he may still respond only to the first and fourth forms on a card. Then he is likely to place his reproduction of the fourth form directly after the first form without leaving a space for the missing second and third forms. He becomes more aware of the way in which he places forms at 7 to 8 years and may query: "Do they have to be in order?" He is told: "No, it doesn't matter." Even if told it did matter, he might well misplace a number of forms at this age. Placement becomes more accurate from 8 years on. On the whole, direction is from left to right, but a fair proportion (11%) progress from right to left at 5 years of age.

As to number of lines used, 5-year-olds as a rule use only one line.

Response at 5½ and 6 years is highly variable. At 7 years and following, however, the majority of children use all four lines on the form sheet. (Clinical experience suggests that this comes in at 6 years.)

ERRORS

A child younger than 5 years of age cannot effectively respond to Visual Three. A young 5-year-old needs kinesthetic reinforcement (he traces form with finger) and makes many vertical reversals. Thus

becomes

The 5-year-old is apt to separate a form into parts if it doesn't seem to him to go together as a whole, e.g.,

becomes

Or he may add to a form after completion. Forms may be at an angle, and many forms are questionable.

At 5 and 6 years of age it is not unusual for a child to shift a horizontal or oblique form to a vertical position. In the 5½-to-6-year realm the desire for symmetry may be so strong that the form is changed to become more symmetric (

becomes   ).

The 6½-year-old often ignores shading and draws only a line of demarcation. Many ask if they have to make the forms in order.

In these same earlier years from 5 to 7, forms are apt to shift. Thus a triangle may be reproduced as a square or a circle; or a triangle, especially at 7, may be reproduced as a diamond. An interesting phenomenon, most likely to occur at 7, is the child's pleasure in making a continuous or continuing stroke. This difficulty in stopping is especially evident in the last form on Card IV (

becomes

).

The 7-year-old often grounds dots

and perseverates or repeats forms.

At 8 years of age there is good awareness of spacing, and a tendency to leave a space for forgotten forms. Outlining of forms may be more common at 5 and again at 9 years, but the younger child does this with less success. Some NINES sketch their forms.

Besides the reversals and errors, the size of the forms and their position within the space allotted may tell much about age and individuality. FIVE's forms may be small and cramped or very irregular in size. SIX's forms tend to be large, filling the whole space of the line. If smaller, they tend to rise to the top of the space. This is not so at 7 and 8 years, when a firm footing in reality, a sure grounding, is desired. SEVENS and EIGHTS tend to place their forms surely on the line, giving them a good base on which to stand.

Figures 12 and 13, which follow, give sample responses to the Visual Three test at approximately yearly intervals from 5 through 10 years of age.

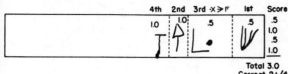

GIRL 4

SCORE: 3.0 (5-year norm 3.5).

CORRECT: $2+/4 = 50\%$ (5½-year norm 54%).

QUALITY: Works from R to L; chooses 3rd or 4th forms.

Chooses one form from each card (5 years).

Good awareness of detail.

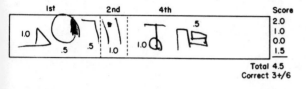

BOY 5[9]

SCORE: 4.5 (5½-year norm 4.5).

CORRECT: $3+/6 = 50\%$ (5½-year norm 54%).

QUALITY: Works from L to R; places all forms in 1 space.

Blackout on Card 3.

Good sense of stretch (3 on Card 1), loss (blackout on Card 3), and recovery (2 on Card 4).

Good awareness of detail.

Forms tend to rise to top of space (5½–6 years).

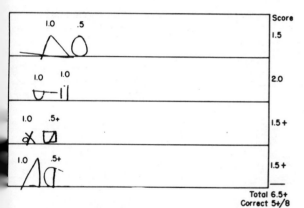

BOY 6[6]

SCORE: $6.5+$ (6½-year norm 6.8).

CORRECT: $5+/8 = 63\%$ (7-year norm 60%).

QUALITY: Uses all 4 spaces (6½ years⁺).

Tries only first 2 forms (restriction).

Irregular size to forms (6 years) or erratic.

Forms are grounded on lines (7–8 years).

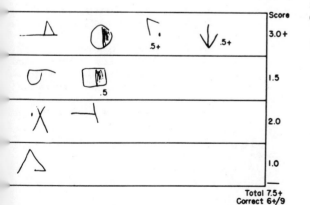

GIRL 7[4]

SCORE: $7.5+$ (7-year norm 7.6).

CORRECT: $6+/9 = 66\%$ (7-year norm 60%).

QUALITY: Uses all 4 spaces.

Good consistency of size (7 years).

Irregular base line; forms tend to rise to top of space (6 years).

Good awareness of detail.

Contracting space placing 1st and 3rd forms of Cards 3 and 4 right after each other (7 years).

Suggestive deficit in pattern; decline in scoring from 3.0⁺ on Card 1 to 1.0 on Card 4 (6 years⁺).

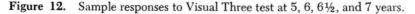

Figure 12. Sample responses to Visual Three test at 5, 6, 6½, and 7 years.

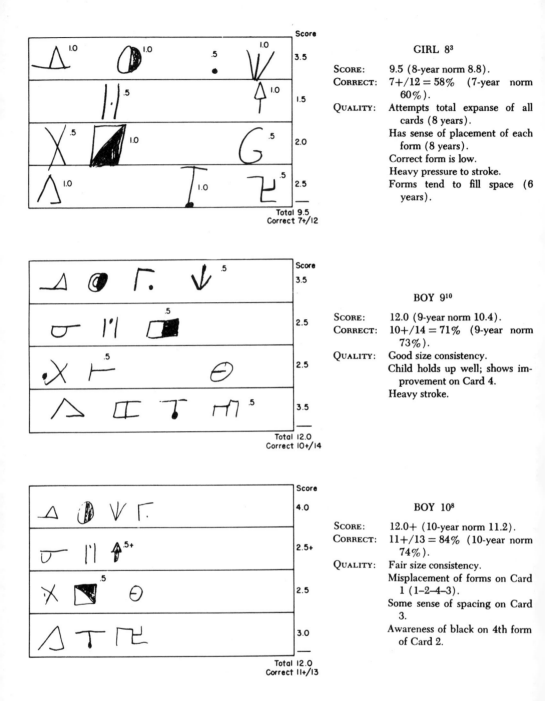

Figure 13. Sample responses to Visual Three test at 8, 9, and 10 years.

CHAPTER 9

NAMING ANIMALS

|||||||||||||||||||||||||||||||||||||||||||||||||||||||||||||||||||||||||||||||

The naming of animals for 60 seconds is an old Binet item. In our use of it over the years we have noted how much children enjoyed this test. They seemed to take it as a mental exercise. Further, this naming gave us clues about the child's tempo, the organization of his thinking, his capacity to range. The very demands of a task that asked the child to sustain for 60 seconds gave us some idea of this important capacity. Since we were also short on language items, we included this task, which we believed to have developmental value.

Administration

MATERIALS
Stopwatch and recording sheet

PROCEDURE
The examiner instructs the child: "Name all the animals you can think of until I tell you to stop." Then examiner begins to time.

If the child has difficulty in starting, the examiner may ask: "What is your favorite animal?" Then, if need be, ask: "Have you ever been to a zoo? What did you see there?" Or ask: "Have you ever been to a farm? What did you see *there?*" Rarely if ever is it necessary to suggest a specific animal. If this should prove necessary, the child is not ready for the test.

Examiner records on recording sheet all the animals named. If the 5- or 5½-year-old stops before one minute, saying: "That's all I can think of," it is usually not useful to urge him to continue, since most do not, even if urged. By 6, however, if the child stops before his minute is up, he should be encouraged to continue for the full time.

The number of seconds the child does sustain should be recorded. If the naming is interrupted by long pauses, note the length of the pauses but do not give extra time beyond the minute.

List animals vertically as the child names them. Record exactly what the child says, including diminutives, as "chickie"; plurals, as "bears"; or word preceded by "a," as "a bear."

SCORING
Add up the number of animals named, and check the number of different categories named.

Findings

TIME

Though this test situation can be presented in the preschool years, as Table 51 indicates, it is not until 5 years of age that even one quarter of boys and girls can sustain their response for the required 60 seconds, and it is at 6 years of age that the response becomes normative. Sex differences are variable. Variability of behavior from child to child in the preschool years is great.

In addition to timing the child's response, the examiner may wish to note the tempo of the child's naming. Some name so rapidly at first that the examiner can barely keep up with them. But this initial speed often slows down well before the minute is over. Others have a nice, steady pace. By 9, some are aware of the examiner's recording and politely ask: "Am I going too fast?"

NUMBER NAMED

Even through 4 and 4½ years of age, the average number of animals named is few. But by 5, the average is a respectable seven animals, and this number increases slowly but steadily from then on. And as Table 51 shows, variability in response from child to child is conspicuously large.

TYPE OF NAMING

Plurals are used infrequently, and more often by girls than by boys, and most frequently in the preschool years, especially when the child is running out of animals to name. In fact, a preschooler may repeat the name of an animal already named, merely adding an *s* to make a plural. Some children precede their animal name with an *a*, and this persists at a fairly high level through 7 years of age and may occur even later than 7. The use of the singular is already normative at 5 years of age, with a steady but slow increase thereafter.

CLASS OF ANIMAL NAMED

To simplify analysis, we have grouped the animals into five different categories: domestic, zoo, intermediate (squirrel, bear, fox, etc.), birds, and fish. As Table 52 indicates, domestic and zoo animals are clearly the

TABLE 51 *Percentage Who Can Name Animals for 60 Seconds, and Number Named*

	3 years G	B	3½ years G	B	4 years G	B	4½ years G	B	5 years G	B	5½ years G	B	6 years G	B	7 years G	B	8 years G	B	9 years G	B
Time: 60 seconds	**6**	**13**	**14**	**13**	**18**	**13**	**6**	**3**	**29**	**28**	**43**	**36**	**64**	**74**	**80**	**88**	**92**	**96**	**90**	**92**
Mean number named	2	2	3	2	5	3	6	5	7	7	8	8	8	9	11	12	12	14	15	14
Range: girls	0–8		0–7		0–15		0–18		0–15		2–19		0–13		7–19		7–21		9–24	
Range: boys	0–10		0–8		0–9		0–13		0–12		4–14		3–16		6–19		6–25		9–22	

TABLE 52   *Naming Animals*
(Percentage of Responses in Each Class)

	5 years		5½ years		6 years		7 years	
	G	B	G	B	G	B	G	B
Domestic	**39.0**	24.2	35.4	27.4	37.2	28.8	**35.5**	27.4
Zoo	35.5	**45.9**	**44.6**	**47.0**	**41.6**	36.9	34.4	**39.7**
Intermediate*	9.0	11.8	5.8	9.9	7.9	8.6	8.8	10.2
Bird	11.0	9.8	7.3	7.8	6.8	11.4	11.6	11.3
Fish	5.0	8.2	6.8	7.8	6.6	14.3	9.8	13.5

	8 years		9 years		10 years	
	G	B	G	B	G	B
Domestic	**40.3**	24.6	**35.6**	24.6	**34.2**	29.4
Zoo	26.7	**35.3**	26.5	**30.8**	29.2	**30.5**
Intermediate*	12.9	13.8	11.4	17.2	13.3	15.3
Bird	13.3	11.6	13.2	12.2	12.5	11.0
Fish	6.5	14.0	13.0	15.0	10.8	13.4

* Squirrel, bear, fox, etc.
NOTE: Boldface figures here are leading, not normative items.

leading classes at every age, though the domestic animals predominate at most ages with girls, and the zoo animals at all ages with boys. (This analysis was not made before 5 years of age simply because responses were so sparse.)

In considering the number of different animals named in each class, few significant findings emerge. Both boys and girls give the greatest variety of zoo animals at 5½ and 6 years of age. Boys name a greater variety of animals than do girls.

NUMBER OF OCCURRENCES OF MOST COMMONLY NAMED ANIMALS

Children do tend to group or classify their responses. Usually at least three animals in a single class—as cat, dog, horse; or lion, tiger, elephant—are named, at least after the preschool years.

Among the domestic animals, dog, cat, and horse lead, in that order. Both cat and dog are more commonly named by girls than by boys. In fact, all the domestic animals are much oftener named by girls than by boys.

The most common zoo animals named are lion, tiger, and elephant. Boys give lions and tigers more often; girls, elephants.

The intermediate animals do not show any strong trends other than that they tend to increase with increasing age. This is also true of birds and fish. With both birds and snakes, boys show a lead over the girls.

In addition to noting timing and the kinds of animals named, the examiner should be aware of the number of categories used and the sequence of naming. When, for example, a child of 7 names only domestic animals, or only barnyard animals, he gives the impression of being close to home, restricted in his behavior. The opposite may be true when only wild, far-off animals are named, with never a cat or a dog mentioned.

When clear-cut classification is evident as early as 7 years, there is good indication of a high intellect. Boys are especially capable in this regard. They may, for instance, name various members of the cat family, various birds, or various snakes.

There are certain qualitative items of which the examiner should be aware. The 5-to-6-year-old might name such things as giant, devil, dragon, or witch. But rarely does he get entirely off the track, as in the case of a child who named "horse, cow, barn, farm."

The naming of young animals (pony, puppy, lamb, colt, calf) shows no clear-cut age trend, though it continues longer in girls than in boys, with 10% of girls giving some diminutive responses as late as 9 years of age. This type of naming suggests a nice differentiation. Naming the male or female animals is less common. The more frequent male animals named are rooster and bull.

Any naming of unusual animals should be noted. A 6-year-old who names armadillo or cougar, a 7-year-old who names vulture or octopus, an 8-year-old who names tapir or okapi, all give evidence of a certain erudition that cannot be equated in averages.

CHAPTER *10*

HOME AND SCHOOL PREFERENCES

||||||||||||||||||||||||||||||||||||||||||||||||||||||||||||||||||||||||||||||||||||

Here we have an opportunity for the child to show us how he expresses himself verbally, rather than a strict test situation as such. We include this item because our test battery at the older ages is rather slim on verbal items. A second reason for its inclusion is that it makes a comfortable conclusion for the testing session.

The first question asked is: "What do you like to do best?" This is followed, in order, by four further questions:

"What do you like to do best indoors at school?"

"What do you like to do best outdoors at school?"

"What do you like to do best indoors at home?"

"What do you like to do best outdoors at home?"

Answers are highly individual and varied. The initial general question is hardest for most. As the questions become more specific as to place, it is easier for most children to respond.

The examiner may be more interested in the *way* the 5-to-10-year-old child expresses himself than in the strict content of the response. Only a few common age trends appear, since responses are highly individual. These will be mentioned. What the examiner really wants to know is how quickly and easily the child gathers his thoughts and expresses himself. Some children cannot give even a single answer to the questions. Others expound at length, and with enthusiasm.

Also, answers reveal the extent to which the child speaks in a manner suitable for his age. Does he pronounce correctly? Does he use correct grammatical construction? Does he answer with real enthusiasm or in a perfunctory manner? That is, does he enjoy this opportunity to share some of his feelings with the examiner, or does he respond to the questions briefly and simply because it is required of him?

The first question—"What do you like to do best?"—should be considered more as a takeoff than as providing a real evaluation of a child's interests, since it is difficult for many children to express this kind of very free choice. FIVE may not even understand what is being asked of him. In fact, he may even think the question means what part of the test battery did he enjoy most.

The 6-year-old, at least, needs to be checked on the validity of his reporting. A 6-year-old girl, for instance, may report that she enjoys horseback riding, though her parents may confirm that she has never been on a horse.

INDOOR PREFERENCES AT SCHOOL

If we group many different sorts of play activities and work activities preferred indoors at school, and if we group all gross motor activities and all kinds of game-playing outdoors at school, certain trends do appear, as Table 53 shows. Thus indoors, 5- and 5½-year-olds tend to like best some

TABLE 53   *School Preferences*

	5 years		5½ years		6 years		7 years		8 years		9 years	
	G	B	G	B	G	B	G	B	G	B	G	B
					Indoor Preferences							
Play	42	55	33	47	25	20	8	11	2	0	0	0
Play games	1	2	4	8	9	15	6	10	6	7	6	6
Work	4	4	12	6	25	35	43	43	75	44	77	61
Creative activity	33	14	27	10	17	17	23	11	11	14	10	16
Other	20	25	24	29	24	13	20	25	6	35	7	17
					Outdoor Preferences							
Gross motor	68	41	58	55	63	34	46	8	40	13	24	9
Play games	4	7	9	7	16	18	27	34	38	42	47	50
Other	28	52	33	38	21	48	27	58	22	45	29	41

sort of play activity. At 6, play and work are mentioned about equally. From 7 on, some sort of "work" prevails, becoming normative by 8 years.

When younger-type responses continue on into the older ages, it may be wise to check. Thus continued preference for play activities after 6 years of age should be investigated to judge the extent of a child's immaturity. Similarly, a persistent interest in trucks by boys after 6 years may indicate immaturity.

Creative activities steadily decrease in girls, though they start at 5 at a rather high level. An interest in books shows a steady rise from 7 through 9 years, with more girls than boys mentioning this interest. Interest in science and social studies becomes stronger at 9 years.

Mention of eating, recess, or doing nothing as preferred interests gives one pause and makes one wonder how well things are going for a child who reports about his school life in this manner. Chances are he may not be doing well. Even the child who reports after 5 years of age that he likes best to help his teacher shows immaturity.

OUTDOOR SCHOOL PREFERENCES

Outdoors at school, some sort of gross motor activity is normative in both sexes at 5½ years and in girls at 5 and 6. Gross motor also leads in girls at 7 and 8. Some sort of playing games increases with age, leading in girls at 9, and becoming normative in 9-year-old boys.

As to separate items, the swing, a favorite of 4-year-olds, remains a high interest at 5 and 5½ years, especially in girls. The interest in the slide is not as strong, but persists through 6 years of age, here again more predominantly in girls. Jungle gym and monkey bars are just as strong in girls as the interest in the slide, and these interests persist in girls 7 and 8 years of age. In the meantime, many boys have shifted to ball play.

INDOOR HOME PREFERENCES

There is not enough consistency in indoor home preferences for us to present these responses in tabular form. Responses are highly individual. Play with some kind of toys is rather strong from 5 through 6 years of age. Many girls and no boys prefer doll play; many boys and no girls prefer to play with trucks. Playing games is mentioned frequently by both sexes, and is especially strong at 9 years of age. Interest in creative play is conspicuous throughout, and watching television is mentioned with increasing frequency as the child grows older.

Reading is coming in at 8 and 9 years as an activity which is mentioned as favored. Doing something with some person or animal shows a steady rise, especially in girls. By 9 years of age, this social interest is twice as common in girls as in boys.

OUTDOOR HOME PREFERENCES

The leading outdoor preference for both girls and boys, through 7 years, is some kind of gross motor activity—seesaw, slide, swing, jungle-gym, bicycle riding, and such. At 8 years, some sort of game-playing—tag, hide-and-seek, hopscotch, jump rope, ball—slightly exceeds general gross motor activity. And at 9 years, game-playing is the leading activity.

Outdoors as indoors, social activity (doing something with somebody) leads, and occurs more in girls than in boys. Seasonal sports are a strong interest, especially at 8 and 9 years of age.

PART III
GENERAL CONSIDERATIONS

CHAPTER *11*

SPECIAL AGE CHARACTERISTICS

Many years of research and clinical work have led us to the conclusion that almost everything the young child does or says reveals not only his individuality but his behavior level as well. Thus even when the young child is not cooperative in responding to our test situations, his very way of refusing tells a good deal that one needs to know. That is, just as test responses change in a patterned, predictable way, so also do the child's ways of refusing the tests.*

Even when a child does cooperate with the examiner, he or she often expresses some behaviors not addressed strictly to the task at hand. These overflow behaviors, as well as actual refusal behaviors, embellish our picture of the child's response and help establish the age level of his behavior. Refusals and other variant or overflow behavior can thus be considered not as apart from or detracting from more positive responses, but as an integral and significant part of the entire response.

With the very young child, the 18-monther and the 2-year-old, motor refusal of a test predominates, chiefly leaving the examining table. Second most common is some kind of emotional refusal, as crying or clinging to mother.

However, even by 30 months, verbal refusals equal in number mere motor refusals and exceed emotional refusals, and by 3 years of age and following, the dominant kind of refusal or variant behavior is verbal.

Figure 14 illustrates the extent to which each of the more common kinds of variant behavior—motor, verbal, emotional, reverted, and perseverative behavior—occurred in a group of fifty subjects each at 18, 24, 30, 36, 42, 48, and 60 months. Motor, verbal, and emotional behavior speak for themselves. Reverted behavior is a kind of response which occurs when a child stays with the test situation (as for instance, Cubes

* Adapted from "Variant Behavior as Revealed by the Gesell Developmental Examination," by Louise Bates Ames and Frances L. Ilg, *Journal of Genetic Psychology*, 1943, *63*, 273–305.

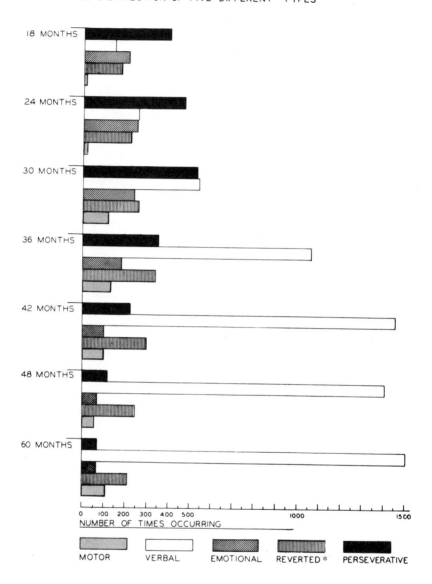

* Reverted behavior is appropriate behavior, but at a lower age level.

Figure 14. Age distribution of different kinds of variant behavior, from 18 months to 5 years

152

or Copy Forms) but behaves in a manner characteristic of a younger child. In perseverative behavior, the child simply goes on and on with some single response.

This chapter describes some of the more common ways in which children at succeeding ages behave during the behavior examination. However, it must be remembered that each child grows at his own rate and in his own way. Even when the sequences we describe hold good, each child has his or her own individual *timetable*. Also, some children seem out of bounds at every age; others are quiet and contained. Thus the descriptions of age levels which follow should be taken only as guidelines, not as gospel.

3 YEARS OF AGE

The 3-year-old, by nature a rather docile and cooperative individual, is much easier to examine than the child just younger. THREE likes people and he wants to please them. He likes to cooperate. Thus in some ways he is an ideal candidate for an examination.

Also, his increased proficiency, and especially his expanding vocabulary and growing control of language, seem to make it easier for him to cope with the examination situation. Particularly does his language interest stand him in good stead. Fatigue or lack of interest can often be countered with "Now let's do it a *different* way."

However, some refusal or inability is still met with, and in the case of a difficult or not too cooperative child, an examiner will do well to preface directions with: "How about doing so-and-so?" rather than giving a direct command.

The total examination, however, is rendered much easier than it has been earlier by the fact that even when the child does not wish to comply, refusals and objections tend to be couched in verbal rather than in motor or emotional terms. The child can say, "I don't know," or "I don't want to" in a gentle way when some one thing is too hard, without disrupting the general flow of the examination.

And you can often bargain with THREE. Thus an examiner may say: "As soon as we do this, we'll do . . ." something else which you hope will appeal to him. Or: "Do this now and then we'll . . ."

The fact that THREE can protect himself verbally makes it unnecessary for him to object to things which are too difficult by leaving the table, crying, fussing, or otherwise behaving disruptively, as he did when younger. Some THREES can be examined without needing their mother beside them. But if mother is requested, best let her be present.

3½ YEARS OF AGE

This tends to be a difficult age for all concerned. Children now tend to be uncertain, insecure, hard to please, anxious, demanding. They want things to be done just right—that is, *their* way. They like to control any situation but actually have little confidence in their own ability. They flutter between "Don't look" and "Look at me"; between "Talk" and "Don't talk."

Fortunately for the examiner, their most difficult behavior occurs at home. Many are relatively docile in an examination situation. They do best if the examiner is fully aware of their inadequacies and sensitivities. At older ages, one can often ride somewhat roughshod over refusals. With the 3½-year-old, one needs to be well aware of things that may go wrong or have started to go wrong, and to guard against them.

The child of this age tends to be sensitive and out of balance both emotionally and motorwise. Thus it is not unusual for hands to tremble, eyes to blink, voice to stutter. A tower that may have stood steady when he built it at 3 years of age now may fall when he erects it; and the child may be unable to judge the distance needed for the base cubes of a bridge which he made easily at 3.

Fortunately, when things do go wrong or are too difficult, the 3½-year-old can express his difficulties verbally. He still may say "No" or "I don't know," as earlier, but now a new phrase has been added to his vocabulary: "I can't." This had better be respected.

Motor ways of refusing—leaving the table, banging things on it, or throwing things—have now sunk to third place as a type of noncooperation. Reverted behavior—that is, staying with the situation but reverting to a more immature way of behaving, such as making a train or tower with the cubes when asked to make a bridge—now comes second.

If one is aware of and makes allowance for uncertainties and insecurities, as a rule the examination goes reasonably well at this age.

4 YEARS OF AGE

The 4-year-old, in the examination as elsewhere, tends to be somewhat out of bounds. As we have noted,[12] he is wild and wonderful. And he tends to be out of bounds in every field of behavior. It is hard for him to sit still; he is very active. His language definitely tends to go out of bounds. In the examination, bathroom language is apt to come in and the Incomplete Man often has a belly button.

His exuberant emotions, too, make themselves evident in the examination. He enjoys it so much, but when tired of it he makes it all too clear that he would like to leave: "Can I go back now?" "When are we going to be through?"

As he approaches the examining room he is likely to run on ahead. He may not want to sit at the table, but once having sat, he may not be able to inhibit himself from picking up the pencil and starting at once, even before the examiner has had a chance to give directions.

His Copy Forms products tend to be expansive; he may need more than one sheet of paper. And throughout the examination, he talks and talks, telling the examiner a great deal about himself and his family and friends. And he is apt to ask quite personal questions of the examiner: "Do you sleep here?" "Do you have any children?"

His enthusiasm makes him, as a rule, a pleasure to examine, but a successful, experienced examiner will anticipate his out-of-bounds tendencies, and will not be overzealous about holding him in line.

4½ YEARS OF AGE

This is a rather strange age, in a way, for it seems not so much to have characteristics of its own as to borrow from the adjacent ages. Sometimes the 4½-year-old is loud, exuberant, and out of bounds like a 4-year-old. Sometimes he is quiet and pulled in like a FIVE.

And this very uncertainty gives this time of life a somewhat uncertain, unstable quality. Its very inconsistency makes the child seem unpredictable. Also, he lacks the bold, secure joyousness of 4 years old; the calm, stable equilibrium and "niceness" of 5.

All this should not give special difficulty in the examination if the examiner is aware in advance that this boy or girl may change before one's eyes; may not end up the examination quite the same person who started it.

5 YEARS OF AGE

This is a pulled-in, focal age of good adjustment. FIVE lives close to home and he wants to be good and to please others. He seems all put together. There is a surety to his movements. Gone are his far-flung, out-of-bounds 4-year-old ways.

FIVE likes to obey and to do what he is told. He is by nature cooperative, and in an examination he likes to follow what he thinks are the rules, to do what the examiner asks of him, to please the examiner.

The child of this age may appear shy when first approached and often the examiner instinctively takes his hand, as she would with a preschooler. He seems compact and pulled-in posturally, and as he walks his arms tend to be held close to his body. Though he responds briefly when directly asked a question, he is not the bubbling-over talker that he was a year earlier.

He recognizes the small chair as his and may sit without being told to. He wants to do what is expected of him and he often looks to the examiner for approval.

FIVE keeps his body and paper straight, picks up his pencil directly and does not transfer it from hand to hand. He moves up close to his work and there is relatively little overflow. The pencil tends to be held in a three-finger grasp, near its tip, with the shaft oblique.

There is marked restraint throughout. FIVE sometimes holds himself rather stiffly in his effort to be "good" and to do what is expected of him. He may occasionally bounce a little in his chair, but seldom stands or asks to finish or to leave the table. His docility and wish to please tend to make him an easy person to examine, though one senses his vulnerability.

Because of this vulnerability, the examiner needs to show great sensitivity. She needs to know how and when to shift her approach and when to give up. It is more important to maintain rapport and to make the child feel that he is doing well than to complete every test or to attain any special response on any one test.

The 5-year-old is often quite easily distracted. Thus at this age perhaps more than others it is important to have an examination room in which outside noises are kept to a minimum.

5½ YEARS OF AGE

Behavior at 5½ tends to be very different from what it was six months earlier. At home, parents note that their child now tends to explode, to oppose, to demand, to strike out and even to strike against. It is as if behavior were loosening up and expanding.

We are not surprised, then, that in the examination, the child of this age is somewhat different from the focal, concerned, trying-to-please person he was at 5. Now he is more ready to speak up, to ask questions if he doesn't understand, to carry out commands with only minimal instruction.

He is also less anxious to please and to do things exactly right. He feels more confidence in himself than he did and is more ready for give-and-take. Though when first approached he may take the examiner's hand, he soon drops it, wishing to be on his own. The examiner is less conscious of needing to protect him. His body now moves with a looseness, having lost the stiffer erectness so characteristic of 5.

The child slips into the chair at the examining table quite naturally, ready and eager for what may come. As he works with paper and pencil, his head often shifts from side to side, which explains in part why letters and numbers are so likely to shift into reversal. The free hand is not held as tight and flat as at 5. The little finger may separate off, moving outward.

Now eyes are less steadily focused on the task at hand. They may sweep boldly over things in the examining room. Overflow is seen in the fact that though the body continues active, as earlier, most total bodily activity is confined to wiggling *in* the chair. The child seldom leaves his seat at the examining table.

As at all ages, there are some verbal digressions, as some comment that things are hard or that he doesn't know, or can't do something requested. Much overflow at this age is in the mouth region. The child's tongue extends and sweeps over his lips, participating fully in the act of writing, and clearly showing points of increased strain.

Paper as a rule is still straight, and if there must be an adjustment, the child shifts his head and not the paper. There is now a better grasp of the pencil.

6 YEARS OF AGE

At 6 the behavior seen in its beginning half a year earlier achieves full expression. The 6-year-old is extremely expansive, enthusiastic, eager. He takes part in an examination eagerly, not so much from a wish to please as because of his enthusiasm for any new adventure. In fact, whatever he does he does with impulsive enthusiasm. His exuberance is contagious.

When approached by an examiner, six responds eagerly and is likely to run ahead to the examining room. It may be hard to keep up with him, not only as he approaches the examining room but as he speeds through the examination.

The child of this age is much concerned with balance, possibly because of his own balance problems. He does not sit quietly, but is likely to balance on the back two legs of the chair. He may even try to balance on only one, and may fall to the floor.

As he works, his head is likely to be tilted to the nondominant side, and he may tilt his paper at an angle. The spread of arms, noted as he walks, may also be observed as he sits at the table with arms outspread. He rotates his hands outward in explanation. Fingers spread as he supports his paper with his nondominant hand.

Eyes sweep up laterally and his tongue may be very active in sweeping over both upper and lower lips. He may try to inhibit this by pushing the tongue against his lower lip or the inside of his mouth.

Fingers are frequently brought to the mouth. The child also chews his pencil or any loose tabs of clothing material. He presses so hard as he writes that he is likely to break his pencil. Throat-clearing can be so marked as to be almost ticlike.

The total body is very active. The child moves in his chair, falls out of his chair. There are many hand-to-mouth gestures: bringing little finger to mouth, chewing on pencil, picking at teeth, or rotating hands outward in an expressive gesture.

A typical 6-year-old response is the use of the expletive "Oh!" which may indicate a sudden insight. He boasts a great deal—"That's easy"— especially when things are actually difficult for him. And he is a glutton for praise. It is hard to praise a 6-year-old too much.

7 YEARS OF AGE

It is a different world at 7 years. The typical 7-year-old is as withdrawn as the 6-year-old is outgoing, as pulled in as the 6-year-old is spread out. Even his posture has changed. Instead of a straight back and symmetrically outflung arms, the arms are pulled in and the head as well as the whole body may be tilted at an angle toward the nondominant side. Even his paper may be highly asymmetric as he slants it on the tabletop.

Tempo is much, much slower than it was just earlier. The child no longer darts ahead of the examiner on the way to the examining room, and his pace as he works tends to be much slower than it was at 6.

In fact, SEVEN may be pulled in almost to the point of withdrawal. He is much less exuberant than he was, has much less to share with the examiner. His expression may be pensive or even slightly sad.

He not only worries about things but has many fears, including, perhaps, the fear that he will not do well in the examination. He tends to think that people don't like him, though this may not extend to the examiner.

Completion is important to the child of 7, and he is so geared to finish that he may continue an activity until he is exhausted. For his own protection he needs to be given limits and stopping points.

SEVEN tends to be a perfectionist and it is in search of perfection that he does so much erasing. In fact, 7 is often termed the "eraser age." And SEVEN tries so hard, works so laboriously, that he tends to take longer than he did when he was 6. He needs to be helped to conclude, and to be satisfied with work that is less than perfect.

The child of this age shows real control in many ways—control of his temper, control of striking out, control of his stroke, and control of his voice. Thus in an examination situation we see fewer tensional outlets; he holds himself more containedly. This may be partly from lesser energy; partly that he actually can inhibit the many extraneous movements which were so characteristic of 6. But he does fatigue easily, and that is why examiner, teacher, or parent must help him stop before fatigue becomes too great.

Eyes, like head and/or total body, may move obliquely. He holds his pencil at its tip, and his nondominant hand anchors his paper. Posture may be so tense that he trembles as he works. The voice may at times drop to a mere whisper. His tongue is less active now, but the lower lip is drawn in, even to the extent that it becomes chapped. SEVEN makes many mouth noises, often to the annoyance of others. There is apt to be much yawning.

8 YEARS OF AGE

As the years go by in their repeated rhythm, with outgoing ages alternating with inwardized ages, 8 brings the customary expansion which follows such extreme inwardization as is customarily seen at 7.

Of the 8-year-old we must say that he is normally speedy, expansive, evaluative, and vulnerable. He expands often beyond his capabilities, evaluates what he has accomplished and often judges it to be wanting. Thus he is extremely dependent on praise. But unlike himself at earlier ages, he now tends to evaluate the praise—so it must be realistic and not excessive.

With his enthusiastic love of adventure and of anything new, the 8-year-old is an ideal candidate for the challenge of a behavior examination. EIGHT has a new ease in meeting any challenging situation. He is ready for the new and the difficult. As he reads, for instance, he can attack a new word effectively, working it out phonetically without losing the meaning of what he is reading, as was apt to be the case at 7. He can also stop in the middle of a passage, talk about its meaning and bring in new material, and then return to his reading without losing the sense of the whole.

The typical 8-year-old likes to be examined. He likes tests. He has acquired a social ease and a more direct approach that makes him a delight to examine. He expresses himself dramatically with his "Yow!" and his "Yikes!" An examiner can be quite natural with him, needing neither to protect him nor to goad him on. EIGHT may be sloppy in his performance, but he is no longer laborious as he was at 7. He is more ready to accept things without straining for perfection, as he did just earlier. He can even sometimes laugh at or shrug off his own mistakes.

Posture, as earlier at 6, tends to be more symmetrical than at 7. The child shifts his paper and also his head slightly to the nondominant side, but he tends to place his paper and also to work opposite his dominant shoulder. There is now much less tension than earlier. The body remains quieter. Any tensional overflow is apt to be expressed verbally rather than with the total body. The mouth, instead of being held tensely, may be so relaxed as to be a bit gaping. The rolling of eyes as he makes some dramatic statement is undoubtedly one form of tensional outlet. If he does feel strain, he is quite capable of verbalizing his difficulties in a matter-of-fact way.

The child now uses his pencil as a tool, more as an extension of his fingers than as a separate object. Grasp is much less awkward than earlier. The 8-year-old can be fun to examine.

9 YEARS OF AGE

It may be the 9-year-old's independence which characterizes him best. He is far less dependent on the adult than he was a year earlier, both at home and at school, and even in an examination situation. He is very much his own person.

The child of this age enjoys competing and trying out new skills. Thus the developmental examination may be accepted as a challenge. He attacks even the difficult parts with interest. Whereas any evidence of a stopwatch, earlier, might have filled the child with concern, the 9-year-old likes the challenge of being timed.

Like 7, 9 is once again an asymmetric age. No longer do we see the symmetry so characteristic of 8. Rather the child shifts his paper more markedly, almost through 90 degrees, thus making the vertical side of his paper parallel with the table edge. At the same time he shifts his trunk so that legs and feet point to the side. His free hand usually steadies his paper halfway down the edge.

Head is initially bent to the nondominant side, but as he writes across the page his head moves through an arc, ending up on the dominant side as he reaches the edge of his paper. This shift in posture repeats itself as he traverses succeeding trips across the page.

Pencil grasp is sure. He shows excellent control of his stroke. Letters and numbers become neater and more accurate.

There is relatively little overflow and what there is occurs in rather small ways. Thus he may pick at his teeth in a precise way. Or he may piano his fingers, but he no longer rolls his eyes as he did at 8, and there is much less explosive dramatic verbalization.

At this point it may be useful for us to suggest just a few of the ways in which children *overplaced* in the early grades show clearly by their school behavior that they *are* overplaced. Almost any experienced teacher will be able to add his or her own signs and clues to this list.

KINDERGARTEN

One of the plainest ways that young children show they are not ready for kindergarten is by crying and clinging to their mothers when it comes time to enter the classroom. Though such behavior is not entirely unheard of even in "ready" children in the first days of school, if it continues for any substantial period of time it should be a warning sign that the child may not be ready for kindergarten.

Certainly any child who has to be dressed and fed and bodily forced onto the school bus is not ready for school.

Unready children find it difficult to take part even in the loose groupings seen in kindergarten. And perhaps most of all, they *bother* the other children. Kindergarten children tend to be permissive about the ways in which their classmates behave, but a child who hurts other children, who throws things, and who destroys the other children's products is saying very clearly that he is not ready.

And then there is a final group, children who may behave very acceptably in school but for whom the lid blows off the minute they reach home. If school attendance causes home behavior to go to pieces, *something* is very wrong.

FIRST GRADE

Unreadiness for first grade is just as likely to be demonstrated at home as at school. In fact, a prime sign of unreadiness here is if the child objects vigorously to going to school, says he hates school and doesn't want to go. A little of this "I don't want to go to school today" behavior is not unusual in any child of any age, but when objection to school persists as a daily matter, and when each morning brings a daily struggle to get the child ready for school and onto the bus, it is obviously a warning sign that something isn't right.

In extreme cases, the child may even be sick to his stomach, or unable to eat any breakfast at all. Such a child is not being bad. He is telling you plainly that the situation is too much for him.

Once in school, unready children show a very short attention span. They are restless. It is hard for them to stay in their seats and they claim that the "work" is too hard. Especially if they are bright, the teacher is likely to complain that "He could do better if he would just try."

Toileting accidents, either in school or on the way home from school, are also good clues that too much is being demanded.

SECOND GRADE

Second-graders quite normally tend to worry that they will be late for school, but when this anxiety is exaggerated it can be a clue that the school situation is demanding too much of a child.

Unready second-graders may still have some trouble remaining in their seats, but more usual clues to unreadiness are that the child talks too much in class or withdraws entirely, bothers the other children, doesn't finish his work. A further good clue to unreadiness is seen if the child is a behavior problem in the playground and demands special and excessive supervision.

THIRD GRADE

Social unhappiness and poor schoolwork are clues that a third-grader might be better off in second grade. The unready third-grader, according to his teacher, "doesn't do his work," and boys especially not only don't do their work but become rebellious and so are punished or isolated. That unhappy-looking third-grader sitting by the teacher's desk, or out in the hall, or in the coatroom, is in all likelihood not so much misbehaving as immature.

And it is not only his academic work which suffers. The unready third-grader often (quite understandably) has a low self-image, has trouble making friends at school and frequently seems tired, irritable, and unhappy at home.

In fact, many ways of behaving which people have punished in the past are now looked on as valuable clues to the fact that something about the school situation is not right for the child. Overplacement is one of the things we think of first.

CHAPTER *12*

GESELL PRESCHOOL TESTS

||||||||||||||||||||||||||||||||||||||||||||||||||||||||||||||||||||||||||||||||||||

School Readiness, admittedly, deals primarily with behavior testing of the school-age child. However, this chapter will discuss testing of the preschooler.

Our preschool tests are discussed here for several reasons. The first is that many 5-year-olds on examination will turn out to be responding not at a full 5-year-old level but more at a 4½- or even 4-year-old level. Thus it is important for examiners to be able to recognize and identify the earlier kinds of response.

Second, any child behavior can have more meaning for an observer if that observer is familiar with its earlier stages. A 5-year-old child's response to Copy Circle, for instance, has more meaning for an examiner who understands that before the child is able to copy in a counterclockwise direction, starting at the top, there are earlier years when the circle is drawn from the bottom up and in a clockwise direction. One tends to have more respect for a mature behavior if one knows what has gone before to make it possible.

And third, many of those who will be using school-age behavior tests—and this is particularly true of psychologists—will also in their practice often find that they are called upon at times to examine preschoolers. This book describes only the preschool response to tests in our school-age battery. For a full discussion of the entire battery of Gesell preschool tests, readers are referred to *The First Five Years of Life,* by Gesell et al.[27] An updating of our preschool tests, by Walker et al.,[51] is currently in preparation.

The Gesell preschool tests have a long history. They were first published by Dr. Arnold Gesell in 1928 in his early book *Infancy and Human Growth.*[23] Dr. Gesell continued his work until he died in 1961, and his colleagues have been working on their refinement ever since.

At their present stage they include many of the tests first proposed, but also some new ones, and norms have been refined substantially. However, they still aim to test four facets of behavior: motor, adaptive, language, and personal-social.

What They Test

It is important to emphasize here the difference between a behavior or developmental test and an intelligence test. An intelligence test purportedly measures the level of the individual's intellectual functioning as such. It tells us how *bright* the person is.

A maturity or developmental test, on the other hand, measures the maturity of the individual's total functioning as a person—that is, it tells us whether or not his behavior is up to that expected of someone of his chronological age.

The Relationship Between Intelligence and Maturity Levels

These two factors, intelligence and maturity, are two separate functions and can develop quite separately, but in infancy there is often a rather close relationship between the two. Thus, though our infant tests do not aim to measure intelligence, to some extent they do give us a clue as to how bright or dull the infant is.

It would be difficult for a dull or defective 6-month-old infant, for example, to rate at or above 6 months on a battery of behavior tests. However, as the child grows older, and especially if IQ is measured on a test which emphasizes verbal over performance items, the gap between a so-called DQ (Developmental Quotient) and the IQ (Intelligence Quotient) can widen. A high IQ does not guarantee that the child will also be up to his age in maturity—in fact, we have a term "superior immature," which designates those children who are bright but at the same time immature.

From the beginning of our work with behavior tests we have emphasized that in obtaining the maturity level of a preschooler we always consider the four separate factors of motor behavior, adaptive behavior, language behavior, and personal-social behavior. Though it is of course possible to average the ratings on all four factors to come up with a single or unitary Developmental Quotient, we are most interested in the child's relative strengths in the different fields. In general, those children whose developmental levels are more or less similar in all four fields may function most comfortably in school and elsewhere.

For those children with some single high point—language, for instance—there is always the danger that school and home will expect them to function in all things at this high level. It is this kind of child of whom school personnel often say, unfairly, "He could do better if he would." Their reason for saying this is that he reads so well, or that his IQ is so high, that he is expected to function equally well in other areas. It is often difficult, in everyday life, to allow for a child's lows as well as his highs.

Predictability of Infant and Preschool Tests

This is a highly debatable question. There are many who maintain that infant and preschool tests are not substantially predictive of later behavior. Dr. Gesell believed that, other things being equal, such tests often could be highly predictive.[26]

Our own most recent study[2] along these lines appears to confirm the Gesell position. Our conclusion was that:

> The present study presents Gesell data to confirm the theoretical position that infant and preschool behavior tests yield scores which are highly predictive of later behavior. This in spite of the fact that infant and preschool tests aim to measure behavior level or developmental level rather than intelligence per se. There is a close, though by no means inevitable, correlation between the two kinds of behavior.
>
> Twenty-one of thirty-three infants, or 63.6% of all, had scores on infant behavior tests which fell within 10 points of a 10 year IQ score. Of these, sixteen (48.5%) fell within 5 points. The mean age for the first infant examination was 33 weeks.
>
> In forty of forty-four preschoolers (91%) preschool and 10 year scores fell within 5 points for the two examinations. The mean age for the first preschool examinations of those examined in preschool only (and not in infancy) was 25.5 months.
>
> Preschool examinations were also available for 32 of the infants examined. Seventy-six percent of all these preschool scores fell within 10 points of the 10-year-old score.
>
> Past experience has suggested that early tests predict most certainly in instances of defect or low intelligence. Such cases were lacking in this present population.

Ways in Which Preschool Tests Can Be Used

It was Dr. Gesell's contention that a behavior test amounted in essence to a neurological evaluation of the maturity level of the individual's nervous system. It told us how far he had proceeded in ability to use the different parts of his body.

One of Dr. Gesell's major professional efforts was to encourage pediatricians to become interested in and knowledgeable about behaviors to be expected at different age levels in infancy and early childhood. As he stated it: "Development as well as disease lies in the province of the pediatrician." That is, he felt it was not enough for the pediatrician to diagnose and treat disease as such, but that he should be concerned with behavior as well.

Thus perhaps *the major use* of infant and preschool tests, by psychologist and pediatrician alike, is in cases where the normality of development is in question, to be able to determine whether or not any given individual is developing normally, whether or not his behavior falls within normal limits.

Diagnosis of itself clearly does not *change* anything, but when a parent is worried unnecessarily about a child's behavior, it can set his mind at rest to know that a child is within normal limits. When the anxiety *is* justified, an evaluation can at least answer the question: How serious or severe is the retardation?

A *second important use* of behavior tests is that they can orient prospective adopting parents as to the developmental level and general potentials of any child they are about to adopt. Many adoption agencies have maintained (*a*) that how an adopted child turns out depends not on his own inherent potentials but on how the parents treat him, and (*b*) that even if his potentials are not the best, he should be adopted anyway.

Our own position has been, and remains, that any couple before adopting a child should require that he or she be examined, to determine both physical status and developmental or intellectual potential. If it is their wish to adopt a child who is handicapped in either dimension, they should do so. But they should *not* do so unknowingly.

Young babies, especially, unless grossly handicapped, may look pretty much alike to the uninitiated, so far as their potentials are concerned. Yet a careful behavior examination can in most instances at least give a warning if and when a candidate for adoption has less than normal potential.

Natural parents, too, may find a preschool examination useful. Since it covers four different and separate fields of behavior, it can tell a parent not only where in general a child is functioning, but it *can also provide a sort of personality profile*. This is a *third* way in which preschool testing can be useful.

Obviously, the child who is advanced in language but below age in motor and/or adaptive behavior is quite different from the child who is advanced in personal-social and perhaps motor behavior but immature in language and adaptive behavior. One's expectations of two such children would be quite different. The first might be a good student but immature in interpersonal relations. The second might be one of the many whom we describe as being "Better at living than at learning."

A *fourth* and to us extremely important use of behavior examinations is that in a school system where children are entered in school and subsequently promoted on the basis of their behavior age rather than their chronological age or IQ, Gesell developmental tests (or similar tests) are vital either in the screening of an entire group of children eligible by birthday age to enter school, or in individual cases where there is a question about or problem as to readiness.

Some children are screened or tested in order to determine readiness as early as four years of age. But since probably more often it is 5- and 6-year-olds with whom such testing is done, this particular use of our tests has been discussed elsewhere.

CHAPTER *13*

SUPPLEMENTARY TESTS USED IN
OUR CLINICAL PRACTICE

|||||||||||||||||||||||||||||||||||||||||||||||||||||||||||||||||||||||||||||||

Behavior tests have been extremely useful to us as the backbone of our clinical service. Especially in the case of children with problems in school, which make up a bulk of this service, the child's developmental or behavior age range is a crucial factor in determining grade placement. And also, as indicated elsewhere, it is our experience that perhaps 50% of school problems can be prevented or cured simply by having the child properly placed.

Other tests or measures which we use to complete our clinical battery include: a standard intelligence test, the Bender Gestalt test of visual-motor integration, a measure of the child's reading level, and an evaluation of his visual behavior. We also use three projective techniques: the Lowenfeld Mosaic test, the Rorschach ink blot test, and the Kinetic Family Drawing test. We then check on the child's teething; and if it seems indicated, refer him elsewhere for help with allergies and endocrine or dietary problems.

INTELLIGENCE TESTING

Though in some cities there is a strong feeling against the use of intelligence tests, we find a knowledge of any child's intellectual level to be vital in arriving at an appreciation of that child's potential. The test which we customarily use is the WISC (Wechsler Intelligence Scale for Children). We use both the verbal and the performance scale, since it is important to know the child's relative ratings on these two scales as well as his total combined score. The WISC is well enough known and widely enough used that it need not be described here.

THE BENDER GESTALT

Though this test has been available for many years, it was not until Elizabeth Koppitz published her book *The Bender Gestalt Test for Young Children*[38] in 1964 that it came into wide use.*

The test material consists of nine 4-by-6-inch cards, each showing a geometric form or forms, such as a circle with touching square, a series of twelve dots in a horizontal line, a series of sets of three small circles appearing slantwise. The child is asked to copy each of these forms on an 8½-by-11-inch sheet of paper.

The test is scored for errors made; obviously, the higher the score, the poorer the response. It attempts to measure four areas of performance or ability in the order in which they are manifested in the child. The first task is to produce the correct number of separate parts of a figure; very young children tend to perseverate or to make too many of anything.

Next comes the ability to reproduce any given figure in its correct orientation. The next most mature ability is that of perceiving and reproducing details—that is, achieving a correct shape. The ability that manifests itself last is the perception and reproduction of relationships, the correct integration of separate figures.

Koppitz's norms and her expectation of the number of errors to be found at any given age are as follows:

TABLE 54   *Koppitz Age Norms for Expected Performance on the Bender Gestalt*

Chronological Age	Mean Number of Errors
5/0 to 5/5	13.5
5/6 to 5/11	9.8
6/0 to 6/5	8.4
6/6 to 6/11	6.4
7/0 to 7/5	4.8
7/6 to 7/11	4.7
8/0 to 8/5	3.7
8/6 to 8/11	2.5
9/0 to 9/5	1.7
9/6 to 9/11	1.6
10/0 to 10/5	1.6
10/6 to 10/11	1.5

Koppitz warns users: "The very fact that the Bender Test is so appealing and so easy to administer presents a certain danger. Because it is so deceptively simple it is probably one of the most over-rated, most misunderstood and most maligned tests currently in use. Psychological

* A second volume was published in 1975.[39]

tests are nothing but tools; and a tool is, of course, only effective if the person handling it is skilled in its use." (Volume II, page 2.)

She emphasizes that "The Bender is NOT a test of visual perception, or a test of motor coordination. Rather, *it is a test of visual-motor integration.* Not *all* children with immature or defective Bender performances necessarily have problems in visual perception. . . . Errors may result from immaturity or from malfunctioning in visual perception, in motor coordination or in the integration of the two. . . . The majority of school age children with immature Benders do *not* have poor visual perception, nor do they show difficulties with motor coordination. Instead they have problems with perceptual-motor integration." (Volume II, pages 3, 5.)

And she gives a further important warning. "Too often it is assumed that children do poorly on the Bender because they have 'perceptual problems' and need special training in this area, when they really need help in slowing down, in developing better inner control, and in improving their work habits."

Koppitz finds that children from deprived areas do relatively less well on the Bender than privileged children until about fourth grade, at which time there is a span of only one or two scoring points for most groups. However, "The Bender performances of young Puerto Ricans, Indian and black children, both advantaged and disadvantaged, seem to mature at a somewhat slower rate than those of white youngsters. On the other hand the rate of maturation seems to be accelerated among Oriental children." (Volume II, page 43.)

And as a last warning, since many people consider the Bender to be a test for brain damage or brain injury, Koppitz states very specifically that a poor Bender may hint at but by no means assures brain damage.

READING LEVEL

After the child has begun to read, it is useful for the examiner to obtain some knowledge of his reading progress. Reading ability is tested not only to secure a reading score, but also to note the quality of the child's method of reading.

We use the Gray Oral Reading test in its original form. It is both easy to administer and easy to score.* The test allows the child to show his level of reading clearly. At the same time, each age group reveals its particular difficulties as well as its own special methods of attack.

Thus the 6-year-old may need to keep his place with his finger. He may lose a line as his eyes drop down too far. (A marker could prevent this.) He is apt to repeat words he has read in a story, such as "little" or

---

* This test and directions for scoring can be ordered from the Bobbs-Merrill Co., Inc., 4300 West 62nd Street, Indianapolis, Ind. 46206.

"long," when they do not recur. He needs considerable help and clearly shows his satiety point.

The 7-year-old has an easier time keeping his place, but as the reading gets harder he tends to hold the page closer to his eyes, revealing focusing difficulty. He often reads in a mechanical way, linking sentence to sentence and paragraph to paragraph. If he does shift his voice at the end of a sentence, his inflection is usually upward. He is especially interested in the meaning of what he is reading and does not wish to linger over difficult words to figure them out. He wants somebody to supply the words he cannot read. Since the meaning of what he reads is more important to him than the exact words, he may translate a word which is hard for him into something he knows, thus reading "birthday" as "surprise." Rather than inserting extra words, as he did at 6, he is more likely to omit words.

By 8 years of age the child is able to read with greater fluidity and inflection. Sentences are now separated naturally, ending with a downward inflection of the voice. EIGHT has a capacity to attack new words and can work over them phonetically. He doesn't lose his contact with the meaning of the story as he stops to work out a word. If he can read the words "Pray, Puss" (paragraph 3 of the Gray Oral test), we judge him to be at a third-grade level. This may seem like an unwarrantedly simple conclusion, but our experience has shown that the ability to read this phrase does reveal that the 8-year-old can accept the unusual and can work it out phonetically as well as in context.

These three capsule age summaries suggest that the child reveals himself in whatever he does. When an 8-year-old is reading like a 7-year-old, he may merely need to progress at a slower rate. He does not necessarily need remedial help. Undoubtedly we are producing many of our reading problems because we do not allow the child to respond from his own base and at his own rate. We may be merely confusing him when we face him with material which is beyond his capacity.

Along with the Gray Oral paragraph reading we use the Iota Word List or any selected list of single words. It is interesting to contrast the child who has an easier time reading within the context of a paragraph and the one who reads single words better. This kind of information about a child can give the teacher a clue to facilitate his reading.

With single words, as with reading in context, the child clearly reveals his age. The 6-year-old either knows a word or doesn't know it. He builds up his knowledge of words by the way they look. Often he gets his clues from the letter they begin with. The 7-year-old has considerable trouble with vowels. "Tap" becomes "tip"; "ball" becomes "bell." He may read words backwards. By 8 years of age, most children are willing to tackle any word; they now have usable phonetic tools. Many get into trouble with silent letters, however.

VISION

Though it is often ignored in clinical testing, no other function can tell us as much about a child's inner workings as his eye measurements and his use of his eyes. Developmental changes in visual behavior can be documented from birth by observation of visual performance. One especially informative kind of observation can be made with the retinoscope during various visual tasks at various distances.

Every child who goes through our clinical service is given a full developmental visual examination. The visual behavior picture usually supports and supplements the findings on the developmental examination, revealing clearly a behavioral age level as well as an individual process of patterning. Such an examination may also indicate specific compensation mechanisms, such as myopia, adverse hyperopia, and astigmatism. Lenses and visual training can often be an important therapeutic consideration in guiding visual behavior, both when actual compensations exist and when only behavior patterns are distorted.

We have come to know that these compensations come about in some children because of the way the child's visual mechanism functions and because of his restricted visual understanding. We wish to know why the child has needed to make these compensations, and we need to help him function more effectively.

Restrictions in function may relate to fixation, to focusing, or to interpreting what is seen and where things are seen. Each of these areas has an age expectancy. The 5-year-old, for instance, should be able to track a moving target. If his eyes cannot posture easily and accurately to fixate the target and hold on to it as it is moved, but rather dart ahead or lag behind or lose contact, then he is in visual trouble.

If the child cannot control and sustain shifts in focusing posture equally in both eyes from a far point such as the chalkboard to the near point of his desk by 8 years of age, he is also in visual difficulty. Misinterpreting what is seen and where things are seen can show up in different ways at any age and needs to be related to the performance patterns of the various age expectancies.

We would like to alert readers to the importance of obtaining careful visual findings. We know that eventually fuller visual coverage will be needed for all children than is now available in most school systems. Information obtained from Snellen Acuity charts barely scratches the surface and reveals only some of the grosser difficulties. We do not consider this test an adequate measure of a child's visual functioning.

For the benefit of readers who may be interested in the whole subject of vision, we should point out that there is considerable disagreement among visual specialists. The major disagreement among professionals relates not so much to whether or not vision is important, as to *how* vision is important. A good deal of this difference focuses around the concept of what vision *is*—a definition of what is *involved* in seeing for human beings. The difference in definition can generally be stated as a difference in the extent to which vision is considered to depend on self-involvement.

On the one hand, vision is regarded as something happening *to* a person, with a minimal degree of self-involvement. This view holds that vision has little or no relationship to a child's scholastic and general behavior and achievement. According to this position, eyes as optical systems respond in a relatively automatic, instinctive manner relatively uninfluenced by the individual doing the seeing. The main concern is getting light and light patterns (images) into the eye in a logical, acceptable manner. When this takes place satisfactorily, and there is no eye damage or disease, the necessary conditions for seeing are generally satisfied within this definition. This is a sight-oriented approach.

A second and contrasting approach holds that what any person sees is highly dependent upon what the person is doing in the act of seeing. Specialists who hold this second view assert that *vision and visual abilities must be considered as one part of total human functioning. They believe that vision is a very important component in the way a child develops, learns, and achieves in school.* They emphasize the need to evaluate the efficiency of the visual system in relation to the activities the child is normally faced with during the course of his or her day. They believe that the eye and body adjustments the individual makes to control and monitor his visual system will affect what he sees. Seeing with meaning and understanding is considered to depend as much upon what the seer is doing as upon what kinds of images are presented to his eyes. Vision is considered to be an involved process, not a passive event.

This viewpoint agrees that it is important to get light and light patterns into the eye in a logical, acceptable manner. But the logic and acceptability are contingent upon the viewer's logic and the viewer's acceptability, as well as on the visual presentation itself. Seeing is thought of as an active process involving patterns that, though instinctive, are subject to modification and change. A changing flexible visual system is considered necessary in order to see both similarities and differences. The modifications and changes necessary depend upon how the individual understands, adjusts, and responds in order to coordinate his active participation with the visual presentation.

These two different definitions of vision admittedly do result in different approaches to vision care. Both approaches emphasize the importance of regular eye and vision examinations and of eye health, and both employ lenses as a major vehicle to help people see. But there will be differences in their decisions as to when and how lenses should be used. There will even be disagreements as to whether or not a child's problems involve his vision. Some practitioners do not even consider or believe in programs of care involving vision training and vision remediation.

These different beliefs within the visual care profession must at times be very confusing to the public, especially to a parent who has received two contradictory opinions and diagnoses from two different vision or eye care specialists.

In general, ophthalmologists hold the first view and practitioners with an optometric background go along with us in favoring the second. However, actual practice often cuts across academic background, since some ophthalmologists take the more active view of what vision is, as we do, and some optometrists do not.

The first viewpoint, that vision is a relatively fixed function predetermined at birth, leads practitioners to make little or no attempt to change vision development, growth, and performance. Their goal is to give the person the best *sight* possible, to get the sharpest picture to his eyes.

Within this viewpoint, vision is considered to be not only predetermined, but a passive function. Seeing happens to one. Accordingly, the major consideration is to get the light focused into the eyes by using either spectacle lenses or contact lenses. When the eyes do not work coordinately as a team, the usual decision is to use prisms or to perform surgery to change the muscles that determine where the eyes point.

The use of lenses, then, is mostly determined in terms of improving acuity. The distance visual acuity is measured at and corrected for is *across the room* twenty feet. When a person has healthy eyes, has 20/20 acuity across the room, and can control his eyes so that they generally point together, vision is considered to be normal. Any problem the person has when these favorable conditions are present or can be achieved with lenses is said not to be a vision problem.

In contrast to this view, the second, expanded, and more involved approach (the approach we ourselves favor) is much more concerned with ways in which vision, vision abilities, and vision performance can be efficiently developed and utilized. It holds that the person himself is involved with a visual system that operates at birth through a series of definable reflexes. But as the child grows older, what he does, how he understands his own reactions in relation to incoming light patterns, will change and will modify the original reflex patterns. To the degree that this is possible, vision may be said to be learnable or adaptable.

Under our approach, lenses, guidance, and vision training are programmed to help the child perform more efficiently and effectively than he may be doing. Visual care is directed toward allowing the child to use vision efficiently to do things, the doing including moving, writing, reading, problem-solving, and even thinking. We now know that when a person holds his eyes "still" and thinks of hitting a ball, or when he works an arithmetic problem in his mind, the eyes change focus in order to do the "thinking." The program of care we favor is designed not just for the now of seeing, but to help promote better vision and visual development.*

THE RIGHT-BRAINED VERSUS THE LEFT-BRAINED INDIVIDUAL

One aspect of individual behavior which we note chiefly by simple observation supplemented by visual testing is the matter of sidedness. The question of so-called mixed dominance has long been a source of disagreement among child specialists. Some believe that any child with mixed dominance (say, a child who is right-eyed and left-handed) will in all likelihood have trouble in school.

Our own point of view goes along with perhaps the majority opinion —that it is *confused* dominance rather than *mixed* dominance that causes difficulty.

With increasing sophistication we have become aware of a further aspect of laterality—the fact that there appear to be marked personality differences between left-brained and right-brained individuals.

It is generally accepted that the left brain controls language functions, verbal communication, analytical, logical, and deductive reasoning. The left-brained individual tends to be well oriented in time. He is usually right-handed. He is effective in talking about things, in describing things. In fact, he may be better at talking about a thing than at doing it.

The right brain, on the other hand, governs visual-spatial configurations and manipulatory performance. The right hemisphere appears to be intuitive, nonverbal, musical, pattern-oriented, spatial, inductive. The right-brained individual may be better at doing things than at talking about them. He tends to be well oriented in space. Some believe that the left-brained person is governed by intellect, the right-brained by emotions.

This information has been available for quite some time, but relatively few parents or teachers have applied the knowledge to children. One exception to this general lack of interest in sidedness is that most people nowadays have come to respect the fact that a child's handedness is determined genetically and should be respected.

Few people today would force a left-handed child to use his or her

---

* Most of this special information about vision has been taken directly from our earlier publication *Stop School Failure*, by Ames, Gillespie, and Streff, Harper & Row, 1972, and was contributed by Dr. John W. Streff, formerly of our vision department.

right hand. But most have not come so far as to appreciate that the right-handed (that is, the left-brained) individual may indeed have quite different personality traits and abilities from those seen in the left-handed (and right-brained) individual.

It is only recently that educators, such as Madeline Hunter of California,[30] have suggested that we keep these differences in mind in our efforts to teach children in school. Dr. Hunter points out that schools for the most part have been beaming most of their instruction through a left-brained input (reading and listening) and a left-brained output (talking and writing), thereby handicapping those who are not good at these skills.

She notes that "Without practice, skills and processes can become stagnant, so the comfort of using the dominant hand (or brain) often results in minimal use of the subordinate hand (or brain). Thus weak inherent ability is emphasized by lack of practice."

She recommends that teachers present information in such a way that students can use both hemispheres either simultaneously or alternately, and then can practice integrating information from *both* hemispheres. When students are "not getting it," teachers should adopt practices that could increase facility in the use of each hemisphere, singly or in concert.

A teacher could present information simultaneously to both hemispheres by doing an example on the chalkboard while at the same time giving a verbal explanation; or she could have a model perform an act while others are hearing the directions.

Further, she might follow one kind of stimulus with another. Or give only one type of stimulus (addressed, say, to the right brain only) so that the left-brained student would be forced, at least on occasion, to use his right brain.

Dr. Hunter gives a good example of the relative abilities of the two kinds of individuals. She points out that the surgeon whose right hemisphere governs would presumably perform an effective operation but might have difficulty describing what he had done. One whose left hemisphere dominates might be better at telling about the operation than at doing it.

At any rate, just recently there has developed considerable interest in the very marked differences in learning ability which exist between left-brained and right-brained individuals, and a beginning willingness to try to see to it that the school situation should be fairer to the right-brained individual. He may be the one of whom we have earlier said: "He is better at living than at learning."

We might also be fairer than we now are to the left-brained person who, because our schools often over-reward his type of ability and aptitude, may seem more superior and more effective than he actually is.

THE LOWENFELD MOSAIC TEST

A test which we use routinely in our own clinical service, though it is not used widely in this country, is Margaret Lowenfeld's Mosaic test.[*]
This test is easy to give, easy to record, and very well received by subjects from preschool right through old age.

Its chief difficulty is that to date no generally accepted formal scoring has been worked out for it. The examiner is therefore required to *evaluate* the child's response rather than simply to score it.

Materials

The standard Mosaic set consists of a box of 456 plastic pieces, $\frac{1}{16}$ inch thick. These pieces come in five different shapes—square, diamond, equilateral triangle, right-angled isosceles triangle, and scalene triangle; and in six different colors—blue, white, red, green, yellow, and black. There are 8 squares of each color; 12 equilateral triangles of each color; 16 diamonds of each color; 16 isosceles triangles of each color; and 24 scalenes of each color. The box is divided in the middle into two equal parts, half of all pieces being included in each half.

The working surface on which the patterns are to be made is a sheet of white paper which covers the surface of a rectangular wooden tray having a raised rim on three sides, with the rimless side placed nearest the subject. The standard size of the working surface is $10\frac{1}{4}$ by $12\frac{3}{8}$ inches.

Administration

The subject should be seated before a table on which is placed, directly in front of him, the tray covered with a piece of white paper. The open box containing the Mosaic pieces is at his left.

The examiner says: "Here is a box of pieces, all different colors and all different shapes. I want you to make something with some of these pieces on the paper, anything you like. But first I'm going to show you all the different kinds."

The examiner demonstrates one piece of each kind. As he holds up each piece, he comments: "This comes in all these different colors"—showing them. After demonstrating and commenting on each shape, the examiner refers to the second half of the box, away from the child: "And here are extra ones in case you need more."

[*] The Mosaic materials can be ordered from Mrs. F. B. Muir, 24 Dickens Chase, Leeds, Nr. Maidstone, Kent, England. Our own rather full discussion of this test will be found in *Mosaic Patterns of American Children*.[6]

He continues: "Now I want you to take some of these pieces out of the box and put them on the paper and make something—anything you like. You may take as long or as short a time as you like. You may use a lot of pieces or just a few. You may make a big thing or a small thing. You may start now."

If the subject hesitates, the examiner may encourage him with: "Which one are you going to start with?" Further encouragement is seldom needed.

The examiner records as much detail as possible, regarding both what the subject does and what he says as he works. When the subject is finished, the examiner says: "Now tell me about what you have made." This should be asked in a friendly and interested way, not in a perplexed manner.

Unless the subject works for more than twenty minutes, he is permitted to take as long as he likes. After the child leaves, the examiner traces around each Mosaic chip the child has placed on the board, indicating its color. The recorded design is then colored in with crayons or pasted over with colored pieces of gummed paper representing the different shapes and the different colors. One of the many advantages of the Mosaic test is that a replica of the child's product is available for analysis.

Findings

Interpretation of Mosaic results does not require the high degree of specialized skill needed for interpretation of the Rorschach. Nevertheless, we recommend that any examiner who intends to use the Mosaic consult our own book on the subject.[6]

Findings are presented here briefly in Table 55. We have also summarized briefly the outstanding kinds of responses which we consider characteristic of the individual at ages 2 through 9.

2½ years old. The child of this age has moved beyond just picking up handfuls of chips and dropping them onto the board. He or she tends to pick chips out of the box one by one and place them at random on the board, with no selection of shape or color.

3 years old. A sizable number still just drop pieces onto the board, but now nearly one fifth of the children are able to make a prefundamental—that is, they can put together, side by side, two pieces of the same shape. A few name a single piece, or a combination of two or more pieces, though there is no relationship between the appearance of the pieces and the name. However, more than half the products are classified as *non-representational without pattern.*

3½ years old. Pieces are still often placed pretty much all over the

TABLE 55 *Mosaic Test: Type of Structure*

	2 years			3 years			4 years			5 years			6 years			7 years			8 years			9 years		
	G	B	All	G	B	All	G	B	All	G	B	All	G	B	All	G	B	All	G	B	All	G	B	All
A. Nonrepresentational without pattern																								
1. Just drop or pile	22	16	38	7	3	10	1	2	3	—	—	—	—	—	—	—	1	1	—	—	—	—	—	—
2. Scatter singly	**24**	**30**	**54**	**18**	10	**28**	5	6	11	1	0	1	—	—	—	—	—	—	—	—	—	—	—	—
3. Prefundamental	4	2	6	6	**12**	18	7	4	11	—	—	—	—	—	—	—	—	—	—	—	—	—	—	—
4. Slab																								
Small	—	—	—	—	—	—	1	2	3	4	1	5	1	0	1	1	1	2	0	1	1	2	2	4
Large	—	—	—	—	—	—	—	—	—	1	3	4	1	3	4	—	1	1	5	3	8	4	3	7
5. Overall	—	—	—	—	—	—	—	—	—	1	0	1	0	2	2	—	—	—	0	2	2	1	0	1
ALL A	50	48	98	31	25	56	14	14	28	7	4	11	2	5	7	1	3	4	5	6	11	7	5	12
B. Nonrepresentational with pattern																								
1. Fundamental	—	—	—	1	2	3	3	4	7	—	—	—	—	—	—	—	—	—	2	0	2	—	—	—
2. Central design	—	—	—	0	2	2	11	6	17	9	6	15	10	3	13	10	3	13	9	4	13	**13**	5	18
3. Design along rim	0	2	2	4	3	7	1	2	3	1	3	4	0	2	2	0	0	0	0	0	0	3	1	4
4. Fills tray																								
Frame and item	—	—	—	6	1	7	0	1	1	3	0	3	1	1	2	2	4	6	5	4	9	2	2	4
Whole pattern	—	—	—	0	0	0	1	0	1	0	1	1	0	0	0	4	1	5	1	1	2	1	3	4
5. Separate designs	—	—	—	1	1	2	0	0	0	3	2	5	5	2	7	5	1	6	0	1	1	2	0	2
ALL B	0	2	2	12	9	21	16	13	29	16	12	28	16	8	24	21	9	30	17	10	27	21	11	32
C. Representational																								
1. Object	—	—	—	7	10	17	**18**	**20**	**38**	**22**	**29**	**51**	**23**	**24**	**47**	11	**18**	29	**14**	**20**	**34**	11	**24**	**35**
2. Scene	—	—	—	0	6	6	0	3	3	3	5	8	9	13	22	**16**	17	**33**	11	14	25	10	10	20
ALL C	—	—	—	7	16	23	18	23	41	25	34	59	32	37	69	27	35	62	25	34	59	21	34	55
D. Mixed, representational and nonrepresentational	—	—	—	—	—	—	2	0	2	2	0	2	—	—	—	1	3	4	3	0	3	1	0	1
Totals	50	50	100	50	50	100	50	50	100	50	50	100	50	50	100	50	50	100	50	50	100	50	50	100

NOTE: Bold face figures are the leading items of each age, rather than normative items.

board, with only minimal attention to shape or pattern. Many now make prefundamentals. Others place pieces around with little attention to shape or color, but name, to their satisfaction, after finishing.

4 years old. This is the first age at which either a nonrepresentational design *with pattern,* or what subjects intend as a *representational object,* predominates over nonrepresentational without pattern. Most characteristic of this age is a hexagon (we call it a "four-year-old circle"), made of six large triangles, but with no attention to color. Other FOURS line up pieces horizontally or vertically. Some manage a small, not very accurate, design with pattern. Naming still tends to be after the fact.

5 years old. A representational object of some kind now becomes normative. Most characteristically it may be a two-piece house made of square and triangle. Some make an elaboration of the hexagon, perhaps making several which interlock. Most products, whether they actually resemble a thing or not, are named as an object. A few, possibly highly creative children use the pieces like paint, piling them onto the paper and then sweeping them into a recognizably structured object. This ability tends to be lost as the child grows older.

5½ to 6 years old. There is a big change here, especially at 6 years of age. By 6, 69% of products are representational, 22% even go beyond the single object and become scenes. Houses are for the most part large and open structures, arrows or boats resemble what they are named to be. Scenes tend to be in layers: blue sky at the top, green grass at the bottom, and houses or flowers or trees in between. Many now pay attention to color.

7 years old. By now all but 4% make either nonrepresentational designs with pattern (30%), or representational objects or scenes. Scenes reach a high point of 33%. Whether scenes, objects, or designs, pieces are placed serially, usually in a horizontal alignment. As at 6, color is used selectively and effectively.

8 years old. Products are becoming larger and more graphic. Some make rather successful designs, but the majority still make either objects or scenes. Color is used selectively. In an effort to attain perspective, some place objects (houses, for example) all over the paper.

9 years old. Though 55% of subjects still make either representational objects or scenes, this is the strongest age to date for nonrepresentational designs with pattern (32%). Subjects tend to go to one of two extremes: they make very small compact designs (often all blue), or extremely large, intricate, and for the most part highly accurate designs.

Fundamentals

A fundamental is the simplest design that can be made from any single shape. In a group of somewhat superior subjects (possibly about one year advanced over a normative rating), we find that a square of four squares is made at 4 years of age; also at that age, a triangle of three large triangles or a hexagon of six large triangles; as well as a square of four equilateral triangles. An arrow of four diamonds can be made at 6; a star of eight diamonds at 7. Either a diamond shape of four scalene triangles or a circle of twelve scalenes is achieved by 8 years of age.

THE RORSCHACH TEST

In any clinical examination we are interested not only in the level of development which any given child may have reached, but also in his or her unique personality or individuality. We are especially anxious, when a child may be in difficulty enough to be brought for a clinical examination, to determine whether problems are actually quite within the limits of supposedly normal behavior, or if the child may be atypical or emotionally disturbed.

One of the most effective tests for making such a determination—though it is a test which can and should be used only by the expert and experienced clinician—is the Rorschach test.

This test, the best-known and most widely used of all so-called projective techniques, has proved remarkably useful in clinical practice, possibly far beyond even the most sanguine hopes of its author, Hermann Rorschach. Like many clinicians, we use it routinely with our clinical cases, where it proves time and again to be one of the most effective and revealing tools in helping us understand the individuality of the growing child.

In the hands of a trained individual it can be a most useful supplement to the usual battery of readiness tests. But since it should be used only by the specialist who will already be familiar with its detail, it will not be described here. Our own method of interpretation has been described fully in an earlier publication.[13] Its strong and weak points are as follows:

STRONG POINTS

1. The Rorschach constitutes an effective supplement to the recommended battery of tests in that it gives good clues to marked immaturity as well as to behavior which is conspicuously advanced.
2. More than other tests in the proposed battery, it reveals the nature of a child's individuality.
3. It can spot emotional disturbance, especially in those children not suited for regular classroom attendance whose problem is emotional rather than one of low intelligence or immaturity.
4. It gives good clues as to the intelligence of subjects.
5. The Rorschach gives certain clues which in any 5-to-7-year-old suggest unreadiness for kindergarten and first grade. The most important of

these is the relation of F% to F+%.* Our experience suggests that an F+% (or correct form percent) which is lower than the F% (form percent) is a clear warning sign that a child is not ready to start first grade.

WEAK POINTS

1. The fact that the Rorschach response requires interpretation by a highly trained person makes it not only impractical, but actually unsafe in unskilled hands.
2. Even the skilled clinician may find it difficult always to distinguish between a response which indicates immaturity and one which indicates merely a limited intelligence.
3. The qualitative aspects of the ages (which give the best clues as to age level of response) tend to show up only in superior or well-endowed children.
4. Unusually high F% or unusually high A% (animal percent), both suspect, may indicate immaturity or they may merely be a sign of a highly restricted individuality.
5. Because of normal variation from age to age, and especially because any given individual sometimes does less well at an older than at a younger age, it is not possible from a single test to be certain whether a given response has never come in, or may have come in at an earlier age and dropped out temporarily. This is especially true in the case of the human movement response on Card III. In some subjects, it is given at 5 years, drops out at 5½. In fact, in 8% of present normative kindergarten girls, in 10% of kindergarten boys, and in 33% of first-grade boys, the Rorschach response on a second examination in sequence is less mature than on a first.
6. Thus a highly enlivened response to the Rorschach tells a good deal, for better or worse, but a record of from 8 to 10 responses with high F% and high A% tells relatively little with regard to school readiness, since this type of response may indicate low intelligence, a restricted psyche, or immaturity. It is often most difficult to make a clear and certain distinction.
7. Also, perhaps more than with other tests, the expected Rorschach response at any given age differs markedly in subjects of different intellectual and social levels.

Unreadiness Signs

Rorschach examiners may also be interested in our list of possible "unreadiness signs"—kinds or levels of response which appear to be sug-

---

* Technical scoring terms are not explained here. Any reader not familiar with these terms who wishes an explanation is referred to Ames et al., *Child Rorschach Responses.*[13]

gestive of unreadiness for first-grade entrance and, in some instances, even for entrance to kindergarten.

Of these signs, the single-word response suggests not only unreadiness for starting first grade, but even for doing kindergarten work. Pure C (color unmodulated by form), C' (black used as color), Cn (color naming), and perseveration occur in both ready and unready kindergarten subjects, but only in unready as opposed to ready first-graders. Thus any of these responses suggests possible unreadiness for first grade.

Other signs of unreadiness for first grade—F% exceeding F+%, fewer than 10 responses, atypical concepts, and preschool confabulation or contamination—are found conspicuously in unready kindergarten subjects and also in unready first-graders. A sC (sum of color responses) greater than M (sum of movement responses) is also suspect.

The Rorschach as Prognostic of Reading Achievement

A study by George Meyer in 1953[41] suggested that the Rorschach if given to kindergarten subjects could distinguish in many instances between those subjects who would later be good readers and those who would not, and also could provide data on first-grade readiness.

We have checked Meyer's findings[14] on a group of 64 public school children for whom both kindergarten Rorschachs and fifth-grade reading test scores were available. Comparison of the early Rorschachs of the later good and poor readers with IQ held constant supported Meyer's findings and added a few further distinguishing signs between the two groups.

Later good readers, as compared to later poor readers, give better-quality W, have a lower W% (percent of whole responses) and higher D% (percent of detail responses), give more introversive responses, and more FM, have a lower F%, a higher F+%, and an F+% which exceeds the F%.

In general, we consider the Rorschach a useful supplementary test to a developmental battery chiefly in that it can provide important clues to a child's basic individuality structure, as well as spotting grossly immature or highly atypical children. It is most useful for this purpose in the 5-to-6-year-old range. By 8 years of age it seems less effective, though at any age it can spot the highly atypical personality.

As a rule the differences between a 7-, 8-, and 9-year-old performance (unless the subject is superior enough to show the characteristic qualitative signs of the age) are not great enough to be consistently helpful in determining developmental level.

Also, owing to the fact that the Rorschach needs to be administered and interpreted by a highly trained person (and even then it is sometimes difficult to interpret just what it has to say about developmental level), we do not recommend that it be given routinely as part of a developmental battery.

KINETIC FAMILY DRAWING

One of the newest, most interesting, and liveliest of the projective techniques is Burns and Kaufman's Kinetic Family Drawing. Anyone wishing to use this test is referred to the two basic books on the subject: *Kinetic Family Drawings* (*K-F-D*), by Robert C. Burns and S. Harvard Kaufman,[15] and *Actions, Styles and Symbols in Kinetic Family Drawings* (*K-F-D*),[16] by the same authors.

The procedure for obtaining a Kinetic Family Drawing is relatively simple. According to the authors:

> The drawings should be obtained from children individually. The child is asked to seat himself at a table of appropriate height. A sheet of plain white, 8½ × 11 inch paper is placed on the table directly in front of him. A No. 2 pencil is placed in the center of the paper and he is asked to "Draw a picture of everyone in your family, including you, DOING something. Try to draw whole people, not cartoons or stick people. Remember, make everyone DOING something—some kind of action."
>
> No time limit is given. Noncompliance is extremely rare. If the child says, "I can't," he is encouraged to try.

Though the task might seem somewhat formidable to the adult, most children from six years of age on respond with alacrity, after perhaps an initial demurral that they don't draw very well. The examiner may tell them that it is not the artistic quality of their product that he is interested in, but rather what it is that the child has the people doing.

In evaluating the response there are many things that one looks for. Primarily, of course, we wish to find out what kind of action the child expresses. Secondary factors are the relationship of the family members to each other. Are they doing things together? Is the atmosphere friendly or hostile? Are they placed near together or are some separated or boxed off or with their backs to each other? The possibilities are almost endless.

Many drawings turn out to be rather bland. Others speak very distinctly of rather specific family or personal problems. The test, as indicated, is still more or less in its infancy, but we anticipate that as it becomes better known, its potential usefulness will be increasingly appreciated.

It provides a lively addition to any test battery and frequently reveals information not obtained in a prolonged personal interview. Also, in drawing, children are often less guarded than they would be if required to make a verbal response in an interview.

TEETH

Since we closely relate function to structure, we have always been aware of the remarkable evidence, so obviously present and clear for all to see, of the differences which exist from child to child in the matter of movement of the loss of baby teeth and their replacement with the permanent teeth. Most parents and others interested in the behavior and growth of infants have already, in the child's first two years of life, been interested in relating his teething to the rest of his growth.

They also note, though often more casually, the falling out of baby teeth and the eruption of the second teeth. But for the most part, people have been very superficial in these appraisals and thus have probably missed many important potential clues that could give much information about any individual child. They may have noted unusual patterns with interest, but somehow failed to relate these patterns to the rest of the child's behavior and growth.

For example, late teething in the infant, with the upper central incisors erupting first, as late as 1 year of age, may seem odd even to the most unschooled. What does it mean? Certainly nearly anyone will suspect that things are topsy-turvy, since the lower teeth are expected to erupt first. Consider the eruption of the lateral upper incisors before the eruption of the central incisors. This again strikes even the untutored eye. Might it imply some difficulty or delay in focal central behavior?

A second set of teeth gives those interested in observing and helping children a second chance to peer into nature's inner workings. We ourselves have become rather self-conscious at the mere mention of teeth, because so many people believe strongly that there is no relationship between structure and behavior—between, for instance, a child's behavior in school and his teething. But our clinical evidence has been piling up over the years to the point that we are convinced that a definitive study should be made of this relationship.

If, for example, an 8-year-old boy is brought to us because of educational difficulties in the third grade and reveals with his smile of greeting that he still has four upper central baby teeth, we are alerted at once that his teething is below a 6½-year-old level. It is natural to question whether this boy is capable even of second-grade work, if the warning of his teeth is taken into consideration. He may more correctly belong at a first-grade level. Fortunately, today's concept of ungraded classes is giving such a child more opportunity to be his biological age, rather than his being pushed into the expectations of his chronological age.

Another example might relate to a *partial* delay in teething. Again let us consider an 8-year-old boy in third grade. This child reveals by his smile that he has his right second central and lateral upper incisors fully erupted, but that his left central and lateral incisors are still his baby teeth. Might this not alert the educator to a potential marked discrepancy in behavior? We have found this kind of eruption to be related to extremes of behavior. In some things the child is right up to his age or better, but he also shows behaviors markedly below his age. This kind of boy will need the stimulation which his advancement requires, but he will at the same time need to be allowed protection to organize through his basic level, which will be much lower.

Anyone interested in the loss and eruption of teeth can witness this drama almost daily in the spring of the kindergarten year. In our Weston study there was clear evidence that the teething schedule of boys was behind that of girls of the same age. Of the 41% of subjects who were behind the average teething schedule, 73% of these were boys. (See Table 56.) We also noted especially that boys more often than girls were likely to erupt their second teeth behind their first teeth without losing their first teeth through the absorption of their roots to facilitate their loss. It is with boys that the dentist more often has to pull the first teeth to give the second teeth space to come into good alignment. Does this mean that boys have greater difficulty in transitions, that they are more apt to hold on to their past?

We include two tables from our Weston study with apologies, since only 80 subjects are covered, without any standardizing controls. The first

TABLE 56   *Average Age of Tooth Eruption*

Age	No Eruption (%)	Beginning Movement (%)	Eruption (%)	Molar (%)	Lower Central Incisor (%)
$5-5^4$	90	25	7	7	7
5^5-5^{10}	50	25	50	25	36
$5^{11}-6^4$	16	14	80	58	78
6^5-6^{10}	5	13	84	81	81
$6^{11}-7^4$	2	0	98	94	98
7^5-7^{10}	0	0	100	98	100
$7^{11}-8^4$	0	0	100	100	100

Age	Upper Central Incisor (%)	Lower Lateral Incisor (%)	Upper Lateral Incisor (%)	Number of Cases
$5-5^4$	0	3	0	28
5^5-5^{10}	7	4	0	68
$5^{11}-6^4$	30	15	5	55
6^5-6^{10}	52	52	18	38
$6^{11}-7^4$	84	72	51	51
7^5-7^{10}	89	80	53	36
$7^{11}-8^4$	96	93	80	29

table gives some idea of normative expectancy. Thus we would anticipate some movement of teeth in the 5½-to-6-year-old, of either the lower central incisors or the 6-year molars (Table 56). By 6 years of age, both lower central incisors and 6-year molars are at a normative level of eruption. Next follow the upper central incisors and lower lateral incisors, by 6½ years of age. By 7 to 7½ years, the upper lateral incisors are erupting. By 8 years of age, one can anticipate four 6-year molars and four upper and lower incisors. This might well be the badge of readiness for entrance to third grade. There are, however, exceptions, as with the 6% of girls who were behind schedule but were capable of top or A group placement. (See Table 57.)

In fact, we should emphasize that in the case of teething as with other aspects of physical growth, though behavioral maturity more often than not does go along with physical maturity just as behavior goes along with chronological age, there can be many exceptions.

Thus a child could conceivably be an early teether and still be slow in his general development. Or he or she could be a late teether and this could be out of line with the general maturity level.

We include a table on correlation between rate of teething and quality of school performance in our Weston subjects. In general, it will

TABLE 57　*Correlation Between Teething and School Performance*

Teething	Number	Total Group (%)	Boys (%)	Girls (%)
Ahead of schedule	25	31	20	**80**
Behind schedule	33	41	**73**	27
Both ahead of and behind	22	28	45	**55**

School Placement	
Those whose teething is ahead of schedule	
Definitely in top group	**60**
Doing well or fairly well	36
Atypical, repeated	4
Those whose teething is behind schedule	
Should have repeated	**54**
(Did repeat)	(22)
Would have profited by repetition	40
Top group—no question of repeating	6 (all girls)
Those whose teething was both ahead of and behind schedule	
Repeated by the school	14
Would have benefited by repeating	**50**
Doing nicely, well placed	
(described as hard workers)	36

be clear from Table 57 that according to our judgments, the majority of those children whose teething was ahead of schedule were doing well in their schoolwork in the grade in which age placed them. Conversely, the majority of those children whose teething was behind schedule were doing less well in school.

THE BODY ITSELF

An adequate understanding of the child's physical body and how it functions, at a deeper and more physiological level than that which many of us test, is at present beyond the scope of all but a few highly skilled clinicians.

However, it is known that many children behave as unsatisfactorily or immaturely as they do because of something wrong in the physical functioning of their bodies. Increasingly, emphasis is moving from the notion that inadequate, ineffective, and even destructive behavior has been caused by something that parent or teacher or society in general has or has not done, and toward the notion that some bodies just don't work right.

Among those physicians who are currently contributing the most along these lines are such individuals as Dr. Lendon H. Smith,[49] Dr. Allan Cott,[20] Dr. Ben F. Feingold,[22] and Dr. Ray C. Wunderlich.[52]

Dr. Smith asks: "Why do so many children turn out so badly, in school and in life?" His answer is that some bodies just don't work right, and the reason they do not work right is that their owners' brains just don't get the proper nourishment. Some individuals *do* manage on an inadequate diet; some don't.

According to him, if the cortex, or forebrain, isn't properly nourished, the animal or emotional brain takes over, and with nothing to prevent it, the child often becomes hyperactive, violent, and aggressive. For instance, he sees a match and nothing tells him *not* to use it to start a fire. Or he feels angry and nothing stops him from launching into violent, aggressive action.

Improper diet, especially the consumption of too much white flour and especially of sugar, *lowers* the blood sugar in the body to the extent that the forebrain does not function.

Among other practical suggestions, Dr. Smith suggests not only the restriction of sugar, but plenty of protein in the form of frequent snacks. He believes that many children would do better with numerous small meals a day in place of the traditional three big ones, since proper food at proper intervals can often improve behavior both at home and at school. Some bodies function in such a way that they just cannot handle the kind of diet that many homes provide.

Dr. Allan Cott, in a series of papers, similarly suggests a biochemical treatment for behavior disorders. He feels that it is time for close scrutiny of the neurological and biochemical processes of the disturbed child and the learning-disabled child. The methods he suggests to parents include restriction of diet, megavitamin treatment, and perceptual-motor training, since he points out that remedial efforts should be directed toward both brain function and body chemistry.

He especially emphasizes the importance of a proper diet since there is coming to be, in the medical profession, an increasing awareness that nutrition operates at all levels of biochemical and metabolic function, and that diet is important in creating an optimum molecular environment for the brain.

He says specifically: "Greater concern must be shown for the quality of the internal environment in which our cells and tissues function because, as in the entire biological world, these environments can vary through the full spectrum of performance—from those which barely keep cells alive up through hundreds of gradations to levels supporting something like optimal performance."

Dr. Ben F. Feingold, like Drs. Smith and Cott, recommends for any children in trouble a high protein/low carbohydrate diet and the exclusion of sugars and sweets. His particular position is that foods and even drugs that are artificially colored and artificially flavored actually cause both hyperkinesis and learning disability. When he has put patients on a synthetic-free diet, not permitting *any* foods or drinks that contain either artificial coloring or artificial flavoring, improvement is reported to be spectacular. Not only did many of his patients calm down and quiet down and respond positively and well in learning situations, but those who had been on drugs on which they had formerly been dependent could do without their medication.

According to Feingold, many hyperactive learning-disabled children are also allergic, but some will respond well to a more careful diet *even without* the treatment of their allergies.

Especially good advice about allergies has been contributed by Dr. Ray C. Wunderlich, who points out: "It works both ways. Allergy can interfere with the function of the brain, and the brain that doesn't work properly can bring on allergy. . . . There is a growing realization that the adjustment problems of children are more often biologically based than was commonly recognized in the past.

"The ability of tranquilizers, anticonvulsants, stimulants, vitamins and minerals to alter brain function leads us to look for further explanation of unsatisfactory behavior *within* the child, at the cellular and subcellular levels."

Wunderlich himself reports remarkable success with school and home behavior problems with the prescription of corticosteroids or megavitamins.

These four researchers, though outstanding, are but a few of those who now suggest that we look inside the child's own body functioning, rather than blaming environmental factors for unsatisfactory behavior. But here, as always, biological and environmental factors must work together, since once we have pinpointed what it is about a body's functioning that is unsatisfactory and what that body needs in the way of diet or medication, it is up to the environment to provide it.

SUMMARY

The range of factors which we consider in a full diagnostic workup is obviously rather extensive. We are casting a very wide net. But all of these tests, measures, observations, are based on our continuing philosophical position, which is that behavior is a function of structure, and that to a large extent the way an individual behaves is the result of a combination of three factors: his basic individuality (based on his physical structure), his developmental or maturity level, and the way he reacts to the environment.

It is also our position that the environment (especially home and school) can act most effectively with regard to any individual child if the other two factors are known.

There are many different and effective tests and kinds of evaluation now available for clinical use. The battery described in this chapter provides the best all-round support for our Gesell behavior tests, which we have found so basic and helpful in appraising any boy's or girl's potential in the age range from 5 through 9 years of age.

CHAPTER 14

THE CHILD IN SCHOOL

|||||||||||||||||||||||||||||||||||||||||||||||||||||||||||||||||||||||||||||||||||||||||

THE IMPORTANCE OF BEHAVIOR TESTING

The field of education today, as most educators know all too well, is somewhat stormy, full of crosscurrents and differing opinions. Wild battles are fought, with the students all too often the victims, and nobody the winner. Postman and Weingartner's lively *The School Book*[46] covers many of the more important areas of controversy.

This chapter does not attempt to deal comprehensively with all these important controversial topics. We merely mention here some which relate most closely to our own greatest interest—the effort to help all children succeed in school.

Since this present volume deals almost entirely with the usefulness of a behavior examination in determining proper school placement, whereas in some quarters there is a feeling that *any* testing in the schools is an invasion of privacy, we might well begin with a brief comment on the importance of behavior testing. It is obvious that we *do* consider it both permissible and essential.

Not only do some consider testing an invasion of privacy; they also believe that any difficulty anybody gets into is a result of something done or not done to him or her by somebody or something in the environment. Thus they feel that any kind of individual diagnosis is unnecessary.

Our own biological point of view holds that to a very large extent, behavior is a function of structure and that the environment can best meet the needs of the individual if we know as much as possible about that individual.

It is our contention that from infancy through college, anyone concerned with fitting the school situation to the child, rather than—as some do—trying to fit the child to the school situation, will be helped by knowing the child's developmental level—that is, knowing the age at which his total body is performing.

Tests are the child specialist's tools, and it is through a knowledgeable use of these tools that we can best help parent and teacher in their joint effort to provide for every child a school situation which will be most suitable.

The importance of a certain amount of physical examination which will lead to a better understanding of how the child's body functions has already been discussed in Chapter 13. As Dr. Ray Wunderlich emphasizes: "Physicians need to know more about educators, as educators need to know more about physicians."[52] Fortunately, to date, physical examination of the child has not been considered an invasion of privacy, so that political objections on that score are seldom met with.

MAINSTREAMING VERSUS SPECIAL CLASSES

A second important question is the matter of mainstreaming versus special classes. This is a matter of particular interest to us.

Historically, the setting up of special classes for those boys and girls who could not comfortably make it in the usual class was a tremendous achievement. Not only educators but parents as well appreciated that there are many children not able to keep up with the demands of the regular classroom.

Such children may be disturbed emotionally, may be of low intelligence, may suffer from some special kind of so-called learning disability. Or their problem may be simply one of immaturity. Our usual finding is that children with a maturity level one or even two years below their chronological age can still fit into the "regular" stream of education if properly placed and allowed to go more slowly than the usual pace. But more than a two-year lag, in our estimation, requires special schooling and attendance in a special class.

We repeat, the setting up of special classes, when it was first achieved, was considered a major victory for all concerned. In recent years, however, some parents and some educators have introduced a concept called mainstreaming. Sharing, perhaps, the same philosophy as those who supported the notion of social promotion for every child,[28] whether or not he or she had actually accomplished the work of a given grade, their apparent aim is to protect children's feelings.

Their argument seems to be that children placed in special classes feel, or are, discriminated against; and that they will be happier if included in the regular classrooms. This kind of thinking ignores the fact that the other children *know* when a child cannot keep up. It ignores the fact that the special child often really *cannot* keep up. It ignores the fact that special teaching, when needed, is a privilege and not a disgrace.

However, we would like to warn against one use of special classes which is often unwarranted and may actually be harmful to the child concerned. In our clinical service it is not unusual for us to examine a child who is being kept in the regular stream of education but is released one or two periods a day for special help in a learning-disability or other special class. All too often our finding, which should be of special interest to readers of this book, is that the child's academic difficulty stems simply from overplacement.

Thus the treatment of choice might best be putting the child back into the grade for which he or she is suited developmentally, rather than continuing him in a too advanced class and then trying to patch things up with special class help.

REPEATING? YES. EARLY COGNITIVE TRAINING? NO. REMEDIAL READING? MAYBE.

Repeating

Should any schoolchild turn out to be overplaced—that is, placed in a grade ahead of the one where he is able to do the work—we recommend that, assuming he appears to be of normal intelligence and without special problems which indicate the need for special class placement, he be allowed to repeat.

We have discussed this matter fully in Chapter 2, but because it is so very important we mention it once again. Ideally, with a good strong developmental placement program, with pre-kindergarten screening, and with a two-level kindergarten and a pre-first grade available for those who need a very slow start, all children should be ready for first grade by the time they reach it, and very little repeating would need to be done.

But if in spite of a school's best efforts a child *must* repeat, research as well as actual practice bears out our contention that with proper handling—a calm but firm approach on the part of both home and school—most children can and do accept the inevitable. And when they find out how much more successful they are, academically and socially, once they are correctly placed, most are as pleased with their corrected placement as are their parents and teachers.

And so our very strong recommendation is: don't be afraid to have a child repeat when repetition seems indicated. But keep in mind that repeating is not magic. It does not necessarily solve *all* of a child's problems.

Early Cognitive Training

An elementary school principal whom we very much respect once gave this advice to his teachers: "Keep those pencils out of their hands and those workbooks off their desks as long as possible."

We would like to underline his advice. In our opinion, all too many first-grade and even kindergarten teachers go much too far in pushing academic instruction. Certainly, unless it is their own spontaneous interest, nursery school, kindergarten, and even beginning first-grade boys and girls don't need to be taught to read. And as to their so-called cognitive development, we sometimes wish the term had never been invented.

Children had minds, and they used them, long before anyone talked about cognition. The child's mind grows and develops and functions from earliest infancy. As Dr. Gesell used to say: "Mind manifests itself in virtually everything the young child does." He learns in many ways other than simply through reading and printing.

We have developed this theme in our own *Don't Push Your Preschooler*,[4] and what is true for preschool is also true for the earliest years of elementary school. All too many small girls and boys, especially boys, are pushed into desk work long before their brains, their bodies, and most especially their eyes are anywhere near ready for it.[28]

Remedial Reading

In this country for many years now, most school systems have on their staffs one or many remedial reading teachers, and such teachers will probably always be needed in the foreseeable future.

However, our experience has been that in communities which maintain good developmental placement programs, relatively few boys and girls have trouble enough with reading to need the help of a remedial reading teacher. That is, we have found that if reading is not started too soon, children rarely become confused enough about reading to need such help. Their pace may be slow. Some boys do not seem fully ready to begin to read till they are as much as 8 years of age. If they are started sooner, they do indeed become confused and need help in overcoming their confusion.

Reports from Scandinavian countries, where children do not start first grade till they are fully seven, and are not pressured to read even in their first year of school if they seem unready, tell us that their schools experience very few reading failures, do not for the most part have on their staffs remedial reading teachers, and do not feel that they have any serious reading problems.

In some schools in this country, developmental placement has reduced the number of children who have trouble with reading to the point that former remedial reading teachers have been released from this aspect of their work and have thus become available to take on the work of developmental examiner.

Certainly it is important to be sure that we are not pushing quite normal but unready children into such early instruction in reading that they unnecessarily become reading failures.

A BOOKLESS CURRICULUM

Regardless of maturity, there are some boys and girls, perhaps those right-brained children who do not learn easily through words and who are not good in verbal pursuits, who do have difficulty in reading. It has been suggested that for such children, at least until they can be helped to read at a simple level, academic material might best be provided through what some call a *bookless curriculum.*

It does seem reasonable that if a child cannot read, or cannot read effectively, it is indeed unfair to present all school material through the printed word.

In the bookless curriculum, any means of conveying knowledge without requiring literacy is acceptable. Such a curriculum will utilize tape recordings, books on records, films, projectors, art, music, role-playing, field trips, discussion, guest lecturers.

At any rate, it has been suggested[48] that the money, time, and brainpower currently being spent in remedial reading might better be focused on less painful ways of presenting a curriculum to a child. And that we might use our efforts to look at ways to expand the curriculum to meet the needs of more children rather than in attempting to find new ways of altering children's behavior to meet the needs of a rigid curriculum.

LEARNING DISABILITIES

There currently looms very large in the field of education the somewhat new concept of learning disabilities. When the term was first introduced, some educators felt that the problem of children having trouble in learning was not new, but rather that our massive concern made it seem like something special.

More recently, Dr. Feingold[22] and others concerned with the influence of the child's diet, health, and body chemistry on his school and general behavior suggest that the problem, if not actually new, is currently much more extensive than in times past.

The notion of learning disabilities looked for a while like an idea whose time had come. Especially as more people became concerned with the academic problems of so-called disadvantaged children as well as those of the middle class, it was increasingly obvious that far too many children in this country were having trouble in school. Unfortunately, the term "learning disabilities," like the equally catchy and equally dangerous term "Right to Read," caught on and swept the country—long before we had reached a really satisfactory definition of what it meant, and certainly long before we knew what to do about it.

The idea in itself is a good one, but (implicitly even if not intentionally) it has brought perhaps too much security and satisfaction. Many a parent today will tell you that his or her child has a learning disability, as if the label itself more or less took care of things. At least, the parent implies, this is a real "thing" the child has, so the parent is not to blame.

Actually, it is extremely important to keep in mind that a learning disability is not a *thing* which can be *cured* if only we go about it right. Many at least now use the plural, "learning disabilities," and that is a step in the right direction.

A second major error characteristic of many in this field today is a total lack of regard for the Law of Parsimony, which requires that one should never give a complicated answer when a simple one will do. Of the supposedly "learning disabled" children brought to our clinic because they are having trouble in school, we find the largest number to be simply overplaced. Thus, inevitably, they fail. In a school community which provides full-time learning-disability classes, they are placed in such a class. In other communities, they remain in the grade which is quite beyond their level of ability, spending an hour or two a day in a learning-disability class.

Another major cause of school failure is that many children cannot be classed as fully defective, but are suffering from the handicap of an IQ in the 80 to 90 range. Such children in most school systems have nowhere to go. Too intelligent for a class for the admittedly retarded, they are still not able to keep up in the "regular" class. They suffer and struggle, flounder and fail, and end up in a learning-disability class, if one is available.

A further group of school failures who all too often end up labeled "L.D." consists of children with overall modest academic ability but unfortunately uneven endowment. These are some of the hardest children to place and to work with. Because they have some single high point (in reading, math, or another subject), school and family insist that such children "could do better if they would," ignoring the fact that their high point is just that, and not a measure of their general level.

Also, those clinics which are fortunate enough to be staffed with vision specialists trained to work with children are frequently amazed to discover the large number with serious visual difficulties. These children, too, are often shoved into a learning-disability class, whereas proper visual help might make it quite possible for them to succeed in the regular stream of education.

And then, of course, there is the tremendous number of boys and girls suffering from allergies of one kind or another, or handicapped by an inadequate behavior chemistry, who *could* be helped in simple physical ways if the true cause of their difficulties were not hidden under the deceptive label of learning disability.

It is true that official definitions of the term have attempted to rule out many or all of these customary causes of learning difficulty. But in actual practice, perhaps half the children classed as L.D. and taught and treated accordingly are actually suffering from some one of these often correctable difficulties. (Even a low intelligence, though it cannot necessarily be improved or changed, can be handled quite effectively in a special class which recognizes that intelligence tests are not merely a basis for discriminating against certain individuals.)

This problem of definition is a serious one. As Hallahan and Kauffman[29] have pointed out:

> Though the formation of ACLD provided a rallying point for parents of children who had been denied services, the orientation of the group has been a factor in the current confusion regarding the *definition* of learning disabilities. Perhaps fearful of the stigma attached to the retarded, ACLD has tended to dissociate itself from the area of mental retardation.
>
> The result has been that the shared characteristics of retarded and learning disabled children and the similarities in services and educational programming for the two groups—*the heritage of the field of learning disabilities*—has been ignored. This zeal to create a separate category with no conceptual ties to other areas has been a primary factor in the rampant confusion regarding the definition of learning disabilities.
>
> Of what use, then, is the term "learning disabilities"? *It is of the utmost use if used as a concept rather than a category.* It is a term indicating learning problems in one or more areas of development or ability, whether ED, LD, or EMR. All these children have learning problems. The basic processes are all the same.

Kirk and Elkins,[37] in their review of 3,000 children enrolled in Child Service Demonstration Centers for Learning Disabilities in twenty-one states, found that *most of the children were general underachievers to a moderate degree in reading, spelling, and arithmetic.* They comment, correctly: "One can raise the question of whether such underachievement actually constitutes a specific learning disability."

In fact, these students on the average tested below an IQ of 90. Before we coined the term "learning disabilities" they would have been classified merely as slow learners or mentally retarded. The fact that the American Association of Mental Deficiency has changed its definition of "retarded" from an IQ of 84 or below to an IQ of 68 or below does not make the child with an IQ of 80 any brighter, or any more of a "special" learning problem than he was before the official change was made. In fact, changing the level was a dubious move, since it did not in any way improve the children and merely led parents, and sometimes teachers, to expect too much of the children in question.

Admittedly, say Kirk and Elkins, the 3,000 children they have checked on did need help, but the help should be an adapted curriculum for *all* areas of education.

So perhaps this is a good place to begin in clearing up an obviously cluttered field. We should differentiate children who are generally underachievers but who with an adapted curriculum could remain in the basic stream of education, from those with *specific* learning disabilities who need *special* education.

And then we might follow this with better diagnostic procedures to precede any placement of any child in a special learning-disability class, for either part or all of the school day. Such diagnostic procedures would rule out, and give special and proper help to, the child who is overplaced, the child with the significantly low IQ, the child who has specific visual problems, and the child whose ineffective school behavior may result from unrecognized allergies or improper diet.

Last of all, we might keep in mind Hallahan and Kauffman's very sensible suggestion that the term "learning disabilities" is indeed of the utmost use *if we consider it as a concept rather than a category.*

Politically the whole notion has been so successful that in some schools, developmental placement examiners are being replaced with learning-disability teachers. This in spite of the fact that one developmental examiner, by correctly placing students to begin with, might "save" perhaps 50% of those who end up in learning-disability classes.

Too many have been too quick to jump on this particular bandwagon. Now it may be time to slow down and figure out where we are going.

HALF-DAY FIRST GRADE

And now for two final topics, both of which seem to us of signal importance—the value of the half-day first grade, and the whole currently highly controversial matter of sex differences in behavior.

Being in the "right" grade is to us perhaps the most important single factor in determining any young child's academic and personal success in school. But also important is being in school for the "right" amount of time. It is generally accepted that kindergarten boys and girls do best with only a half day of school attendance.

For many years now thoughtful educators have suggested that most first-graders, too, have a limited endurance and that many if not most might do better with a half-day rather than a full-day program. A few communities have tried this half-day program for first-graders with success. Four states report that the shortened school day program has been implemented in some of their districts. Two further states indicate that a shortened school day has been used either one day a month or as an orientation program at the beginning of the school year.

However, until very recently there has been no formal research evaluation of such programs. We are thus pleased to report here a current study carried out by Principal John C. Mulrain of Woodbridge, Connecticut.[43] Dr. Mulrain and Suprintendent of Schools Alexander M. Raffone have long been advocates of the half-day first grade, and have carried on such a program for many years with good results. Dr. Mulrain's research, carried out at Temple University, now supports his (and our) contention that most first-graders do best with a half-day first grade.

His research method was to check the effect of the shortened school day by analyzing the acquisition of basic skills at the third- and sixth-grade levels of children who *had* experienced the half-day first grade, as compared with children in the same school system who had *not* experienced the half day.

Statistical analysis of data indicates that academically *there was no significant difference between the two groups* in vocabulary and reading skills, in language and work-study skills, arithmetic concept skills or arithmetic problem-solving skills. Children on the shortened school day did just as well academically as did those who had been subjected to a full day in first grade.

Teachers' and parents' responses as to the effect of the shortened day tended to be extremely positive. Ninety-nine of the teacher respondents had had two or more years experience in the shortened school day program. Of the teachers interviewed, 93% considered that the shortened school day resulted in less pupil fatigue; 92% felt that it lessened pupil frustration; 79% thought the children's attention span was improved by a shorter day. And 53% of teachers considered that it improved work habits, though 36% took a neutral position in this area.

Further, 85% of teachers perceived the positive effects of the shortened school day program in the area of pupil enthusiasm. Also, large majorities of teachers found that the shortened day resulted in less fatigue and more enthusiasm on the part of the teachers, and improved the teachers' ability to meet the academic needs of their pupils.

As for the parents, 87% felt that the shortened day had met the academic needs of their children, and 88% thought that the shortened day had no negative relationship to the child's acquisition of basic skills.

That the shorter day had met their child's social needs and also that their child's attitude toward the shorter day had been positive was claimed by 82% of parents; 84% of them recommended the continuation of the shortened school day program.

It is our hope that, perhaps encouraged by these positive findings, more school communities will at least try a shortened day for all first-graders.

SEX DIFFERENCES

It is important for every examiner to keep in mind that though behavior differences very often cross sex lines, on the average boys in the present age range tend to develop a little more slowly than do girls—on the average there is about a six-month difference.

Though on certain of our tests—as Naming Animals, Right and Left, Visual Three—sex differences are small, on other tests rather substantial differences do occur.

Thus on the Incomplete Man, at all ages until 6 years, girls add substantially more parts than do boys, and the addition of extra marks and parts drops out sooner in girls. As to individual parts, in most cases where there is a difference, girls respond somewhat earlier and somewhat more correctly than do boys. Good placement and good length of leg comes earlier in girls. Placing the eyes evenly and matching them as to type occurs sooner in girls than in boys. Completion of the neck area occurs first in girls. But boys are ahead of girls in moving the arm into the upper third of the body line and in correctly placing the ear.

In Copy Forms, too, girls are generally ahead of boys. Thus copying a circle from the top down, counterclockwise, is normative in girls at 5 years of age, in boys not till 5½, and at every age till 8 more girls than boys make this "correct" kind of circle. Though both sexes copy a recognizable cross or better at 3½ years of age, 70% of girls achieve this level of success, only 50% of boys.

A counterclockwise square is normative in girls at 5 years of age, in boys not till 5½. Girls copy a recognizable triangle or better at 4½ years of age, boys not till 5. However a well-proportioned triangle is normative in boys at 6, in girls not until 7.

As to organization of forms on the page, girls are somewhat ahead of boys at every age level in the number of forms which are of an even size. A (good) horizontal arrangement of figures is normative in girls at 7 years, in boys not even by 9. However, at 7 years (only), using less than half a page is normative in boys. At no age is it normative in girls.

And there are small sex differences in writing name, numbers, address. At 5 years of age, 70% of girls but only 56% of boys are making first name or better. So far as quality of printing or writing is concerned, girls in general are somewhat more advanced. Thus at 7 years, 82% of girls but only 56% of boys make medium-sized letters. Also at 7 years, 72% of girls but only 54% of boys make letters of a consistently even size. An even baseline is normative in girls sooner than it is in boys.

Sex differences are especially conspicuous in the test situation in which the child is asked to tell his or her age. A correct response is normative in girls at 3 years of age, in boys not until 4.

A perhaps more important, and more impressive, expression of sex differences was demonstrated when we analyzed our data from children seen at the Hurlbutt School in Weston, Connecticut, as described in Chapter 2. Data from this study show that not only were girls in general more advanced on individual tests, but that more girls in any grade were judged by us to be fully ready for the work of the grade than were the boys.

Thus, as Table 58 shows, almost twice as many girls in kindergarten and second grade were ready for their grade than were boys in the same classes, while nearly twice as many boys as girls were questionably ready, and four times as many boys as girls were judged to be unready.

TABLE 58   *Sex Differences in Readiness for the Grade in Which Age Alone Placed Them of Subjects Who Remained Consistently Ready, Questionable, or Unready over a Three-Year Period (Weston)*

Original Group	Ready		Questionable		Unready	
	G	B	G	B	G	B
54 Kindergarteners	22	9	6	11	1	5
21 First-graders	6	6	3	4	0	2
23 Second-graders	5	3	2	6	2	5
Total	**33**	**18**	**11**	**21**	**3**	**12**

In order to make an even more specific comparison, again using our Weston subjects, we matched as many girl-boy pairs as possible with relation to WISC IQ, age in months, and socioeconomic status, and compared responses of each girl-boy pair on the Incomplete Man test, on Visual Three, and on the Mosaic and Rorschach tests.[9] Table 59 shows the percentage of these matched pairs in which either girl or boy gives the better performance. As this table indicates, regardless of test used and regardless of age of subjects, for nearly every test at every age it is the scores of girls which are superior and show greater maturity of response.

There is today great concern in some quarters about any data which imply that there may be a difference between the behavior of girls and that of boys other than that which society has imposed. A recent memo from the State Department of Education in Connecticut indicates that "A question is now being raised as to the discriminatory effects of the use of psychological tests that provide norms based on sex." If it is upsetting to any school system which uses our behavior tests that norms are given for boys and girls separately, our best recommendation is that the examiner average these norms and thus obscure the differences.

TABLE 59   *Percentage of Matched Pairs in Which Either Sex Gives the More Advanced Performance (Weston)*

	Kindergarten Test Number			First Grade Test Number			Second Grade Test Number		
	1	2	3	1	2	3	1	2	3
Incomplete Man									
Number of pairs	18	18	17	6	6	6	7	7	7
Girls more advanced	83	83	76	67	100	67	71	86	100
Boys more advanced	17	17	24	33	0	33	29	14	0
Visual Three									
Number of pairs	16	15	14	6	6	6	7	7	7
Girls more advanced	81	53	57	50	83	83	43	28	57
Boys more advanced	19	47	43	50	17	17	57	72	43
*Mosaic**									
Number of pairs	18	18	17	6	6		9	9	9
Girls more advanced	72	55	53	50	33		66	55	66
Boys more advanced	28	17	29	12	66		33	11	11
Rorschach									
Number of pairs	17			6			7		
Girls more advanced	53			83			57		
Boys more advanced	47			17			43		

* Not all percentages add up to 100% since performance of some pairs was judged to be equal.

But politics to the contrary, any experienced teacher or examiner may continue to observe that there is on the average a tendency for girls to be more advanced on a behavior examination than are boys.

THE DEVELOPMENTAL EXAMINER AS POSSIBLE CHILD ADVOCATE

Equally controversial as the matter of whether sex differences are biologically determined, or are caused by the way we as a society treat boys and girls, is the whole matter of children's rights and child advocacy. Child advocacy has been defined as "a rapidly evolving social movement for children much as civil rights is for blacks and consumer advocacy is for the American buyer."[44]

The child advocate takes as his task the mutual adaptation of children and their environment. The feeling among those who propose the need of an individual agency to stand as child advocate is that "we have lost our heroes in the helping professions. The teacher in the one-room school, a respected ally of the parent in imparting certain behavior and ethical codes as well as the three R's, has no contemporary counterpart."

Nor, some feel, does the old-time general practitioner of medicine or the known and respected lawyer have a counterpart among today's professional people. Thus a new professional role, some feel, must be created, though just what this should be, where he (or she) would be based, what exactly he would do, how be trained, are at present all rather ambiguous.

Without questioning the need for child advocacy, we can suggest that it might be possible for those within professions which now exist to do even more than they now are doing to serve as advocates for the child.

In our experience, one such person who so far can and does play a very flexible and useful part is the developmental examiner. In school systems—as, for instance, formerly in Cheshire, Connecticut—in which each primary school was fortunate enough to have its own developmental examiner, here was a person ready and made to order to serve as a child advocate.

This individual, concerned primarily with the welfare and proper placement of the child, inevitably puts the child's welfare first in his or her concern, and by the very nature of the role mediates among parent, teacher, and school administration.

Because he or she does or can have status in the eyes of the existing community, many of the hazards which so far seem inevitable in the role of the child advocate can be by-passed.

In our eyes, the role of developmental examiner fits superbly into today's culture—a culture which is becoming increasingly concerned about the rights of every child to be provided with a situation, in school as at home, which fits his or her individual and very special needs.

These are obviously but a few of the many important issues which concern parents, teachers, and all who are interested in the welfare of school children today. To discuss all the issues which must be kept in mind by those who would like to see every child have the best possible schooling would take a book in itself.

Education today is a rapidly changing field, a field in which political and theoretical issues as well as a genuine concern for the welfare of the individual child play a prominent role. Those who are informed about what these issues are will be in the best position to help things move in a direction which will be to the best advantage of our school-age girls and boys.

This chapter has discussed what we consider some of the most vital and most controversial. It suggests that whereas correct grade placement, as made possible or at least substantially aided by the developmental placement examination, is basic to school success, it does not stand alone.

In the final analysis, effective teaching depends on a good teacher teaching a group of children who are ready for the level and kind of instruction being given. Correct grade placement, which is what this book is all about, is but one of the essential ingredients.

APPENDIX A

SAMPLES OF TEST RECORD FORMS

Face Sheet   Name

Final thumb-nail summary of behavior   Age   b. d.

                                    Date

                                    School

                                    Teacher

                                    Group

Recommended group   Examiner

_____

Total impression and summary

Teachers comments

206

Initial Interview

How old are you?

When is your birthday? _____ Month? _____ Day? _____ ____

Did you have a party? (who came)

      What did you like to do best?

      What was your favorite present?

How many brothers and sisters?
     (Names, ages)

What does your daddy do?
     (Where does he work?)

207

Write letters or name, last name (6-7 yrs), date (7-8 yrs),   Name

                      address (8-9 yrs)

           1st name with non- dominant hand.   Age

Copy forms   R _____   L _____

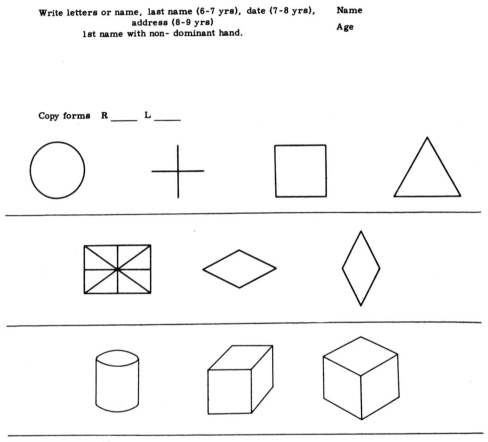

Write numbers 1 to 20 -

Incomplete Man (look like; order of parts & comments)   Facial Expression (How can you tell?)

How does he look?

How does he feel inside?

Happy or sad?

How can you tell?

209

Age

Naming parts of body

1. Eye
2. Eyebrow
3. Palm

4. Elbow

Naming fingers () 5 yr.

(1) Thumb
2 Index (pter)
(3) Middle (2-2)
4 Ring (wear)
(5) Little

Naming R & L

R hand (point to child's R hand)

Show me your R hand (if can't name R hand)

How do you know?

L hand (point to child's L hand)

Ex-er's R hand (show)

How do you know?

Single Commands () 5 yr. items

		Seconds	Method
(1)	Eye	_____	
2	Index	_____	
3	Ring	_____	
4	Middle	_____	
(5)	Cl. eyes, bend head	_____	
(6)	Bend head, tap fl. with heel	_____	
7	Raise head, open mouth	_____	
(8)	R ear	_____	
(9)	R thumb	_____	
(10)	L index (5 yrs-L big)	_____	
	Total	_____ Av. _____	

Double Command () 5 yr. items

		Seconds	Method
(1)	R thumb-R little	_____	
2	L hand-L knee	_____	
3	L ring-R eyebrow	_____	
4	R elbow-palm L hand	_____	
5	R middle-L cheek	_____	
6	L thumb-R thumb	_____	
(7)	R middle-L little	_____	
8	R little-L ring	_____	
9	L middle-R index	_____	
10	L thumb-R ring	_____	
	Total	_____ Av. _____	

Summary Comments:

210

Visual Test 1
Matching Forms

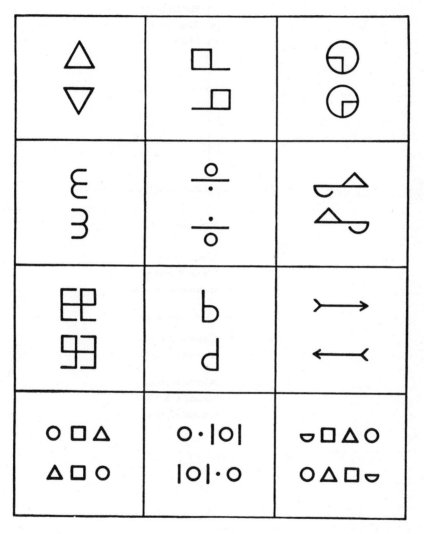

211

Visual 1

○ ○ ○
○ ○ ○
○ ○ ○
○ ○ ○

Visual 3

1.

2.

3.

4.

Name

Age

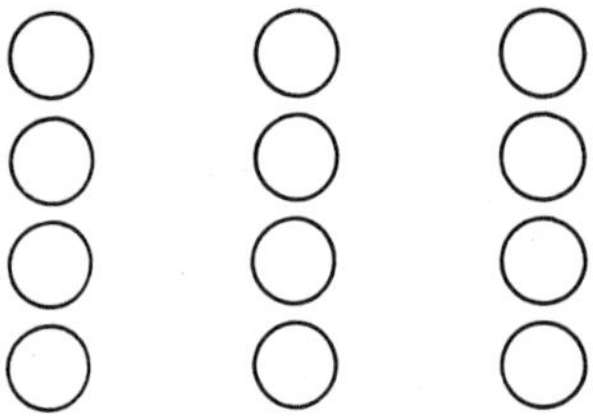

Comments on Visual 1 and 3

Visual 3 - Projections

Card 1

△

◐

Γ.

∨

Card 2

ᘉ

|•|

◧

⇧

Card 3

✕

◪

⊣

⊖

Card 4

△

⊏⊐

⊤

⊓

212

Visual 3

213

Animals and Interests

Name

Age

Naming animals (60°)

Interests - what do you like to do best?

At school indoors:

At school outdoors:

At home indoors:

At home outdoors:

Tooth eruption   Physical items: (fat, muscular, slender, etc.)

R.   Upper   L.

12 6 M M	2nd B	1st B	C	LI CI	CI LI	C	1st 2nd B B	6 12 M M		

Lower

214

A P P E N D I X   B

SUBJECTS AND MATERIALS

||||||||||||||||||||||||||||||||||||||||||||||||||||||||||||||||||||||||||||||||||||||

SUBJECTS

PRESCHOOL

Eighty children (40 girls and 40 boys) were tested at each of ages 3, $3\frac{1}{2}$, 4, and $4\frac{1}{2}$ years, each within a month of his/her yearly or half-yearly birthday. Children were chosen according to their fathers' occupations, to match the proportional distribution of employed men in the 1970 U.S. Census. Equal numbers of boys and girls were chosen at each level. About 8% of the children tested were black, the remainder were white. All children tested resided in New England.

SCHOOL AGE

Subjects for ages 5 through 9, whose responses constitute the main part of this volume, are the children on whose performance we reported in our 1965 edition of *School Readiness*. Children came from the public schools of our neighboring town, North Haven. We examined in two school districts (Center and Montowese), each of which had around 100 children at each grade level.

In our standardization study the age ranges for each age level were as follows: the 5-year-old could be from 4^{11} to 5^4; the $5\frac{1}{2}$-year-old from 5^6 to 5^{10}; the 6-year-old from 6^0 to 6^8; and similarly for ages 7, 8, 9, and 10.*

Since we knew that a fair number of children would be lost to the study, especially through moving away, we examined 65 boys and 65 girls at each age level. Our goal was to examine as many of the subjects as possible at *successive* age levels. Since the entire examining program was

* Though data were originally gathered for 10-year-olds, these are not included in the present revision, since after 9 years of age this type of developmental evaluation seems effective only if a child is extremely immature.

conducted over a period of four school years, not all subjects could be followed longitudinally. However, we arranged it so that one group of 65 subjects of each sex was seen at 5, 5½, 6, and 7 years; another group of the same size was seen at 6, 7, and 8 years; and still a third group at 8, 9, and 10 years.

To be certain of having 50 cases of each sex at each age level, we added 200 extra cases at the ages 5, 5½, 9, and 10—cases which did not overlap as in our longitudinal planning. These extra cases were examined only once each.

All subjects to be examined were selected at random (other than that age was checked) from class lists. Since most subjects were seen at more than one age, 301 different children gave us the 700 records needed.

The final decision of the 100 records at each age level which were to be analyzed was made on the basis of completeness of recording.

INTELLIGENCE

The subjects were above average in intelligence, with a mean IQ of 117.4 (standard deviation 13.3) for both boys and girls on the California Mental Maturity Scale (CMMS), the one used by the schools. However, when this score was corrected for a sample of the children to a score on the Wechsler Intelligence Scale for Children (WISC), the mean IQ for girls was 104.8 and that for boys 106. (See Appendix C.) The California scale is considered by many psychologists to be a less effective measure of intelligence and it also gives a less consistent rating from year to year than the Wechsler. It usually scores at least 10 points higher than other tests, such as the WISC. The WISC scores here are more in keeping with our own subjective impression of the present subjects.

SOCIOECONOMIC STATUS

The socioeconomic status of these older subjects has been rated on both the U.S. Government Scale (1961) and the Minnesota Scale of Parental Occupations. We have given both scales since there is considerable difference in classification.

According to the U.S. Government Scale, the highest percentage of fathers (34%) fall in Class I or within the professional grouping, with 13% in Class II, semiprofessional or managerial. This gives 47% in either Class I or Class II, as opposed to the Minnesota rating of only 27% in Classes I and II. On the Minnesota Scale, the majority (40%) fall within Class III—the clerical, skilled labor, or retail business grouping.

In our opinion, the U.S. Government Scale has some of the same flaws as the California Mental Maturity Scale. The ratings of both are too high. Along with the choice of the WISC, we would prefer to use the Minnesota Scale, in which the majority of parents fall chiefly in Class III.

Since readers will for the most part be primarily interested in school-age performance, when data at 4½ are available for North Haven or so-called *School Readiness* subjects, in order to provide as much continuity as possible we have used the North Haven 4½-year-olds rather than the newer preschool data.

MATERIALS*

PAPER
Green letter-size Hammermill bond No. 16, on which child can write letters, numbers, name, address, date.

COPY FORMS
White 7½-by-5-inch cards with the following forms outlined in black in the center of each card—*circle:* diameter 8 cm.; *cross:* lines at right angles, 7.5 cm.; *square:* 7 cm.; *triangle:* equilateral, 9.5 cm.; *divided rectangle:* rectangle 10 × 6.5 cm. with two diagonals and a perpendicular to the center of each side; *diamond:* horizontal—5.5 cm. each side, top angle 125°; vertical—same size.

THREE-DIMENSIONAL FORMS
Two three-dimensional objects. A 1.5-inch cylinder and a 1.5-inch cube, of red-painted wood.

INCOMPLETE MAN
Blue letter-size paper with drawing of unfinished man.

VISUAL ONE
Material for this test is in two parts. The first part is a record form sheet, 8½ by 11 inches, marked off into twelve small squares, three across and four down. In each square are two paired but opposed figures. (The child has to choose which of these figures matches one shown him on a separate card.)
The second part of the test material is a set of twelve cards, each 8½ by 5½ inches in size. On each is printed a figure which resembles one of the two shown on the record sheet.

VISUAL THREE
Material for this test is also in two parts. There is a (pink) record sheet, 8½ by 11 inches in size, marked off into four horizontal lines. On each line are to be reproduced as many forms as a subject can remember. The second part of the material is a set of four cards, 11 by 8½ inches in size. On each are printed, in horizontal alignment, four black geometric forms.

RIGHT AND LEFT DIRECTION CARDS
Small cards on which are printed commands which examiner gives to subject for (1) naming parts of the examiner's body; (2) naming right and left, own and examiner's; (3) single commands; (4) double commands.

---

* Test materials can be obtained from Programs for Education, 101 Park Avenue, Suite 1236, New York, N.Y. 10017. All test materials are illustrated in Appendix A.

IDENTIFYING LETTERS AND NUMBERS

An 8½-by-11-inch card with capital letters, out of sequence, on one side; small letters, out of sequence, on the other. A second card, same size with numbers from 1 to 12, out of sequence.

MATERIAL FOR SUPPLEMENTARY TESTS

GRAY ORAL READING TEST

This is a standardized individual reading test consisting of a series of paragraphs of graduated difficulty. Available from the Bobbs-Merrill Co., Inc., 4300 West 62nd Street, Indianapolis, Ind. 46206.

RORSCHACH CARDS

A set of ten 9½-by-6½-inch cards on each of which is printed a symmetric ink blot; some are in color, some in black-and-white. Available to qualified psychologists through the Psychological Corporation, 304 East 45th Street, New York, N.Y. 10017.

LOWENFELD MOSAIC TEST

Box of 456 plastic pieces, ⅟₁₆ inch thick. Pieces are in six colors and five shapes. This box can be obtained from Mrs. F. B. Muir, 24 Dickens Chase, Leeds, Nr. Maidstone, Kent, England. (The large box of 456 pieces is $55.00; the smaller half-box is $35.00.)

The working surface on which patterns are to be made is a sheet of white paper which covers a rectangular wooden tray having a raised rim on three sides, the side to be placed nearest the subject being rimless. The standard size of this working surface is 10¼ by 12⅜ inches.

RECORDING SHEETS (OR TEST RECORD FORMS)

Test Record Forms, which, like the test materials themselves, can be obtained from Programs for Education, are illustrated in Appendix A.

SPECIAL NORMS FOR SPECIAL SITUATIONS

Unless each school in a school system has its own developmental examiner, many an examiner will find herself or himself pressed for time. However, for those special schools which do provide their own examiner, such an individual as time goes on may like to save data from year to year and eventually work up for any or all of our tests a set of norms which are uniquely appropriate to the special subjects with whom he or she works. *Obviously, for good developmental placement, there are no norms quite as useful as those which apply to the exact population with which one is working.*

INTELLIGENCE SCORES FOR SELECTED SUBJECTS

TABLE 60   *Intelligence Scores for 25 Selected Girls Compared on the*
California Mental Maturity Scale and Wechsler Intelligence Scale for
Children (or Stanford Binet)

| Name | Age | Intelligence Scores Compared for | |
		CMM	WISC or Stanford Binet
6 years			
Girl A	6^6	129	111
Girl B	6^5	122	92
Girl C	6^6	128	92
Girl D	6^6	110	103
Girl E	6^2	122	96
7 years			
Girl F	7^3	102	92
Girl G	6^{11}	107	97
Girl H	7^5	130	121
Girl I	7^3	132	108
Girl J	7^{10}	110	84
8 years			
Girl K	8^5	115	96
Girl L	8^1	125	100
Girl M	8^4	108	95
Girl N	8^7	121	123
Girl O	8^2	111	109
9 years			
Girl P	8^{11}	132	116
Girl Q	8^{11}	118	106
Girl R	9^0	119	126
Girl S	9^6	115	105
Girl T	9^5	120	89
10 years			
Girl U	10^2	119	125
Girl V	10^6	114	105
Girl W	10^0	128	115
Girl X	10^6	124	129
Girl Y	10^5	105	85

	Mean	Median	
CMM	118.7	122.0	
WISC	104.8	105.0	

TABLE 61   *Intelligence Scores for 25 Selected Boys Compared on the California Mental Maturity Scale and Wechsler Intelligence Scale for Children (or Stanford Binet)*

Name	Age	Intelligence Scores Compared for	
		CMM	WISC or Stanford Binet
6 years			
Boy A	6^2	122	89
Boy B	6^6	122	100
Boy C	6^6	114	95
Boy D	6^5	124	110
Boy E	6^7	117	99
7 years			
Boy F	7^0	125	108
Boy G	7^0	126	110
Boy H	7^7	120	101
Boy I	7^0	134	103
Boy J	7^3	110	116
8 years			
Boy K	8^1	112	107
Boy L	8^1	112	104
Boy M	7^{11}	129	106
Boy N	8^9	127	125
Boy O	8^7	119	120
9 years			
Boy P	8^{11}	111	104
Boy Q	9^3	117	107
Boy R	8^{11}	111	111
Boy S	9^4	118	104
Boy T	9^8	115	109
10 years			
Boy U	9^{11}	120	105
Boy V	10^5	115	101
Boy W	10^1	116	111
Boy X	10^3	109	96
Boy Y	10^9	111	103
		Mean	Median
CMM		118	118
WISC		106	106

REFERENCES

||||||||||||||||||||||||||||||||||||||||||||||||||||||||||||||||||

1. Ames, Louise B. *Parents Ask*. A syndicated daily newspaper column. New Haven: Gesell Institute, 1952–.
2. ———. "Predictive Value of Infant Behavior Examinations." Chapter in *The Exceptional Infant: The Normal Infant*, vol. I, 1967, 209–239.
3. ———. *Is Your Child in the Wrong Grade?* New York: Harper & Row, 1967.
4. Ames, Louise B., and Chase, Joan Ames. *Don't Push Your Preschooler*. New York: Harper & Row, 1975.
5. Ames, Louise B.; Gillespie, Clyde; and Streff, John W. *Stop School Failure*. New York: Harper & Row, 1972.
6. Ames, Louise B., and Ilg, Frances L. *Mosaic Patterns of American Children*. New York: Hoeber/Harper, 1962.
7. ———. "Variant Behavior as Revealed by the Gesell Developmental Examination." *J. Genet. Psychol.* 63 (1943): 273–305.
8. ———. "Every Child in the Right Grade: Behavioral Age Rather Than Age in Years the Best Clue to Correct Grade Placement." *The Instructor*, 73, no. 3 (November 1963): 7 ff.
9. ———. "Sex Differences in Test Performance of Matched Girl and Boy Pairs in the 5- to 9-Year-Old Age Range." *J. Genet. Psychol.* 104 (1964): 25–34.
10. ———. *Your Two Year Old: Terrible or Tender?* New York: Delacorte, 1976.
11. ———. *Your Three Year Old: Friend or Enemy?* New York: Delacorte, 1976.
12. ———. *Your Four Year Old: Wild and Wonderful*. New York: Delacorte, 1976.
13. Ames, Louise B.; Rodell, Janet; Métraux, Ruth; and Walker, Richard N. *Child Rorschach Responses*. Rev. ed. New York: Brunner/Mazel, 1974.
14. Ames, Louise B., and Walker, Richard N. "Prediction of Later Reading Ability from Kindergarten Rorschach and I.Q. Scores." *J. Educ. Psychol.* 55, no. 6 (1964): 309–313.

15. Burns, Robert C., and Kaufman, S. Harvard. *Kinetic Family Drawings (K-F-D)*. New York: Brunner/Mazel, 1970.

16. ———. *Actions, Styles and Symbols in Kinetic Family Drawings (K-F-D)*. New York: Brunner/Mazel, 1972.

17. Carll, Barbara, and Richard, Nancy. *One Piece of the Puzzle: A School Readiness Manual*. Moravia, New York: Athena Publications, 1977.

18. Chase, Joan Ames. "A Study of the Impact of Grade Retention on Primary School Children." *J. Psychology* 70 (1968): 169–177.

19. ———. "Differential Behavior Characteristics of Non-Promoted Children." *Genet. Psychol. Monog.* 86 (1972): 219–277.

20. Cott, Allan. "Megavitamins: The Orthomolecular Approach to Behavior Disorders and Learning Disabilities." *Academic Therapy Quarterly* 7 (1972): 3.

21. Delacato, Carl. *A New Start for the Child with Reading Problems*. New York: McKay, 1974.

22. Feingold, Ben F. *Why Your Child Is Hyperactive*. New York: Random House, 1975.

23. Gesell, Arnold. *Infancy and Human Growth*. New York: Macmillan, 1928.

24. ———. *Mental Growth of the Preschool Child*. New York: Macmillan, 1930.

25. ———. "The Stability of Mental Growth Careers." Pages 149–160 in *Intelligence: Its Nature and Nurture*. Bloomington, Ill.: The Public School Publishing Co., 1940.

26. Gesell, Arnold, et al. *Biographies of Child Development*. New York: Hoeber/Harper, 1939.

27. ———. *The First Five Years of Life*. New York: Harper & Brothers, 1940.

28. Hedges, William D. *At What Age Should Children Enter First Grade: A Comprehensive Review of the Research*. Ann Arbor, Michigan: University Microfilms International, 1977.

29. Hallahan, Daniel P., and Kauffman, James. *Introduction to Learning Disabilities*. Englewood Cliffs, N.J.: Prentice-Hall, 1976.

30. Hunter, Madeline. "Right-Brained Kids in Left-Brained Schools." *Today's Education*, November/December, 1976.

31. Ilg, Frances L., and Ames, Louise B. *Child Behavior*. New York: Harper & Brothers, 1955.

32. Ilg, Frances L.; Ames, Louise B.; and Apell, Richard J. "School Readiness as Evaluated by Gesell Developmental, Visual and Projective Tests." *Genet. Psychol. Monog.* 71 (1965): 61–91.

33. Jacobson, J. Robert. "A Method of Psychobiologic Evaluation." *Am. J. Psychiatry* 109 (1949): 330–346.

34. Jacobson, J. Robert, and Pratt, Helen Gay. "Psychobiological Dysfunction in Children." *J. Nerv. and Ment. Dis.* 109 (1949): 4.

35. Jensen, Arthur R. *Understanding Readiness: An Occasional Paper*. Urbana, Ill.: ERIC Clearing House in Early Childhood Education, 1969.

36. Kaufman, Alan J. "Piaget and Gesell: A Psychometric Analysis of Tests Built from Their Tasks." *Child Development* 42 (1971): 1341–1360.

37. Kirk, Samuel A., and Elkins, John. "Learning Disabilities: Characteristics of

Children Enrolled in the Child Service Demonstration Centers." *J. Learning Disabilities* 8 (1975): 630–637.

38. Koppitz, Elizabeth. *The Bender Gestalt Test for Young Children.* New York: Grune & Stratton, 1964.

39. ———. *The Bender Gestalt Test for Young Children.* vol. II. *Research and Applications, 1963–1973.* New York: Grune & Stratton, 1975.

40. Lewis, Verne. "Parents' Evaluations of the Effects on Their Children of Repeating." Unpublished paper.

41. Meyer, George. "Some Relationships Between Rorschach Scores in Kindergarten and Reading in the Primary Grades." *J. Proj. Tech.* 17, no. 4 (1953): 414–425.

42. Monroe, Marion. *Growing into Reading.* Glenville, Ill.: Scott, Foresman, 1951.

43. Mulrain, John C. "The Effectiveness of a Shortened School Day Program for First Graders: A Follow-Up Study." Dissertation at Graduate School, Temple University, 1977.

44. Paul, James L.; Neufeld, G. Ronald; and Pelosi, John W., eds. *Child Advocacy Within the System.* Syracuse, N.Y.: Syracuse University Press, 1977.

45. Pitcher, Evelyn G., and Ames, Louise B. *The Guidance Nursery School.* Rev. ed. New York: Harper & Row, 1975.

46. Postman, Neil, and Weingartner, Charles. *The School Book: For People Who Want to Know What All the Hollering Is About.* New York: Delacorte, 1973.

47. Scott, Betty A., and Ames, Louise B. "Improved Academic, Personal and Social Adjustment in Selected Primary School Repeaters." *Elementary School Journal* 69 (1969): 431–439.

48. Silberberg, Norman E., and Silberberg, Margaret. "The Bookless Curriculum: An Educational Alternative." *J. Learning Disabilities* 2 (1969): 302–307.

49. Smith, Lendon H. *Improving Your Child's Behavior Chemistry.* Englewood Cliffs, N.J.: Prentice-Hall, 1976.

50. Stringer, Lorene A. "Report on a Retention Program." *Elementary School Journal* 60 (1960): 370–375.

51. Walker, Richard N., and others. *Gesell Preschool Norms Revised.* (In preparation).

52. Wunderlich, Ray C. *Allergy, Brains and Children Coping.* St. Petersburg, Fla.: Johnny Reads Press, 1973.

INDEX